LORD MINIMUS

LORD MINIMUS, JEFFREY HUDSON

LORD MINIMUS

The Extraordinary Life of Britain's Smallest Man

NICK PAGE

St. Martin's Press ⚜ New York

www.stmartins.com

Illustrations
Frontispiece from Silvester Harding, *The Biographical Mirror* (London, 1810).
(Based on an original painting by Daniel Mytens.)
Chapter heading illustration from James Caulfield, *Portraits, Memoirs and Characters of Remarkable Persons, from the Reign of Edward III to the Revolution* (London, 1813). (Based on the original by Nicholas Droeshutt in *The New Yeare's Gift*, 1636.)

ISBN 0-312-29161-2

First published in Great Britain by HarperCollins*Publishers*

First U.S. Edition: August 2002

10 9 8 7 6 5 4 3 2 1

For Claire

CONTENTS

The Story of the Pie 1
The Receipt 4
The Butcher's Son 10
The Duke's Gift 26
The Queen's Dwarf 46
The Pirate Captive 69
The Little Courtier 80
The Wonder of the Age 97
The Mistaken Prince 132
The Captain of Horse 153
The Fatal Duellist 166
The Abandoned Slave 180
The Lost Son 206
The Wronged Catholic 216

APPENDIX 1
Fuller's Biography of Jeffrey Hudson 235

APPENDIX 2
James Wright's Account of Jeffrey Hudson 237

APPENDIX 3
Sir Geoffrey Hudson and *Peveril of the Peak* 240

SOURCES 243

INDEX 257

THE
STORY OF THE PIE

IN 1626, GEORGE VILLIERS, DUKE OF BUCKINGHAM, hosted a royal banquet. The guests of honour were King Charles I and his new young wife Henrietta Maria. The Duke had a special, indeed unique, gift – a veritable 'rarity of nature' – for the Queen, and it was to be delivered to Henrietta Maria in a manner which she would never forget.

Buckingham was, if nothing else, a showman. His evenings usually featured a show or an entertainment, but that night he had planned something different. As the feast reached its climax, the trumpets blared and the crowded hall fell silent.

Two footmen entered, carrying between them a platter on which stood a large pie. It was a fine example of the master-cook's art, some two feet long and a foot high, its pastry gilded with gold leaf and glistening in the candle-light. They carried it with great solemnity through the crowded banqueting hall, past tables groaning under the weight of salmon and stewed carp, venison, capons and whole geese, right to where the guests of honour were seated on a raised dais. With great ceremony the pie was set down in front of the young Queen.

The Duke turned to Henrietta Maria, bowed low and

handed her a knife. She must have been puzzled. It was a pie. A little large, to be sure, and extravagantly decorated, but nothing out of the ordinary, and certainly not the gourmet fare that was already before her. And was he really inviting her to cut it? Was this presumptuous man really asking the Queen of England to serve herself? Mystified, she went along with the game. She took the knife and rose, preparing to cut into the pie.

It was just as she was about to cut into the crust that she noticed the pie was moving. The crust was rising, being lifted from within. A hand appeared – a tiny hand, smaller than a child's, more like that of a baby. Two eyes peeped out, then a face, tinier than any doll's and framed by a miniature helmet. Finally, before the entranced Queen's gaze, the crust was thrown back and a tiny figure emerged.

It was a boy – the smallest human being that anyone had ever seen – perfectly proportioned and dressed in a suit of miniature armour.

He climbed out of the pie and stood shyly on the table in front of the Queen. Then, as if remembering the script, he started to march up and down, and wave his flag, weaving around the gold plates, the ornate salt cellar and the fine Venetian glassware, acknowledging the rapturous applause of the court. Then, as the applause died away, he stood in front of the Queen, and bowed low.

The Queen gazed at the little boy adoringly. Only fifteen, alone in a foreign country and trapped in an apparently loveless marriage, she surrounded herself with pets: monkeys, dogs and birds in cages. Now here was the ultimate present – a little man to call her own.

The Duke smiled graciously. Everything had worked flawlessly – the perfect present delivered in the perfect manner. The young Queen laughed and clapped in delight.

The crowd cheered. The little boy looked around him in wonder.

His name was Jeffrey Hudson.

He was seven years old and only eighteen inches high.

And his life is one of the most remarkable stories of the seventeenth century.

THE
RECEIPT

ALL WE HAVE IS A RECEIPT. IT IS NOT MUCH IN TERMS of historical documents. Just a receipt, signed 'Geoffrie Hudson', acknowledging a gift of five pounds.

But for me, when I unearthed it on a spring day in the Public Record Office in London, it was like the Holy Grail. For here, at last, was something from his own hands. Here was something that he had touched, that he had written himself: a receipt for five pounds, signed in a shaking tremulous hand. Here, at last, was a personal memento of Jeffrey Hudson, the Queen's Dwarf, the Hero of the Pie, the smallest man in England, and one of the most remarkable characters of the seventeenth century.

He is written about by others, he appears in paintings, poems and plays, his actions are reported in official dispatches, even in the very early newspapers. But from his own hand we have nothing. Nothing, that is, except a receipt for five pounds, signed when he was tired and old and forgotten.

Strange as it may seem, looking at that signature in the cold spring light brought it home to me. This was a man. He had actually lived.

And his story was true.

*   *   *

This is the tale of the tiniest man in England. It will take us from the heart of the English countryside to the edges of the known world; from the lowest social stratum to the seats of king and princes. It is a tale of pirates and princes, playwrights and poets; of soldiers and courtiers, of shipwreck, slavery and imprisonment. It is a remarkable life, given that Jeffrey was largely a peripheral figure. He was not a great statesman, not an orator or an artist. He spent much of his life standing in the corner, observing.

Yet the times he lived through and the events on which he looked were some of the most significant in history. The wars and the adventures, the triumphs and the tragedies of the seventeenth century had profound consequence, not just for England, but for Europe and the world. And through all this, Jeffrey was *there*. He was the friend of queens and kings; his life was lived both in palaces and prisons. He was a courtier, slave, soldier and criminal. He was painted by great artists and celebrated in verse by court poets. He made people laugh and cry. He was one of the wonders of his age.

Over time his story has become distorted, fiction has been taken for fact. It is not surprising that this is so, for, from his first appearance, Jeffrey the Dwarf was always seen as a miraculous, almost fictional creature. What is, perhaps, more surprising is that his life was so bizarre that any fictional add-ons are simply not necessary.

There are two main contemporary accounts of Jeffrey's life. The earliest is in Thomas Fuller's *The Worthies of England*, published in 1662. The account is incomplete and lacks certain details – Fuller does not know Jeffrey's surname, for example – but, as will be shown, it is substantially correct.

The second account is by James Wright in his *Histories*

and Antiquities of the County of Rutland, published in 1684 after Jeffrey's death. Wright's history is unique, because he actually knew and spoke to Jeffrey.

These are the only two contemporary narratives, and together they do not add up to more than a few hundred words. The rest of Jeffrey's story must be drawn from other sources: diaries, letters, diplomatic reports, poems, plays, even early newspapers. And, of course, receipts. There are, however, two more accounts of Jeffrey's life, both of which are more remarkable for the effect that they had on subsequent historians than for the accuracy of their portrayal.

The first of these was written by Henry Stonecastle of Northumberland, owner and publisher of and chief contributor to *The Universal Spectator and Weekly Journal*. Stonecastle claims that his biography has the benefit of some 'short-hand notes which were taken of this diminutive Hero, by a curious Micrographer and F.R.S. [Fellow of the Royal Society] of the last century'.

However, Stonecastle does not give the name of his source, and the 'short-hand' pun undermines the seriousness of his work. However, while Stonecastle's narrative reads as if it was written with a smirk, it does show signs of some original research. He gives us some plausible details of John Hudson's role at Burley, and some insight into the character of Jeffrey's parents. The problem is winnowing out those real events from what appear to be apocryphal anecdotes and plain myths.

The second account is by Sir Walter Scott, the novelist. In 1822 he published *Peveril of the Peak*, a historical novel set in the time of Charles II. Jeffrey appears as 'Sir Geoffrey Hudson', and tells the hero, young Julian Peveril, details of his life story. We need not go into those details here, but what is remarkable is the way in which Scott's account – his invented words and imagined history – became accepted fact. By 1910 a Rutland historian was able to state with certainty, for example, that Jeffrey fought alongside Prince Rupert at the Battle of Newbury, and even what he said to the troops there. Neither of these facts is historically verifiable. Both were invented by Walter Scott. To Scott, as well, we owe the often used title of 'Sir' Jeffrey Hudson. Jeffrey was never knighted. He was certainly a Captain of Horse, and proudly used the title in later life, but he was never 'Sir' Jeffrey Hudson.

For over three hundred years writers have added incredible events and unbelievable details to Jeffrey's life story. But the truly amazing thing about Jeffrey is that his life needed no embellishing. It was fantastic enough already.

*　　*　　*

One of the first issues I had to face in telling this story, was one of terminology. To many people the term 'dwarf' is seen as offensive, a label reflecting discrimination and prejudice. Whilst I appreciate their feelings, I feel that alternatives such as 'Little Person' or 'Person of Limited Stature' would be both unwieldy and unhelpful. Jeffrey was, throughout his life, referred to as a 'dwarf' and that is the description I have used in this book. He certainly experienced and fought, prejudice and ignorance, but he was the Queen's Dwarf and this was the common term used in his day.

I faced similar difficulties when trying to decide how to spell his name. In seventeenth-century England, spelling was not an exact science, especially when it came to names. Most people could neither read nor write, and even those who could were entirely at the mercy of clerks and officials, who would simply put down the name as they thought it should be spelled. Jeffrey's mother, for example, was written down as 'Luce', the clerk's spelling of the name Lucy.

Jeffrey seems to have had many variants. He appears in records as 'Jeffrey', 'Jeffry', 'Jeffery', 'Geoffrey', 'Geoffry',

'Geffry' and 'Geoffrie'. In France he is referred to as 'Joffroy'. The record of his baptism in the parish register spells his name 'Jefery' and, in his only signature, he signed himself 'Geffrie'. In the accounts of his life he has generally been called 'Jeffrey Hudson' and that is the convention I have used throughout this book.

Similarly, I have altered the dating system. In the seventeenth century, Britain was still using the Julian Calendar, in which the new year began on 25 March. That means that a date which they called, say, February 1626, we would call February 1627. Historians usually use the convention February 1626/7, but for simplicity's sake, I have taken January as the beginning of the year.

Finally, with regard to sums of money and relative values, any attempt to translate these into modern equivalents is fraught with difficulties because of the large number of variables involved. It is not a matter of simply multiplying the sum by a certain amount. The prices of commodities such as grain, clothing, meat, land and property have all fluctuated greatly in the past four hundred years. The laws of supply and demand, combined with advances in technology and agriculture mean that certain items now cost less in real terms than they did in the seventeenth century. Buying patterns have changed: in Jeffrey's day oysters were a common food, and lemons a rarity. Likewise, we now have entirely different standards of living from those of our predecessors – a farm labourer of the present day lives in a manner that his seventeenth-century equivalent would regard as positively palatial.

Nevertheless, some indication of the relative value of the sums mentioned in this book can be obtained by bearing in mind that between thirty and forty-five pounds per year constituted a very substantial wage. Certainly a gentleman with an income of forty-five pounds had no need to work for a living, while a farm labourer earning between five and ten pounds a year would have found it hard to support his family.

*   *   *

There are still many gaps to fill in Jeffrey's story. So much is still supposition or assumption. So much has to be deduced from scraps and fragments. At times, therefore, my quest has been less like biography and more like archaeology, like the piecing together of shattered fragments, the unearthing of a lost portrait.

We know the facts of Jeffrey's life but, without any personal reminiscences, without any letters or diaries, we cannot tell what he was thinking or feeling. In such cases, interpretation and supposition are inevitable, but not, I trust, irresponsible. In all cases, I hope, the suppositions and interpretations are based on facts and contemporary accounts. I have avoided filling the pages with detailed notes and references, but the general sources at the back of the book will tell the reader more about where I have found the information.

In the end, all we have from his own hand is a receipt, signed in his later years, when the glory of life at Court had been overtaken by decades of poverty, imprisonment and neglect.

Not much. But when you understand that piece of paper, when you know what he went through before he came to put his signature to the document, then that simple receipt becomes more significant. Far from being a throwaway scrap, it becomes a mute testimony to one man's courage and perseverance, to his determination to overcome his physical limitations and live life to the full.

Jeffrey Hudson was a remarkable man. And his story deserves to be told.

THE
BUTCHER'S SON

Yet you may find Magnum in Parvo, that great excellency in sundry little things.

The New Yeare's Gift

THE BIG MAN ARRIVED IN OAKHAM IN 1611. Broad-shouldered, or 'of a lusty stature' as he was later described, he was a cheerful man, gregarious and outgoing.

Oakham, the town to which he had come, was the centre of the cattle trade for the tiny county of Rutland, the smallest county in England. Indeed, it was the presence of the cattle that had brought him here, for he was a butcher and slaughterman by trade, and each day he would walk from his meagre cottage, through the town, past the new Butter Cross and into the Shambles, just off the market square.

Every town in England had its Shambles – an area where livestock was slaughtered, carved up and sold – and that in Oakham was no different to those elsewhere. Each Saturday the town had a market, and the Shambles was filled with grunting and lowing and the squeals of animals being herded into their pens, unaware, as yet, of their fate. For the rest of the week, the air was foetid with the stench of blood, the stone streets slippery with gore, the flies buzz-

ing endlessly around the joints of meat hanging in the
slaughterhouses. Standards of hygiene were not impressive.
In an era without refrigeration, and where every street was
little more than an open sewer filled with slops and human
waste, the seventeenth century was a great time to be a fly.

In the shambles, housewives, innkeepers and cooks could
buy the staples of seventeenth-century meat: sides of
mutton, joints of beef, whole veal calves, even a whole kid
for as little as ten pennies. Meat was expensive however;
it had steadily risen in price for years. Many of the poorer
families could not afford so much beef as they would like;
they had to content themselves with sparrows, which could
be had for twopence. A dozen.

The big man soon established himself in the town. He
was poor, it is true; he and his family lived in a one-roomed
cottage that was little more than a hovel, but he was popular and friendly. He was no craftsman or artist, unless you
count it artistry to slit an animal's throat with one swift
movement, or butcher a pig so that not a single part of the
valuable animal is wasted. But he made friends, and even
found a girl to marry. The name of this simple butcher
was John Hudson and on 20 June 1611, he married Mary
Browne in the church of All Saints, Oakham.

We don't know when, exactly, John Hudson came to
Oakham, but he is not mentioned in parish records before
his marriage, and he does not appear to have had family
living in the area; there are no brothers or sisters in the
records and no mention of parents being buried. So he
must have moved into the town from elsewhere. Whatever
the case, he settled down with Mary and, four years later
in June 1615, she gave birth to their first child, Joan. The
birth was evidently difficult, for Mary Hudson died a
month later.

It was not, alas, an unusual occurrence. Death during

childbirth was a common hazard of the seventeenth century, a natural result of poor diet, primitive midwifery and insanitary conditions. Generally speaking, if the birth was not straightforward, then either the mother or child would die. Although the Barber Surgeons Guild started to license surgeons to attend difficult births in 1610, the practice was not widespread and, anyway, even if a surgeon did attend that was no guarantee of success. Caesarean sections were inevitably fatal for the mother, and were in fact only performed to save the child.

More frequently, it was the child who did not survive. The rates of death were appalling. In London and the bigger cities, where disease was rife and conditions squalid, only one in three children survived their first year; those that died in their first month were the chrisom children – so called because they were buried in the chrisom cloth used for their baptism. The chance of a child reaching its fifth year was only about eleven per cent. The net result of this was that few families had more than three children alive at any one time.

In the seventeenth century, whether you were prince or pauper, death was always a close neighbour. The bereft parents or lone spouse might grieve, but the only thing to do was to move on.

With a month-old baby on his hands and no wife, John Hudson was forced to look for a new wife and mother for his child. He found that person in Lucy Royce, whom he married seven months later.

Lucy was a twenty-one-year-old girl from a well-established local family. They married in January 1616, and a few months later Lucy was pregnant. In December 1616 she gave birth to a son, named after his father John and in July 1618, they had a daughter, Annis, who died at birth.

Then on 14 June 1619, a second son was born. Like most children of the time, he was probably christened the day of his birth, in case he did not survive.

They called him Jeffrey.

Every writer, from Fuller onwards, has been keen to point out the coincidence of Jeffrey's birthplace. For the smallest man in England was born in Rutland, the smallest county in the land. Indeed, the county's motto, 'Multum in Parvo' – 'Much in Little' – could sum up Jeffrey's life.

Rutland is still proud of its famous son. Even today, one can walk through Oakham and see 'the Dwarf's Cottage', the house in which, reputedly, Jeffrey was born. It is a small thatched cottage on a busy road. With its tiny windows and doors it looks the ideal setting for the birth of a dwarf; it's just a shame that the place has probably nothing to do with Jeffrey.

There are a number of reasons for rejecting the identification. The first, and perhaps most compelling, is that the house is not mentioned until the twentieth century. The earliest reference to it I can find is in a Rutland publication of around 1910 where it is described as being 'opposite the White Lion Hotel'. (The home of another famous Oakham man, Titus Oates, is described in another early twentieth-century publication as being 'opposite the Crown Hotel'. It was a happy coincidence for the nineteenth-century Rutland tourist industry that both of their birthplaces should be so close to hotels.)

The house was probably chosen because of its low ceilings. However, as we have seen, Jeffrey's father was a big man, so it is hardly likely that he would have chosen this house in which to live. In fact, it is hardly likely he would have been able to afford this house. For what we think of today as 'typical' seventeenth-century cottages were originally dwellings for the relatively well-off, and were generally beyond the means of poor working folk.

Jeffrey was born into a far more humble dwelling. Despite his appointment by the Duke, John was by no means prosperous. He was described as 'a person of very mean condition'. He died a pauper and Fuller says that Jeffrey was originally 'one degree above rags'. His birth-place would therefore not have been the picture-book country cottage of 'Olde England'. Far more likely it was a one-room hovel, a roughly built dwelling with a single room, the house-room, where the family ate, drank, slept and played. If his father had prospered then he might have added another room on the side, an 'outshut' which might be used as a buttery or larder, or if it were bigger partitioned off with pieces of cloth into sleeping cubicles.

John Hudson and his family were poor. Perhaps his trade would have given him some access to cheap meat, but for the most part poor families existed mainly on soups, broths, rye or barley bread and cheese. If they were better off they might have some chickens or a pig, or maybe even a cow housed in a barn attached to the house.

A little while after Jeffrey's birth, a buzz went round the town. The country house that overlooked Oakham, the great hunting lodge of Burley on the Hill, had been sold. And the new buyer was George Villiers, Duke of Buckingham, the most powerful man in the land. Burley cost Villiers a lot of money – some twenty-one thousand pounds – but financial matters did not worry him, for he was the star of the moment, a parvenu and adventurer who in a short time had become the favourite of King James I.

From the moment Villiers appeared at Court he made an impact. His first introduction into favour was from 'the handsomeness of his person', wrote Clarendon, whose pen-portrait of Buckingham remains the most perceptive. 'His ascent was so quick, that it seemed rather a flight than a growth ... as if he had been born a favourite, he was supreme the first month he came to Court.'

The King was besotted with the young man. He would hang his arms around his beloved 'Steenie', as he called Villiers, slobbering him with kisses and scandalizing the whole Court with his behaviour. Whether the relationship was physically consummated in any way is not clear, but it was obviously homoerotic.

'The love the King showed was as amorously conveyed as if he had mistaken their sex ...' wrote Osborne. 'For the King's kissing them after so lascivious a model ... prompted many to imagine some things done in the tyring-house that exceed my expressions no less than they do my experience.'

In rapid succession Villiers became Gentleman of the Bedchamber, Knight of the Order of the Garter, a Baron, Viscount, an Earl, a Marquis and finally Duke of Buckingham. He married the daughter of the Earl of Rutland, a charming girl who brought with her a considerable dowry.

His ascent disgusted veterans of Elizabeth's court. In 1611 Lord Howard wrote a letter to Sir John Harington lamenting the decline of the learned and artistic courtier and the rise of the mere 'favourite'. If Harington was to receive advancement at Court, Howard told him, he must learn to lie, to praise the King's latest favourite (or even his favourite horse), to agree, if necessary, that 'the moon shineth all summer'.

Alas, Harington never learnt the skills. He died a bankrupt man and George Villiers, the favourite of favourites, bought his house at Burley on the Hill.

*　　*　　*

Burley was the Duke's country retreat. The real business of his life went on in London and it was there that Villiers spent most of his time. But during the hunting season the house came into its own. Standing a mile above the county town of Oakham, surrounded by woods and rivers and fertile land, it was ideally placed to offer guests a wide range of entertainment. They could walk in the gardens and admire the rare plants which the Duke's gardener, the famous John Tradescant, had collected from throughout the world. They could ride any of the forty horses in the superb stable block, a building which Fuller was to describe as 'the best accommodated in England'. Guests could go hunting hares on nearby Empingham Heath, or deer in nearby woods. Inside the walls of the park, there were even more activities on offer, from fishing in the artificial ponds to playing bowls on the bowling green.

James Wright described the park:

Those who love exercise and healthy game,
For chase, or flight, or of what other Name,
Meet here those manly sports in such excess,
Envy herself must certainly confess,
This single park may with some Forests vie,
As well for Store as for Variety.
What Admiration to the place is due,
That's a vast garden for its pleasing view,
And for its game a little forest too.

Buckingham's guests were members of the nobility, used to the attractions of London, where there were plays and tournaments and all manner of spectacles. So when they came to Burley, the Duke, with his love of hospitality, was determined that they should not find the entertainment lacking. Along with the hunting, fishing and riding, the

Duke introduced one of his favourite pastimes, bull-baiting. And the person ordered to arrange the spectacle – to select the bull and recruit the participants – was Jeffrey's father, John Hudson.

Bull-baiting – where dogs attack a bull – was one of the most popular spectator sports of the time. James I, Buckingham's lord and master, disapproved of the sport; he forbade bull-baiting on Sundays, and made great attempts to discourage it altogether, but obviously the King's favourite, like the majority of the country, had no such scruples and bull-baiting became a regular feature of the entertainment for his guests.

The event was simple enough: a rope was tied around the root of the bull's horns and tethered to an iron ring fixed to a stake, effectively limiting the bull to a space of about thirty feet in diameter.

The bull-wards – who were, like John Hudson, usually butchers – then released their dogs one at a time. The dogs were the original British 'bulldogs', working dogs, owned by the butchers and used during slaughtering to catch and throw down refractory cattle. They were stocky and powerful and their jaws possessed a legendary grip.

Each dog would be released in turn. The bull was not supposed to gore his attacker – indeed, bulls whose horns were considered too sharp were given a wooden or metal sheath. Instead the poor animal tried to get his horns under the attacking dog and toss or 'hike' the dog into the air, when it might be injured or break its neck in the fall.

To protect his animal, the owner would run to get underneath the dog and bend down, offering his own broad back as a cushion to the injured dog. Bulldogs, unless completely stunned or otherwise injured, would then return to the fray. 'Unless he is totally stunned with the fall,' wrote one observer, the dog was 'sure to crawl again towards the bull, come on't what will.'

The dog would try to clamp its jaws on to the hapless bull – usually on the nose. Once a dog's jaws were clamped they did not open. No matter how the poor bull raged and bellowed and thrashed, the dog would not loose its grip. Either the flesh would be bitten off, or the owners would have to lever the dog's jaws open with a cudgel. Sometimes, to increase the fun, the bull was hung with squibs – small fireworks – which were let off just as the dog attacked.

In the end the bull would die through loss of blood and other injuries. Naturally, the participants being butchers, the animal was then cut up and either sold or served at a feast. The meat was much valued, as a line in the seventeenth-century play *A Rogue Well Basted* shows: 'Trust me, I have a conscience as tender as a stake from a baited bull.'

The meat may have been tender, but the suffering was cruel; suffering on both sides, for the dogs would be horribly injured by their falls, the bulls terribly maimed by the relentless jaws of the dogs. Occasionally a bull would break its shackles and burst into the crowd causing further injury and death. It was a horrific spectacle, yet it remained a favourite spectator sport for many years. Kings, queens, princesses all attended. Not until 1835 was effective legislation brought in to defeat it, but even then bull-baitings continued in some areas, finally dying out in the 1840s.

John Hudson's job as the bull-ward was to select the bulls, to choose animals that would give 'good sport'. A cowardly animal would die too quickly, a mean-spirited bull might hurt too many dogs. Particularly good performers might be kept for several baitings. Occasionally a trial baiting took place the night before the main event, to test the animal's demeanour. The important thing was the spectacle, and that was John Hudson's responsibility. He was a showman, an organizer, a slaughterman strong enough to catch his bulldog on his back after the poor creature was tossed.

By the latter half of 1620 it must have started to become apparent that Jeffrey was different. John and Lucy Hudson probably did not notice anything immediately; Jeffrey was, after all, perfectly proportioned. Perhaps he was small – one account implies that he was born 'beforehand', that is prematurely – but it was probably not until he started to grow – or rather *not* to grow – that his parents noticed there was anything different about him.

He remained tiny. He survived the first year, but he did not grow, at least not at the rate of other children. Happy, healthy, alert and intelligent, he might have been; but he was not growing.

To the seventeenth-century writers Jeffrey Hudson was a marvel, a miracle of nature, one of the wonders of the age. They marvelled at the disparity between his size and that of his parents. They came up with the most remarkable theories to explain his birth.

Henry Stonecastle, for example, tells us that Jeffrey's mother had 'an uncommon straitness in her throat' which caused her to choke on a pickled gherkin. 'This happening about the time of her pregnancy,' writes Stonecastle, 'some thought this smaller kind of that Fruit might, through sympathy, or other influence of the Imagination have some Effect on the Infant, not to mention certain other reasons that were offer'd from the sourness of the Pickle itself, vinegar being, as all know, a very great Astringent.'

'It seems that families sometimes are chequered, as in brains so in bulk,' writes Thomas Fuller, the earliest of his biographers, and that is the truth. To the seventeenth-century enquirer there was no reason to it, just the simple fact. A big father had sired a tiny son. Today Jeffrey's condition is far more easily identifiable and, with injections, curable. It was not a case of choking on cucumbers or the astringency of vinegar. Jeffrey suffered from growth-hormone deficiency.

In most cases of dwarfism the condition is one of skeletal dysplasia, where the trunk is normal size, but the limbs are extremely short. Typically the individual is disproportionately shaped, often with a larger than normal head. With growth-hormone deficiency the person's head, trunk, and limbs are in the same proportion, but the overall stature is small. The problem is caused by either a deficient or a totally non-functioning pituitary gland, the organ which releases the growth hormone.

Nowadays the condition is treatable by injections of the necessary growth hormone, but even today it is not certain what causes it. Certainly many hypopituitaristic dwarfs have suffered problems during or before the birth; perhaps Jeffrey was starved of oxygen, particularly likely if he was 'beforehand'.

Jeffrey was wholly proportionate and very good-looking. Like many hypopituitaristic dwarfs he was a little tubby – the condition often results in extra abdominal fat – but most of his appeal lay in the fact that he was a perfect 'little man'. Thomas Fuller describes him: 'He was, without any deformity, wholly proportionable, whereas often dwarfs, pigmies in one part, are giants in another.'

While Thomas Heywood, who must have seen Jeffrey at Court describes him as 'one of the prettiest, neatest, and well-proportioned small men that ever Nature bred, or was ever seene, or heard of beyond the memory of man.'

Whatever the cause, growth failure is usually noticeable by the end of the first year. At that time Jeffrey must have stopped almost completely, for the thing that made everyone stare, the factor that made Jeffrey a 'wonder', was his remarkable size. He was astonishingly tiny; by the age of seven he was no more than eighteen inches high.

It seems incredible, but the key point to remember is that height can be verified. We patronize the past. In our age of science we tend to look on all previous ages as fundamentally ignorant. So it is easy to think that the observers of the time must have been mistaken, that his height was a mere fable, a tale spun by a century which wholeheartedly believed in witches and goblins, in unicorns and mermaids. Whilst the seventeenth century had more than its share of credulous minds, they did, at least, know how to measure. While many men clung to a belief in alchemy and sorcery, they also built fine houses and powerful ships. They constructed ornate and intricate stage machinery, built siege engines and artillery, bridges and roads, all of which required precise and accurate measurement.

Jeffrey's height was verifiable. Indeed there are at least two independent witnesses to Jeffrey's height; the first is given by Fuller in his *Worthies* in 1662. Fuller cites 'credible persons then and there present, and still alive' for his evidence as to Jeffrey's height, even giving a name: John Armstrong of Cheshunt.

The second reference comes from a letter written in 1629, where the writer refers to 'sesquipedalian Jeffrey'. Sesquipedal means, literally, a foot and a half. Although the word later came to mean 'long words', this cannot be the meaning here. For a start, when the writer was writing about Jeffrey, the boy was only ten, hardly an age when one is likely to be using a huge vocabulary. No, the meaning is clear. The letter-writer may not have known Jeffrey, but he knew his reputation; he knew that the boy was supposed to be only eighteen inches tall.

Wright, too, the only biographer who actually knew and spoke to Jeffrey, records that he was 'above seven years old and scarce 18 inches in highth'.

There have, after all, been other instances. Demaillet, a consul at Cairo, claimed to have measured a dwarf of the same height as Jeffrey. Virrey, in his *Dictionnaire des Sciences*, tells of a German girl only eighteen inches high, and she was nine, two years older than Jeffrey when his size was first documented. And whilst there are no recent instances, part of that may be because humans generally are now taller than their ancestors.

Was he really that tiny? Today we have no real way of knowing. But had he been markedly taller, then even in the seventeenth century the fable would surely have been exposed, for the Court was full of men with enough education to reveal the truth.

He must, therefore; at the very least have been close to the height, and, given the witnesses and the references, there is every possibility that the fable was true; that Jeffrey by the age of seven had only reached some eighteen inches in height. He was sesquipedalian Jeffrey: a foot and a half, no more.

There was another rumour about how Jeffrey came to be so small – a more disquieting piece of gossip than gherkins and vinegar. Stonecastle writes:

> Tis thought the parents were cunning enough to humour the caprice of nature in this diminutive production by Art, either in the dress of the child, as the Chinese women acquire little feet; or else in his diet as our Ladies stint the growth of their Lap-Dogs, in order, I suppose, to make a penny out of him when he grew old enough by showing him about in a Box or Bird-Cage.

There were many ways that they could have gone about this. As Stonecastle says, they might have put him in tight clothes or bandages. His diet would have been meagre enough anyway.

They might even have used more esoteric, not to say quack approaches, applying traditional 'magical' treatments. A work entitled *Miscellanea Curiosa, Medica, Physicam* published at Leipzig in 1670 tells of a way of dwarfing men by rubbing their backbones in their infancy with the grease of moles, bats and dormice.

Of course, this is probably nothing more than a cruel rumour. But it is true that, later in life, there was a coldness between Jeffrey and his father. Fuller cites it as proof of Jeffrey's pride, implying that if he could grow big no other way, he had at least grown too big for his boots. But maybe there is another explanation. Perhaps if your parents treated you as another bull to be tied up before the Duke, there is a reason for this coldness.

John Hudson, after all, provided his patron – the Duke – with animals to provide a spectacle. Here, perhaps, was something he could display, something he could show. Here was a 'freak of nature' that could be turned to value. Even if they did treat the child in some way to discourage growth, that does not imply a coldness or callousness but a recognition of the harsh realities. Perhaps John was merely recognizing that Jeffrey's very future lay in being 'different', that his only real option for survival lay in literally making an exhibition of himself. This, after all, was an era when 'naturals' – those people we would describe as having learning difficulties – often ended up in the roles of fools or jesters at the big houses. It was a time when the mentally ill and the inhabitants of asylums were routinely seen as sources of laughter and entertainment.

For a dwarf – certainly one of Jeffrey's size – the future

was pretty much assured and the chances are that, from very early on in his life, he would have been 'displayed'. Certainly by the age of six or seven he would have been expected to make a contribution to the family coffers. In poorer families, most children of this age were considered old enough to start learning an 'arte'. This might mean working the fields, or even engaging in some form of manufacturing: the children in Norwich, for example, were employed knitting socks for rich Londoners to buy. How was an eighteen-inch-high child going to help the family in any practical way, except by earning a few pennies at country fairs and markets? By the time he was old enough, he would have been taken along to one of Oakham's annual fairs – on the feast of St Mark the Evangelist or the eve of the feast of St John the Baptist – and he would probably have climbed up on a table and danced or sung or simply stood there while the locals laughed and those from out of town gaped in astonishment.

Jeffrey was eventually to become a 'wonder' at Court, but had he not ended up on display in London, he would have just become a curiosity among the fairgoers in the provinces. The fairs were venues not only for the sale of goods, trinkets and livestock, but for displays of 'freaks' and 'rarities'. They were a kind of cross between a country market and a circus, full of people like Jeffrey: the different, the outlandish, the downright weird.

Bartholomew Fair was the most famous, the most popular fair in England; here curious customers could see such things as 'a child with 3 legs' or 'the Indian King' – a tall Negro who had previously been a slave. They could marvel at 'a tall englishman eight feet high, and but seventeen years of age'; they could see a man with one head and two bodies (or, if they preferred it, 'a woman with one body & two heads, one above the other').

And they could always see dwarfs. Frequently the little people were caged like animals, like the Italian who was 'not above a cubit high' (that is eighteen inches) and carried about in a parrot's cage. Another, 'a Frenchman of Limosin', used to be brought out in his cage, from which he would emerge to play an instrument.

Dwarfs, with their air of mystery, of 'otherness', were often displayed as changelings, tapping into the seventeenth-century belief that sometimes the fairies stole human children and left fairy children or 'changelings' in their place. At Bartholomew Fair in the late seventeenth century was displayed a creature described as 'a little farey woman, lately came from italy, being but two foot two inches high, and in no way deformed'.

It is difficult not to believe that had things turned out differently for Jeffrey, he would have been advertised in broadsheets and hand-outs as a little 'farey man', that he would have been carried about in a cage, a miraculous changeling, only eighteen inches high and 'in no way deformed'.

The birth of Jeffrey was followed two years later by another son, Samuel. They played together, these two – even though the younger brother quickly outgrew his elder sibling. Whilst later in life they cannot have had much contact, Samuel remained Jeffrey's closest relative.

Samuel was followed in 1624 by Theophilus who was to die when he was just eighteen. This then was his family: half-sister Joan, brothers John, Samuel and Theophilus. This up until the age of seven was all that he knew.

But 1626 was to be a year of dramatic change for Jeffrey; a year which would see him leave Oakham and find himself adopted into another, far greater family.

THE
DUKE'S GIFT

He is one of the prettiest, neatest, and well-proportioned small men that ever Nature bred, or was ever seene, or heard of beyond the memory of man . . .

Thomas Heywood, *The Three Wonders*

PRETTY SOON, NEWS OF THE BOY SPREAD AROUND THE district and when he was just seven, he was summoned to Burley. The Duchess of Buckingham wanted to see for herself.

Wright records that 'Being above seven years old and scarce 18 inches in highth, he was taken to the Family of the late Duke of Buckingham at Burly on the Hill, in this county, as a Rarity of Nature.'

Fuller, likewise, tells us that he was first presented to the Duchess.

Thus it was that his parents dressed him up in his best clothes, such as they were, and he and his father walked the mile up the hill to the great house. From the first, Katharine, Duchess of Buckingham, was entranced. She offered John a place for his son in her household. The clothes on his back would be replaced by velvets and satins

and silks. Two servants would attend to all his needs.
Above all, he would live in the great hall, in Burley on the
Hill. No more cold nights in the butcher's cottage. No
more frugal broths and dry bread. There really was no
choice. Whatever Jeffrey thought about it all – and there
is no indication that he ever regretted the decision – the
best move for the boy would be to leave his home. John
Hudson agreed, so Jeffrey left his family in Oakham and
moved into the big house.

It must have seemed another world for the butcher's son
from the town at the bottom of the hill. With footmen to
attend on him, dressed in specially designed livery, in
Fuller's words, 'Instantly Jeffery was heightened (not in
stature) but in condition, from one degree above rags into
silk and satin, and two tall men to attend him.'

Fuller is making a comic effect; throughout his portrait
of Jeffrey there runs the theme of the little man with high
aspirations, but there is no doubt that Jeffrey's status was
completely altered. Life as part of the Burley household
would have been utterly different to his life in Oakham.
Here there were no cramped conditions. He had a room
of his own, no chores to attend to, no duties to perform.
He was on display, it is true, but there was a big difference
between dancing in front of the Duchess and dancing on
a table at the local fair.

In the end he was not to stay at Burley for long. The
only mention of any incident from his time in service at
Burley is a rather gruesome and incredible story. It was
recounted by Stonecastle in his 1732 *Universal Spectator*
article, and tells how some wags stole an old woman's cat
called Rutterkin, killed and flayed it and dressed Jeffrey in
the skin. When the old woman offered her cat a piece of
cheese, Jeffrey is supposed to have answered 'Rutterkin
can help himself when he is hungry' and ran off downstairs.

The woman was accused of being a witch and having a talking cat, before the truth emerged.

It is a ludicrous and slightly repulsive story. Even at his smallest, Jeffrey would not have been able to fit in the skin of a cat. Whilst it is true that the period was rife with stories of sorcery and there was a widespread belief in the witch and her familiars, it is difficult to imagine how anyone could be fooled by a dwarf in a cat costume. However, like so much of Jeffrey's story, once the myth was printed it found its way into subsequent histories. Whether Stonecastle invented it himself, or whether it had become a local legend in Oakham is impossible to say. But it probably never happened.

Other than that, there is no record of Jeffrey's brief stay at Burley, for as soon as he had arrived he was to move on. The Duke of Buckingham soon got to hear of this rarity of nature. And he had other plans for the seven-year-old-boy.

In late 1626, George Villiers, Duke of Buckingham, was in a difficult position. Hugely unpopular with the people, he was in danger of being impeached by Parliament and sent for trial in the House of Lords.

Villiers's problem was that the skills he needed were not the skills he possessed. His real skill lay in being a 'favourite', indeed, he was so good at this that he achieved the unprecedented feat of being a favourite under two successive monarchs. James I had always doted on his 'Steenie' (even though wagging tongues claimed that his appeal was diminishing by the end), but James's son, Charles, came to rely on the Duke every bit as much as his father. Charles was a shy, stumbling boy, aloof and remote and as refined as his father had been coarse. Lonely and distant from those around him, Buckingham was his only real friend, the only person he could confide in.

In many ways it was an unfortunate choice, for although Villiers excelled at being a favourite, virtually everything else he attempted – every attempt to move beyond that role – resulted in disaster.

The half-baked plan to go to Spain and negotiate a marriage with the King of Spain's daughter ended in ignominious rebuttal. His foreign policy only succeeded in isolating England and making an enemy of both Spain *and* France. His declaration of support for the High Church alienated the Puritans and his failings as Lord High Admiral enraged Parliament. He was a favourite at Court, but everyone else hated him.

In the end, Parliament decided to impeach Buckingham on charges ranging from embezzlement to ineptitude. For good measure they even threw in a hint that he might have poisoned his old master King James. The threat was real, but Buckingham remained confident. Let them show their jealousy; he retained the unwavering support of the King. Buckingham understood that others would be jealous – that went with the territory. For there was only ever room for one favourite, and that man must be prepared to make any sacrifice, offer total obedience and dedication. Always be there for your master. And always, always, watch your back.

By 1626 the Duke's back was in real danger. He was, as ever, in need of money to finance his lavish lifestyle, art collecting and house improvements. The army and navy were near rioting because their wages had not been paid. Several soldiers even broke into his house and confronted him, forcing him to place an armed guard at the gates. The fleet was lying at Gravesend, running out of supplies.

To counter this he decided to do what all good English statesmen have done when their popularity runs low; he attacked the French. The problem with this policy – one of the *many* problems with this policy – was that attacking the French meant going to war with the Queen's brother.

Princess Henrietta Maria of France married King Charles of England in May 1625. She was a tiny girl, accomplished at dancing and madly enthusiastic about the theatre. Despite the fact that she was a Catholic, most people seemed pleased with the match, and she was universally praised for her poise and good looks. (Well, not quite universally; her niece once said that her teeth protruded from her mouth like guns from a fortress.) Her English subjects, with their usual insularity, found her foreign name impossible to pronounce and settled for calling her Queen Mary.

It soon became clear, however, that 'Queen Mary' was, like her sixteenth-century namesake, an ardent, even zealous Catholic. Charles and his advisers had expected her to be discreet about her faith, but she regarded herself as a sort of Catholic crusader, a guardian angel sent to rally English Catholics to the cause and to initiate a Counter-Reformation. Her mother, the strong-willed and wrong-headed Marie de Medici, had instilled in her fifteen-year-old daughter a belief in her destiny, an underlying stubbornness, and an almost complete inability to recognize when she was out of her depth.

It was not long before she and the Duke were in direct competition for the favours of the King. This conflict eventually boiled over in the matter of the number of French people at her Court.

The marriage agreement stipulated that Henrietta Maria was to be allowed sixty French members of her household. Somehow she had managed to bring over the slightly higher number of four hundred and fifty, sixty of whom were priests. They were costing the country two hundred and forty pounds per day.

It was not merely the numbers either, but the way in which they behaved. Her confessor had a shouting match with the King's chaplain over who was to say grace before the meals. When a Protestant ceremony was being held, the Queen and several of her ladies had loudly and ostentatiously walked through the congregation, laughing and talking. She behaved, in short, like what she was: a spoilt teenager.

Worst of all, she was advised not to attend the King's coronation on the grounds that it was part of the heretical rites of the Anglican Church. She watched the King enter the abbey from a window in a nearby building. This act, more than any other, was to come to haunt her, for she was never in fact crowned. From that time on she was perceived by many of her Protestant subjects as an enemy. By 1626, the marriage had descended into a drawn-out series of petty squabbles. At its absolute lowest, the French ambassador was called in to settle an argument over whether or not it was raining.

The culminating row led to her isolation. On 1 August 1626, Charles sent for the Queen who refused to come, pleading a toothache. Charles, accompanied by the entire Privy Council, angrily marched to her chambers to find the Queen slumped on a chair with her servants 'unreverently dancing and cavorting in her presence'. After abruptly expelling her attendants, he told the Queen that he was going to send all of her French servants back to France, 'for the good of herself and the nation'. Henrietta Maria sobbed throughout his lecture, and then flung herself on her knees and begged him not to send them all away. He refused. She rushed to the window and smashed the glass with her bare hands, screaming to her unhappy servants as they were filing away. Charles pursued her, and dragged her away from the window with such force that she tore her gown and bruised and cut her hands. Her women howled and wailed, but were pushed out of the door by the King's yeomen and the door was locked after them. Henrietta Maria shut herself away, weeping so uncontrollably that some thought she would cry herself to death.

The whole affair is more akin to a father scolding his adolescent daughter. Which is hardly surprising for that is what Henrietta Maria was. It took another month for the French entourage to leave. On the day of their departure, they still refused to go, because they did not think the departure was being performed 'with proper punctilio'. Heralds and trumpeters were sent, along with yeomen to throw them out bodily if necessary. In a remarkable show of ingratitude, the departing servants pilfered most of Henrietta Maria's wardrobe as well as trying to embezzle the King for monies they claimed to have spent on the Queen's behalf. Henrietta's chief chaplain was allowed to leave London at midnight to escape the ridicule of the mob. Masses of Londoners turned out to watch the French depart. The Queen was left with a lady-in-waiting, a nurse, four dressers and a priest.

Isolated and alone, trapped in a loveless marriage, the young girl surrounded herself with pets – monkeys, dogs, birds – animals that would give her the affection she so desperately craved.

She certainly felt that the King was lacking in all tenderness towards her. His love, his affection was centred on Buckingham, who from the first regarded Henrietta Maria as at best an irritation and at worst a rival. In the first few months of her marriage, he treated her with a marked disrespect, continually reminding her that he held the real power, and even warning the poor girl that he could make her the unhappiest woman in the world. He told her 'to beware how she behaved, for in England queens had had their heads cut off before now'. He took advantage of the bad advice her French advisers had given her since she entered the country and used her youthful naïveté against her.

The in-laws were soon involved. The formidable Marie de Medici wrote to say that she had not been so upset since the assassination of her husband. Her son the King sent over a special ambassador, Marshal de Bassompierre.

Bassompierre was magnificently diplomatic and impartial. He listened to both the King's and Queen's sides of the story, in fact to all three sides of the story, for Buckingham had his say as well. Bassompierre managed to bring about some change in the relationships. He chided the Queen for 'picking a quarrel', and brought in Buckingham who, according to Bassompierre's own account, 'made his peace with her which I had brought about with infinite trouble'. The King, too, was reconciled to his young wife.

It didn't last, of course, and within a fortnight Henrietta Maria had fallen out again with both parties. But Bassompierre persevered and over subsequent months there is evidence of a change in the relationship between Henrietta Maria and the Duke of Buckingham. They were never friends but, in the latter part of 1626, there is evidence that the Queen was growing up a little, and the Duke was making an effort.

While in part this was due to the influence of Bassompierre, in part it must also have been driven by Buckingham's own needs, for by late 1626 he needed all the supporters he could get. And he could afford to be magnanimous – after all the Queen had lost the battle over the servants. She was in a weak position now. Perhaps it was time to reconsider his alliances. Perhaps it was time for a charm offensive.

He managed to get the King to reinstate some of her

exiled staff. A letter dated 11 November 1626 tells how 'The Duke . . . hath, on the Queen's behalf, obtained from the King the readmission of twelve French priests, and chamberlain, and some other officers to attend her.' Another letter puts the figure at 'ten French priests, with a bishop, or supervisor, and lord Chamberlain, a secretary, two ladies of the bedchamber, two maids of honour, and one Frenchman in every office to be readmitted.'

Above all, Buckingham decided to do what he did best. He would stage a series of banquets, not only for the King and Queen, but also for the new French ambassador. They would be lavish and luxurious. They would show Bassompierre that everything was really all right. The Queen would be showered with gifts, there would be plays and pageants, music and marvels. Yes, marvels; had not his wife recently acquired one of these? A dwarf, a tiny boy only eighteen inches high. What better present for the Queen with her monkeys and her dogs than a little human, all of her own?

The date and place of Jeffrey's presentation to the Queen is a matter of conjecture. We know that by Christmas 1626 Jeffrey Hudson was at Denmark House, the home of the Queen. Wright records that he was presented to the Queen when he was 'above seven years old', which would place us after June 1626. He states also that the presentation was at Burley on the Hill, but there are no records of the Court being at Burley during 1626.

The nearest they reached was Wellingborough, where the King and Queen stayed during the summer of 1626. London was infected with the plague and the Queen, as she was to do throughout her life, decided to take a dose of spa waters. They stayed near the spa called the 'Red Well', sleeping in three sumptuous marquees set out in the meadows nearby. However, this was at a low point in the relationship, when the trouble over the Queen's servants was brewing. It is hard to imagine Buckingham giving her any kind of present at this stage.

The Duke himself does not seem to have been at Burley, save for a fleeting visit. With Parliament in London, with all the business over the Queen's household and with the preparation of plans to make war on the French, it seems unlikely that he left the capital for more than a few days at a time.

Fuller does not give the place of his presentation. Stonecastle writes unhelpfully 'whether about this time the Court was in progress at Burly or the Duke's Family at London is not very material'.

What we do know is that during the early part of November 1626, the Duke of Buckingham threw a series of banquets at his London home, York House. York House was perhaps the most magnificent private house in Europe. It had originally been the London home of Francis Bacon, before the Chancellor's fall from grace, and had then been granted by James I to Buckingham. Villiers had spent a fortune on the house, turning it into a palace fit for a King. Today, all trace of the house has vanished, save for the Water Gate (which stands rather forlornly behind Charing Cross Station) and the street names: Villiers Street and Buckingham Street.

Given such sumptuous surroundings, the entertainment had a lot to live up to. But Buckingham did not let his guests down. The banqueters were 'entertained royally with plays and desports'; the food was the finest in the land, the guests of honour were showered with gifts.

And one of these 'gifts', the strangest gift of all, was a little man. If the King and Queen did not go to Burley, then Jeffrey must have come to them. Probably, therefore, it was in early November 1626 that Jeffrey boarded one of the Duke's coaches at the door of Burley on the Hill and began the long journey to London.

The journey took several days. From Burley, the coach would have taken Jeffrey and other members of the Duke's family and household to Stamford and then south, down the Great North Road until the coaches crested the hill and entered the village of Hampstead. There below them in the distance was London.

London at this time was still two towns, 'the City' and Westminster, the two joined by a narrow thread of roadways along which lay some of the greatest houses in the land. Hampstead, Highgate and Hackney were all still villages and the church of St Martin-in-the-Fields was literally still that – a church surrounded by pastures and market gardens. It was still a green place where it was possible to wander in the countryside whilst enjoying a view of the Tower.

To a boy from rural Rutland, however, the spectacle must have been astonishing. As the coaches paused among the windmills of Hampstead, there was the city spread out before him. Small spires and steeples studded the view. Smoke rose steadily from the thousands of chimneys. To the east the pale cube of the Tower surrounded by turrets and walls; to the west the distant Abbey of Westminster, separated from the city by green fields and the gardens of great houses. And straight ahead, the massive bulk of St Paul's, surrounded by houses, which clustered against it in their thousands, washing up against the cathedral like waves against the rocks.

It is difficult now to imagine the size of the original St Paul's. The building was one and a half times the length of the current one and its original spire was over one hundred and fifty feet higher than the existing dome. It was in many ways the heart of the city, not only in religious terms, but in social terms as well. It was a meeting place for the city, where all day, every day, a great deal of serious business was conducted. Porters and carriers of ale, beer, bread and other foods took a short cut through the aisles, drunkards lay sleeping on the floor, some had even gone so far as to set up shops within the church. Dekker mentions booksellers, as well as seamstresses and 'the new tobacco office'. Parts of the vault were occupied by a carpenter and a wine cellar, houses were built against the outer walls and for a small fee the bell-ringers allowed tourists to climb the tower to shout and throw small stones at the passers-by. It was even the scene of shows and exhibitions, such as when a Dutchman climbed to the top of the weathercock and waved a banner. The strangest event surely was when a man called Bankes led his horse Marocco to the top of the tower in 1600. The horse could count and Bankes eventually took it to Paris and Rome. Tragically, in Rome both he and the horse were burnt for witchcraft. As Ben Jonson observed, 'he had better stayed at home'.

Beyond the huge bulk of St Pauls was the Thames, alive with boatmen and ships. It was spanned by a single bridge – London Bridge – heavy with houses and shops of all shapes and sizes. In the centre of the bridge, glinting in the pale November light, was the gilded splendour of Nonsuch House, composed entirely of fantastically carved wood which was said to have been brought from Holland and assembled entirely by means of wooden pegs. Its golden turrets were crowned with domes and surmounted by gilt weathercocks.

Beyond the river were the boroughs of Lambeth and Southwark, where the traveller could make out the flags fluttering on top of the cylindrical theatres and bear-pits of the south bank.

For a boy who had never been beyond his little town it must have been as if all the houses in the world had suddenly swum into his vision. Where he came from there was only one church, one noble house. Here there were hundreds of churches and anyone who was anyone had a palace.

It was the greatest city in the world. Andrew Boorde called London 'a city which excelleth all others ... For Constantinople, Venice, Rome, Florence cannot be compared to London.'

It was to be Jeffrey's home for the next fifteen years.

From Hampstead, the coaches descended the hill until they eventually arrived in the narrow streets of the city, passing along the Strand until they reached their destination: York House, London home of the Duke of Buckingham. The main gate to York House stood on the south side of the Strand, where carriages wheeled in to a fine walled courtyard. Ahead of them stood the house itself, a tall, stately, rectangular building with two towers at the east end.

The exterior was magnificent enough, but it was the interior which made all visitors stop and stare. It was more like a palace than a house, for everywhere there were fine pictures and beautiful statues. Buckingham, like Charles I, was a passionate collector of art. His agent Nicholas Gerbier wrote to him that 'out of all the amateurs and Princes and Kings there is not one who has collected in forty years as many pictures as your excellency has collected in five'. His gallery had, according to Rubens, the finest collection of pictures he had ever seen. The walls were rich with tapestries and golden with fine carvings. There were busts and statues from ancient Rome; in the garden stood the statue of Cain and Abel by John de Bolognas which was given by the King of Spain to Charles, who passed it on to his favourite. The ceilings of the rooms were by the Court painter Orazio Gentileschi. In the ceiling of the Duke's private apartments was a huge panel by Rubens, showing Buckingham being taken into the Temple of Virtue by the Goddesses of Wisdom and Fame, while 'Envy' attempted to grab his heel and pull him down. Even in his private moments, the Duke never forgot the danger of envy and malice.

Jeffrey was probably taken through to the back of the great hall, where the plans for the banquet were being finalized. From the banqueting room above he would have heard the sound of hammering and sawing as workmen finished the special effects which would entertain the guests. Seamstresses and tailors were busy making costumes, and wig-makers brought specially prepared wigs for fittings. This was going to be a feast to remember.

The master of ceremonies was there, ordering and arranging, fine-tuning the special displays for tonight's meal. The boy was probably given a costume such as a soldier's uniform with a bright, shiny breastplate, a tiny helmet surmounted by a plume, a sword and a tiny banner. Finally it was four o'clock. Distantly, Jeffrey could hear the trumpets perform a fanfare. The guests of honour had arrived and the feast was about to begin.

Buckingham's banquets were legendary. He might be inept as a military commander and foolish as a statesman, but he was a superb host. The trumpets sounded. The King and Queen came through the doors. Behind them, the Duke and Bassompierre, the French ambassador. They crossed the room to the raised dais where they were to sit.

The trumpets blared again and the noise dwindled to a hush. The curtains at the end of the room drew back to reveal a huge backdrop, painted with the blue of the sky;

against it, high up, were large clouds of white muslin. From behind the scenes came the sound of machinery, the creaking of ropes and pulleys, and slowly the clouds began to descend.

They lowered to the ground, stopped and then, from behind them, to the applause and wonder of the diners, emerged servants with the first dishes. It was a masterpiece of theatricality. Buckingham, it seemed, was serving his guests the food of the gods.

Throughout the evening, every 'service' or course was delivered, as it were, from above, with the clouds rising and lowering. As a letter-writer described it the following Saturday: 'Last Sunday at night, the duke's grace entertained their majesties and the French ambassador at York House with great feasting and show, where all things came down in clouds . . .'

The meal was as sumptuous as ever. The 'sallets' of green leaves and vegetables were followed by fricasees of eggs, bacon, beef or young pork. There were Tansies – strange concoctions of scrambled egg, the juices of wheat blades, violets, strawberry leaves, spinach and walnut buds, plus breadcrumbs, cinnamon, nutmeg and salt. Each guest sprinkled his Tansy with sugar before eating. Every table had a mix of sweet and savoury in each course, a range of different dishes, each brought to the table in an ascending order of merit.

As the evening wore on, the clouds moved again and again, each time bringing new delights. There were cooked meats, in broths and stews, and 'Carbonardoes', barbecued over hot coals. The meat ascended through the orders, first the domestic fowl, then the lesser fowl (mallard, teal, snipe); the lesser land fowl (chickens, pigeons, partridge); until on great platters of silver and gold arrived the greater fowl – bittern, shoveler, and peacock. Finally it was time for one of the climaxes of the dinner itself, a huge marrow-bone pie, constructed of alternate layers of artichokes, currants, dates, sliced sweet potato, candied sea holly roots and marrow, sweetened with sugar.

The Stuarts were renowned for the length and extent of their feasts. Although those of James's era were largely about gluttony, in the more refined atmosphere of Charles's court something more than just over-eating and getting drunk was required of a royal occasion. The King frowned on drunkenness and debauchery. What he demanded was taste and elegance.

Stuart feasts were as much about the visible as the edible. They were frequently accompanied by shows and 'ballets'. The highlight of the feast was the 'banquet' which was separate to the dinner itself. The dinner was the main meal, but after the dinner the guests, already bloated by the dishes they had consumed, would move into a special banqueting hall where an array of mainly sweet dishes would await them.

The banquet ran according to strict rules. It was dominated by 'march pane' (from which we get our marzipan), which was carved into ornate and wonderful shapes. Like the pie, the showpiece of the banquet was a culinary special effect, a piece designed for show or surprise. This was not intended to be eaten (indeed, some of the set-pieces were kept as props and wheeled out at successive events), but was to impress the guests. Markham describes it as 'made for shew only, such as beast, bird, fowl, fish according to invention'. The showpiece dish was followed by march pane and then fruits, comfits, slices of lemons and oranges, cakes, preserved fruits and marmalades.

The 'banquet house' could be a part of the house itself, or could be in the gardens, a long way from the kitchen.

Houses were often specially designed, often in places which would afford the guests a spectacular view of the surrounding countryside or gardens. At houses such as Longleat, Worksop Manor and Hardwick Hall, banqueting rooms were built on the roof, or in turrets and towers.

So it was that the master-cook of the Caroline Court was as much a showman as chef. Ben Jonson describes the role in his masque, *Neptune's Triumph*:

> . . . he designs, he draws
> He paints, he carves, he builds, he fortifies.
> Makes citadels of curious fowl and fish,
> Some he dry ditches, some moats round with broths;
> Mounts marrow-bones, cuts fifty angled custards;
> Rears bulwark pies; and for his outer works,
> He raiseth ramparts of immortal crust.

Part of the cook's armoury, as mentioned by Jonson, was the huge 'bulwark pie' with its ramparts of raised pastry. The pie was not necessarily part of the meal, just as frequently it was a special effect, concealing something to amuse the guests. These pies were also known as 'coffins' – hence Shakespeare's grim pun in *Titus Andronicus*, 'a coffin I will rear', meaning the pie in which Titus has cooked the children of his enemies. Master-cooks would have appreciated Shakespeare's pun, even though they might have baulked at his choice of filling. Mostly they contented themselves with the more prosaic, such as the Italian recipe book which gave minute instructions for making a pie containing live blackbirds, although this was somewhat passé by the early seventeenth century.

There are, alas, no descriptions of the moment itself; no accounts of that instant when the crust began to rise and the little man climbed out. However, we can make some guesses as to the scene, for there are precedents.

There is an account, for example, of one Russian banquet where two pies were brought to the table, from which a male and female dwarf climbed out and proceeded to dance a minuet together. Similarly, in 1568 at a grand festival in honour of William, Duke of Bavaria and the Princess Renata of Lorraine, a fully armed dwarf leapt out of a pie, waving a banner and marching around the table, and paid merry compliments to the august and delighted guests. It is therefore most likely that Buckingham simply adapted the idea.

The pie, huge and glistening, was carried to the table and set before the Queen. Then, at some pre-determined signal, the crust began to lift. A hand emerged, an arm, a small, bewildered face peering out from beneath a shiny helmet. And then the boy himself, as tiny and as delicate as a doll. No doubt, schooled by Buckingham, Jeffrey would have played his part. He would have bowed to the Queen, marched up and down the table, waved a flag, maybe even made a speech. Whatever his instructions, it is not hard to imagine the applause and gasps of wonder as the revellers had their first sight of Master Jeffrey Hudson, one of the wonders of the age.

And, of course, Buckingham's brilliance lay not only in the presentation, but also in choosing exactly the right gift. For the childlike Queen, with her love of theatricals, what could be better than a pie that was also a jack-in-the-box? For the girl who liked pets, what could be better than a pet human of her very own?

Whatever the details of his surprise appearance, the Queen was enraptured and from the moment he stepped out of the pie and onto the table, Jeffrey Hudson became 'The Queen's Dwarf.'

*   *   *

The rest of the evening passed in a whirl. After the pie was produced there were further courses brought from among the clouds, rare dishes, swan and sturgeon and even porpoise. And following these gastronomic delights there was the show.

The clouds parted for the final time and there in front of the delighted Queen were actors, carefully made-up and dressed to represent members of the French Court. There in front of the Queen and her new dwarf, were her father and mother and all their principal attendants, 'and so to the life that the Queen's majesty could name them'.

Henrietta Maria must have had mixed feelings about this display. Clever as it was, the tableau, with all its detail of her former Court, must have brought home just how alone she really was. Her family were many miles away. She was in London, sitting between the scheming Duke and her cold distant husband.

Small wonder that she surrounded herself with monkeys and dogs and dwarfs. They at least loved her. And Jeffrey loved her as well. For the next twenty years he was to serve her loyally through triumph and disaster. In the end, when they were forced to part, it was only because it was the only way to save his life.

But that was in the future. For now, the revelries continued. The King in particular was in a buoyant and cheerful mood. He was as merry as his courtiers had ever seen him. The banquet went on until four o'clock in the morning, by which time the royal couple, too tired to return home, decided to take up the Duke's offer of a bed for the night. The guard was discharged and they retired to their quarters. The event was so unusual that it caused some cynics to observe that the King must be in very great favour with the Duke. The banquet was estimated to have cost the Duke five or six thousand pounds. From its evident success, he must have thought it was money well spent.

They stayed there nearly all the next day, dining again on Monday afternoon and dancing from four o'clock until eight. Then it was time to go home. The King went to Whitehall. The Queen, her ladies-in-waiting, her dogs, monkeys, negro servants and her new dwarf went to Denmark House.

THE
QUEEN'S DWARF

Had you been Bigge and Great ten to one you never had prooved a Courtier; 'twas onely your littlenesse preferr'd you.

The New Yeare's Gift

THEY WALKED OUT OF THE BACK OF YORK HOUSE AND through the gardens, down to the magnificent water gate designed by Inigo Jones. It had three archways, each surmounted by lions holding a shield with an anchor on it, a reference to Buckingham's role as Lord High Admiral. Through the central archway, a flight of steps led down to the Thames, where the Royal Barge was docked. There, Henrietta Maria's boatmen were waiting to row the party the few hundred yards downriver to her own palace, Denmark House.

The Thames was, as ever, alive with traffic. As the barge moved out into the water, Jeffrey could see the lights on the other boats out across the river. They drifted downstream, past other great palaces and buildings; Durham House, Russell House, the dark, medieval mass of the Savoy Hospital, all of them served by similarly grand water gates. In London, anyone who was anyone had a palace with a river gate. The streets were too crowded, dirty and noisy to allow for easy transportation. The Thames was the main artery of the city and with all the major residences in the city spread out south of the Strand and along the river, all points were within easy reach of a boat.

Those who could not afford a boat of their own had to rely on the services of the ferrymen, a group noted for the robustness of their language and wit. 'There's no talking to these ferrymen, they will have the last word,' complained Ben Jonson, himself no slouch when it came to verbal sparring. Indeed, it was customary for the passengers to join in and those being transported often passed the time by shouting abuse at passers-by in the most inventive language they could manage. (Even as late as in the time of Samuel Johnson the practice persisted: when one traveller attacked him with what Boswell called 'coarse raillery', it drew from the great Doctor the wonderful retort, 'Sir, your wife, under pretence of keeping a bawdy-house, is a receiver of stolen goods.')

It was not just travellers that packed the Thames, for the river was also provider for the city. Holinshed in his *Chronicles* talks of 'fat and sweet salmons, dailie taken in this streame' as well as 'barbels, trout, chevins, perches, smelts, breames, roches, daces, gudgings, flounders, shrimps &c.' It was common custom for the Thames fishermen to carry the first salmon of the season to the King's table. Any sturgeon caught below London Bridge was taken to the Lord Mayor, above the bridge to the table of the King or the Lord High Admiral.

This, then, was the highway along which Jeffrey was taken to his new home. After a brief journey downstream, the boatmen raised their oars, and the Queen's barge docked at the water gate of Denmark House, the great London palace of Queen Henrietta Maria.

*   *   *

Denmark House was once Somerset House, built by the Duke of Somerset, who came into power on Henry VIII's death as Lord Protector. It was the first Renaissance palace in England, a hugely important architectural statement, with a classical, Italianate design and clean white stone.

It was a large house, some five hundred feet from front to back, with a river frontage of six hundred feet. While the plan remained fundamentally that of a late medieval palace, complete with gatehouse, courtyard and great hall, the detail pointed to a different age – an age which had rediscovered the classical lines, for Somerset House featured a Roman triumphal arch, columned bays surrounding the courtyard and widely spaced windows. It was a thoroughly modern palace, based on thoroughly ancient architecture.

The palace was hugely expensive to build, even though Somerset economized by trying to steal as much stone as possible. His workmen filched from a variety of sources including the collapsed great cloister on the north side of Old St Paul's and the priory church of the Knights Hospitallers at Clerkenwell. They also tried to loot stone from the church of St Margaret's Westminster, but they were repulsed by the angry parishioners, who turned out with clubs and bows to defend their property.

Alas, Somerset himself never finished his new home. The office of Lord Protector was a notoriously greasy pole, and in 1552 Somerset fell off with a crash. He was executed and the unfinished house was forfeited to the crown. Up until the accession of James I, the house was similarly out of favour. It was occupied by minor court officials until King James granted it to his wife, Anne of Denmark. 'Somerset' House became 'Denmark' House and when Henrietta Maria married Charles I she, in turn, was granted its use for her private residence.

Under Henrietta Maria, Denmark House was to gain a unique status. It was to be more than a royal residence, more even than an architectural statement. It was to become a symbol, a building so closely associated with the Roman Catholic cause that it achieved an almost mythical status among Londoners. For the hard-pressed English Catholics, Denmark House was a place of hope, a place where Catholics could gather in peace to worship, a place where the flame of the true faith still burned, ready to burst out, to spread once more throughout England. For the vast majority of Londoners, however, it was not so much a candle of hope but a fire-risk. The flickering flame of Popishness was exactly why they hated the place so. In one location they found the two things they hated most: 'Popery' and 'Frenchness'.

The only thing the London mob liked about Denmark House was the seafood. Henrietta's taste for shellfish meant that a thriving seafood market grew up opposite the gates. At least the citizens could enjoy their Colchester oysters and gilt gingerbread, their Venus cockles, mussels and scallops, even if it did mean that across the street, behind the high walls, suspicious foreigners were observing their evil Romish rituals.

Jeffrey was not the only marvel at Court, as he found out as soon as the boat docked. At Denmark House there was another 'wonder of nature', another *lusus naturae* waiting for him, but this marvel was at the opposite end of the scale. His name was William Evans, he was the porter of the backstairs and he was seven feet six inches tall.

Evans was born in Monmouthshire, Wales and took over the post of King's porter from another giant, Walter Persons. Although generally referred to as the King's porter, he was actually a part of the Queen's establishment as the Denmark House account books show. From 1630 he appears as 'porter of the backstairs', his annual payment of twenty-five pounds acknowledged with an 'X'. At seven feet six he was two inches taller than his predecessor, but he presented a less attractive figure. Fuller describes him as 'what the Latines call compernis, knocking his knees together, and going out squalling with his feet, but also haulted [limped] a little'.

This, then, was the figure who opened the great door to greet the Queen and her new companion: a knock-kneed, splay-footed and slightly limping giant. There were times when living in Denmark House must have been like living in a bizarre version of fairyland.

Jeffrey's first recorded encounter with the giant occurred only a few weeks after his arrival at Court. For, in what may have been another attempt to heal the breach between the royal couple, a masque was being held in honour of the Queen's birthday.

The masque was a unique art form. It was part-play, part-dance, part-opera and all spectacle. It was primarily a visual entertainment, a parade of special effects and spectacular costumes, set against a background of ornate scenery and specially commissioned music. It was very much an aristocratic art form – the participants were generally from the highly educated aristocracy with the King, Queen and princes often taking roles. The subject matter was drawn from classical mythology, but as time went on the content became more overtly political, the 'inventors' of the masque using classical allusions to present reassuring, royalist political statements.

Fundamentally, however, the masque's purpose was to allow the nobility to dress up and 'play pretend'. It may well have had a sophisticated script by Ben Jonson, John Milton or Thomas Campion, but its participants really just wanted to dress in lovely clothes and take to the stage.

The masque reached its high point in the reign of Charles I. Although his father commissioned masques James was usually too drunk to enjoy them properly; frequently he fell asleep, several times he lost patience completely and stopped the thing halfway through. He only ever tolerated them because his wife, Anne of Denmark, so enjoyed acting in them. Anne's successor at Denmark House was even more of a fan. Henrietta Maria was passionate about acting and dancing, and throughout her reign Denmark House and Whitehall were seldom without a theatrical production or a masque in preparation. Her husband, although initially somewhat disapproving, eventually became a strong supporter of masques, particularly if they had more sophisticated plots and allusions and especially if the political message helped to reinforce his blinkered view of the world.

Compared to later productions (as we shall see), the Queen's masque of 23 November 1626 was a simple affair. The large room in Denmark House was covered with 'a floor of green cotton' secured by two thousand black tacks. The warrant for the costumes records outfits for poets, postillions, 'Lutanists' and 'Valting Masters' or acrobats. Although no script, or even title, survives, it appears to have contained a large chunk of broad comedy, notably in the scenes where William Evans, that 'overgrown Janitor' as one correspondent described him, played the part of the giant Gargantua, from Rabelais's *Gargantua and Pantagruel*.

In the masque, Gargantua is supposed to be instructed by three tutors, all played by members of the King's Privy Council. The Duke of Buckingham, perhaps emboldened by the success of his recent entertainments, played the role of a fencing master, trying to teach Evans how to 'skirmish'. He was accompanied by Lord Holland, who played a mathematics tutor, and Sir George Goring who tried to teach the giant to dance.

After all this slapstick, the giant sat down on the edge of the stage. From one enormous pocket of his coat, he drew a loaf of bread. Then he reached into the other pocket and brought out, not a piece of cheese, but Jeffrey. The little dwarf was wearing a suit and cloak specially made for the occasion. It had cost twenty shillings to make.

Just two weeks after appearing from a pie, Jeffrey made another unexpected appearance. Evans, the knock-knee'd, seven-foot porter and little Jeffrey, eighteen inches high and only seven years old – the picture caught the imagination not only of the Court at the masque, but of society as a whole. William Evans and Jeffrey Hudson were in later years to appear together in books and engravings and even carved in stone, the Porter and the Dwarf, the huge, ungainly, shuffling Welshman, and the tiny, nimble, elegant Jeffrey.

I first came across this incident in Fuller's account of William Evans. After his description of the porter's appearance, Fuller tells us that 'he made a shift to dance in an Antimask at Court, where he drew little Jeffrey the Dwarf out of his pocket, first to the wonder, then to the laughter of the beholders'.

I thought this story another of the myths about Jeffrey because, although Jeffrey appears in three other masques, none of them features Evans. But the proof that they shared a stage together in a masque is found in a warrant for costumes in the Public Record Office. Dated 'Christmas 1627', the warrant lists both 'a suite and Cloke for Ieffry the Dwarfe' and 'a sute for the Great Porter'.

This does not prove, of course, that the event took place

exactly as Fuller describes it, but it certainly fits the character of the Rabelaisian scenes, and with the memory of the pie only a few weeks old, it must have been a simple and obvious jest.

Only a few weeks later, on 14 January 1627, Jeffrey was a spectator at another masque, this time acted by the King and Queen. It was a hugely drawn-out affair, lasting from three in the afternoon till four next morning. The King was intimately involved with this production, placing, we are told, 'the ladies' gentlewomen with his own hand'. The masque concluded with the Duke of Buckingham, fourteen noblemen, the Queen and the King joining the masquers in a dance.

'Doubtless it cost abundance,' wrote one witness sourly. 'It was said one Mr Chalmer sold 1000 yards of taffety and satin towards it.'

Masques, of course, were only one part of the entertainments at Court. There were gambling games, especially dice games like in-and-in, passage and hazard. Huge sums could be won or lost on these games – on one night the King won £1,850 at dice and the Queen £900. Indeed, gambling was something of an addiction at Court; even the apparently sedate game of bowls was a magnet for gambling, resulting in some very underhand skulduggery. Edward Somerset, Marquis of Worcester, wrote a book called *A Century of Inventions* in which he gave helpful advice on how to create a 'deceitful Bowl to play withal' by inserting discs of lead. No one seems to have thought badly of the Marquis for suggesting this; his book was even dedicated to the King.

The Queen also played billiards, and took to carrying her own billiard table around with her when she travelled throughout the country. There was even a large-scale version, 'trucks', which was more lively and required a larger table, balls the size of tennis balls, and iron-tipped cues. Whether she cunningly weighted the billiard balls is not recorded.

In April 1627, Jeffrey accompanied Henrietta Maria to Whitehall for another popular pastime – and one which would have been very familiar to him: bull-baiting. Whitehall was the other great royal palace of London. It was a massive, sprawling ramshackle collection of buildings, the largest palace in the known world, so big that the main street from Charing Cross to Westminster ran through the centre, spanned by two archways. It was largely a maze of red brick buildings, hemming in gardens and courtyards, ancient tilt-yards and a cock-pit where the bull- and bear-baiting took place.

Whitehall, despite numerous attempts, stubbornly resisted modernization. The only major new building of the time was the magnificent Banqueting House, designed by Inigo Jones and completed in 1622. On the ceiling Rubens had painted nine panels representing peace and prosperity. Charles was so proud of Rubens's work, he banned all performances in the Banqueting House lest the smoke from the candles ruin the paintings. Today, the Banqueting House is all that is left of the great palace of Whitehall. It was Charles's finest building. It was the scene of his greatest banquets, his finest state occasions and also, in the end, his execution.

Whitehall, like Denmark House, was a world within a world, a society with its own social order and ways of doing things. If Denmark House was the unacceptable face of royalty, with its fancy foreign ways and pro-Catholic style, then Whitehall was what you might call 'Old Monarchy'. It was a feudal place – a knight could always get a free meal in Whitehall, for even when he was away, the

King kept open house. All the knight had to do was turn up at the door and a meal would be waiting for him. In one year, the cooks in the Whitehall kitchens cooked 1,500 oxen, 7,000 sheep, 6,800 lambs, 1,200 calves, 400 'young beefs', 300 pigs, 26 boars and 24,000 pieces of poultry. Not to mention various quantities of venison, game and masses of fish. All this was washed down with 600 tuns of wine and 1,700 tuns of beer.

The palace was also famous as a centre of entertainment and revelry. As well as bull-baiting, it was a venue for plays and performances. The Revels Account tells us that plays such as 'The Moor of Venis', 'Mesur for Mesur', 'the plaie of Errors' and 'the Martchant of Venis' had been performed there – all by the celebrated playwright 'Shaxberd'.

Meanwhile, Jeffrey was settling in at Denmark House. He was given a servant to look after him, a man whom the household books list as Jeremy Griggory, but who signed himself 'Jerome Gregoire'. He was French, no doubt one of the servants brought over by Henrietta Maria from France in 1625, and one of the few she was allowed to retain. Jerome was to remain with Jeffrey for the next fifteen years. In the early days, Jerome was paid directly by the Queen's Treasurer. Once Jeffrey became an adult, however, he took over administering his servant's pay.

There are no records of Jeffrey's education, but no doubt he was given basic schooling by the resident schoolmaster at Denmark House. He could certainly read and write, and he would have learnt to speak French; Henrietta Maria herself never spoke very good English and with a French servant as well, Jeffrey must have mastered the language rapidly. Indeed, he was surrounded by French people, for his other main supervisor was Madame Garnier, the Queen's nurse. She was allowed a hundred pounds a year to look after the dwarves, for Jeffrey was not the only dwarf at Court.

We know of at least three other dwarfs at Court during Jeffrey's time. A little while after he joined Henrietta Maria's Court, another dwarf arrived, a girl named Sara Holton. She was looked after by a series of female servants, one of whom, named in the accounts as 'Anne Gregory', appears to have married Jeffrey's servant Jerome. Sara was at Court at least until 1640.

There was also Anne Shepherd and the King's dwarf Richard Gibson. Gibson was a few years older than Jeffrey, born in 1615. Originally he was in the service of a lady at Mortlake; she noticed he had a talent for drawing and sent him to study under De Cleyn, director of the Mortlake tapestry works. He also studied with Sir Peter Lely, whose portraits he learned to copy. De Cleyn supplied tapestries to the crown, and it is this link that must have brought Richard to the attention of Charles I. He was taken to Court, where he became the King's dwarf, and where he continued his artistic career. In later life he became, without, it seems, any trace of irony, a talented miniaturist, specializing in those miniature portraits of which the period was so fond, and which, with their portability, served the purpose that photographs serve today.

Gibson's works were highly valuable – so much so that one of them inspired a tragedy. A painting of the Lost Sheep was highly prized by Charles I who gave it into the care of one Vanderwort, the Keeper of the Royal Pictures. In obedience to strict injunctions to take care of it, Vanderwort put the picture away in a safe place, but when the King asked for it later, he could not remember where he had put it. In a blind panic, and afraid to say he had lost it, Vanderwort hanged himself. A few days later the picture was discovered where he had placed it.

Gibson was appointed page to the backstairs and later married another of Queen Henrietta Maria's dwarfs, Anne Shepherd. Anne was Jeffrey's contemporary, born in 1620, and her marriage to Richard was a great event.

One can easily imagine Henrietta Maria's excitement. What could be better than two of her little doll-people marrying? What could be more charming, more picturesque? Indeed, the entire Court threw themselves into the idea. Charles gave away the bride and the Queen presented her with a diamond ring as a bridal gift. The Court poet Edmund Waller even wrote a poem *On the Marriage of the Dwarfs* which begins with the lines: 'Design or chance make others wive; / But nature did this match contrive.'

Given Henrietta Maria's involvement, one might be forgiven for suspecting that nature alone was not entirely responsible. Nevertheless the couple were happy and produced nine children, five of whom lived to maturity. All grew to full height. Gibson went on to thrive under the Protectorate, painting a portrait of Cromwell as well. He died in 1690 at the age of seventy-five, Anne outlived him by nearly twenty years, dying in 1709 at the ripe old age of eighty-nine.

The role of the King at this wedding ceremony – standing in for Anne's father – illustrates well his relationship with his servants. The seventeenth-century view of servants – and it was particularly strongly held by Charles – was that they were part of an extended family with the King and Queen *in loco parentis*. Books of household government at the time likened the relationship between master and servants to that between parents and children.

Charles took a keen interest in his servants' welfare. Petitions addressed to him were normally passed straight on to the relevant minister; but those petitions from his servants he dealt with himself, usually endorsing them in the servants' favour.

For Jeffrey, indeed, who came to the Court aged only seven, Henrietta Maria took the place of his mother. At some time during his first years at Court, however, his real father came to visit.

Fuller describes the meeting, stating how Jeffrey

... ever after lived (whilst the court lived) in great plenty therein, wanting nothing but humility (high mind in a low body) which made him that he did not know himself, and would not know his father, and which by the king's command caused justly his sound correction.

There is no other evidence of this visit, but no doubt his parents did visit Jeffrey, perhaps during one of Henrietta Maria's annual excursions to Wellingborough. Fuller, as we have seen, paints a comic portrait of Jeffrey, stressing the difference between the height of Jeffrey's aspirations and the shortness of his stature. It suits him to paint the picture of the 'high and mighty' dwarf, especially in his interpretation of later events in Jeffrey's life.

However, that doesn't mean that the incident didn't take place. It may well be that John Hudson visited his son, if not in London, then when the Court was on progress through the country. And it may equally be that Jeffrey disdained to meet him. We know that the rest of Fuller's account is substantially correct. Jeffrey was living a different life now, a life of elegance and refinement, among those of aristocratic descent, so he may not have been enthusiastic to see the butcher from Oakham. But it is telling that it is the King who steps in to settle the dispute, the real father-figure. The incident, if nothing else, amply illustrates the patriarchal nature of the Court.

Tragically for Charles, however, the Court was the only place where he was viewed in this way. He would have loved to be the stern but loving patriarch of his people, but they never recognized that side of him. In the public forum he came across as merely aloof and demanding. He stood so much on his honour that no one ever saw the more human side of the man. The Court saw him enjoying himself. It saw a different Charles; a relaxed, calm and confident father-figure, who granted favours and received love in return. If he could be a somewhat formal and correct parent, he was nevertheless kind and caring. And he was loved by his servants in a way that he was never loved by his Parliament or his people.

Jeffrey emerged from the pie into a new family. His real parents were part of the past now, he had a new adoptive mother and father. In particular, Jeffrey had a special relationship with Henrietta Maria. She delighted in the little man, loved showing him off to visitors and courtiers, worried about him and fussed over him, like a mother over her son. One incident from 1627 illustrates how intensely she felt.

For a tiny man like Jeffrey, the seventeenth-century house was full of potential dangers, but if one is to believe all that was written about him, one would have to conclude that he was the most accident-prone human being in London. Some of these stories appear to be inventions, but enough of them are true to indicate that he did live an incredibly disaster-prone life. He was always a spirited and curious individual, willing to attempt things that others of his condition would never have thought of trying. As later events will bear out, sometimes these attempts brought tragic consequences.

His history of misadventures begins some seven months after he arrived at Denmark House, when on 17 June 1627 he fell out of a window.

The incident is recorded in a contemporary letter: 'Little Geffry, the Queen's dwarfe fell last day out of the window at Denmark House; The Queene tooke it soe heavily that she attyred not her selfe that day . . .'

The Queen was utterly distraught. The entire day was disrupted because of the accident. All visits were cancelled, all engagements scrapped. Henrietta Maria was never reluctant to turn a drama into a crisis, but given Jeffrey's size and stature, this could easily have brought an abrupt end to his career at Court. Or, indeed, his career anywhere.

It is not hard to see how it happened. There are not many pictures of the interior of Denmark House, but one from the the earlier years of the century shows a window reaching to just above floor level with a small, square pane open. It would have been impossible for a fully grown man to fall through such a gap, but for a dwarf – and more importantly an excited and curious little boy – standing on the window ledge, staring out across the gardens to the Thames and the bankside beyond, the danger would have been only too real.

The Queen need not have worried. Jeffrey appears to have made a complete and rapid recovery. Where he fell from, and what he landed on we do not know. One presumes it cannot have been on to the main courtyard, but it must have been on to the gardens or flower beds.

This incident gave rise to other similar tales, although of less historical veracity. Stonecastle mentions two other incidents which were both supposed to have occurred during Jeffrey's early years at Denmark House. Both are more than faintly ridiculous. The first of these is probably a garbled version of the fall from the Denmark House window:

> Once he was washing his hands and Face, he had like to be drown'd in his Bason, her Majesty would not suffer him afterwards to have anything bigger than a Coffee Cup.

Since coffee didn't arrive in England until the middle of the century (the first coffee house was opened in Oxford in 1650, according to Oxford scholar Anthony Wood, the first London house opening two years later), the Queen would have had to have been several decades ahead of fashion when it came to her crockery. Even assuming he is speaking figuratively, the story is incredible; basins were not that big and Jeffrey, for all his rarity, was not that small.

The second incident related by Stonecastle shows Jeffrey becoming the hero of someone else's story:

> Another time when in a blustering Day, the friendly Arms of a spreading shrub have sav'd him from being blown into the Thames, the Queen, after a full Council, gave strict orders that he should never go abroad in windy Weather without his Leaden-heel'd shoes.

This is a retelling of an old story. Aelian, the classical writer, tells of a poet called Philetus during the reign of Alexander the Great. Philetus was reputedly so small that he always carried piece of lead in his pocket to prevent himself from being blown away by the wind. All that Stonecastle has done is take the story of Philetus and give it a modern setting.

However, once again he may be basing the story on the original incident. Perhaps it was a freak gust of wind which took Jeffrey out of the window, and perhaps it was a shrub that broke his fall. Whatever the case, there is no evidence that he wore weighted boots either then, or at any time afterwards.

Jeffrey had a special status at Court. It was not only his unique size, his boyish charm, his perfect proportion, and doll-like looks; it was that he soon learned the skills that Buckingham had demonstrated. He learned not only how to look charming, but how to *be* charming. He looked quaint and sweet, and he learnt how to act that way as well.

Henrietta Maria adored him. There were other dwarfs at Court, but none of them was fêted like Jeffrey. No one else had books and poems written about him. Henrietta Maria commissioned no paintings of her other dwarfs. Only Jeffrey was rewarded this way. Only the most small, the most wonderful of her *lusus naturae*.

There are three major paintings of Jeffrey, and two in which he appears as an incidental character. Nearly all of these – with one notable exception – date from his first years at Denmark House. During May 1628, Jeffrey stood for his first portrait, standing for hours posing for the Court painter, Daniel Mytens. Mytens was a man of limited artistic abilities. Technically adept, his paintings are frequently stiff and formal. He captures the appearance, but only rarely do his portraits give us any insight into the character of the subject.

The painting was delivered on 25 June 1628, Mytens submitting a warrant for ninety-five pounds 'for 2 pictures by him viz. For one great one of ye Queene and ye Dwarfe, both in one peece delivered at Whitehall ye 25th June 1628 by his majesties command to my Lord Carleton to be sent to ye Queene of Bohemia . . .'

This seems to imply that Mytens made one great picture

in two pieces, one part of which was sent abroad, no doubt to show other nobility the rarity of nature that England could now boast. A further copy of this picture was made in August 1628 to be 'carryed to the Duchess of Saxe beyond the seas'.

Identifying this picture is not easy. It may be the picture of Jeffrey holding a dog, which was later engraved by James Stow in 1810. Jeffrey, in hunting gear, holds the leash of a spaniel. He stares directly ahead, solemn, unsmiling. His hair is straight, and hangs down by his shoulders and in his right hand he clutches a rose.

Mytens painted Jeffrey several times. In two of his pictures – *Charles I and Henrietta Maria Departing for the Chase*, and *An Interior With Charles I, Henrietta Maria, The Earls of Pembroke and Jeffrey Hudson* – Jeffrey is an incidental figure. In each painting Mytens has Jeffrey in the same pose, leaning back, a ludicrously tiny doll straining to hold back a small hunting dog. Something about Jeffrey is beyond Mytens's ability. His appearance seems to defeat the painter. He could cope with powerful figures in formal finery, but this prodigy of nature was beyond him. Mytens made several attempts to paint Jeffrey, only the last of which came close to penetrating the mystique. It would take a greater painter than Mytens to show us the truth about Jeffrey and Henrietta Maria.

In late summer 1627 Buckingham, in one last desperate attempt to salvage his popularity, attacked the French at Rochelle and the Isle of Rhé. Henrietta Maria's brother, the French King Louis XIII, was besieging the Protestant Huguenots on the island. His father had granted toleration to the French Protestants, but Louis reopened the conflicts and sought to drive the 'heretics' out of France. It must have seemed a good idea at the time: attack the French and rescue Protestants, two of the most popular things any seventeenth-century government could do. But it was a gamble. The Duke, for all his undoubted courage, was no military commander, and years of wrangling between King and Parliament had led to a serious weakening of the English forces and fleet.

Significantly, while he was away the King and Queen had their best months since the beginning of the marriage. Charles wrote to Buckingham expressing his delight at how responsive the Queen was and how much he was enjoying her company:

> I cannot omit to tell you that my wife and I were never on better terms; she upon this action of yours, showing herself so loving to me by her discretion on all occasions, that it makes us all wonder and esteem her.

Typically, he lacked the insight to ask himself just why they should be getting along so well.

The adventure ended tragically. The expedition was a disaster: two thousand men lay dead on the island's narrow causeway along which the Duke had fled in chaos and retreat. Buckingham's plans for glory and popularity, for the victory that would force Parliament to obey him, were in ruins.

He returned from France on 11 November 1627. Charles, as myopic as ever, blamed everyone except the real culprit, and immediately called Parliament with the aim of raising money for a second expedition. The second expedition to Rochelle began to muster in Portsmouth in August 1628.

Buckingham's star, so long in the ascendant, was now in free fall. Leaflets against him were distributed in the streets of London. When his portrait fell with a crash from the wall of the High Commission in Lambeth, people took it as a prophecy of his imminent demise.

On Tuesday 19 August, John Felton, an unemployed officer, asked his mother to lend him some money. He packed up his few belongings and left his lodgings above a barber's shop in Fleet Street. He went to a shop in Tower Street and purchased a ten-penny knife which he strapped to his right-hand pocket so that he could draw it without having to use his crippled left hand.

Then he set out for Portsmouth.

He had already encountered the Duke the previous year, when he had begged Buckingham for the command of a company.

'Without such a position I cannot live!' he claimed.

Buckingham looked at him coolly. 'In that case,' he replied, 'you had better go hang.'

It was the kind of cheap joke that comes to haunt a man.

Felton arrived at the Duke's Portsmouth lodgings on Saturday 23 August, and waited for him to appear. When Buckingham emerged from the house, the crippled man moved forward swiftly, leant over the shoulder of Sir Thomas Fryer and stabbed Buckingham through the left breast. The Duke pulled out the weapon and cried, 'Traitor, thou hast killed me!' His wife rushed out from her bedroom in her nightdress. It was too late. Buckingham died in his doctor's arms.

Charles was at prayers when he heard the news. Mustering all his self-control, he remained kneeling until the service concluded, then he went to his room, flung himself on to his bed and burst into tears.

Jeffrey was at Wellingborough with Henrietta Maria when the news of Buckingham's death came through. Henrietta Maria hurriedly abandoned her stay and the entire Court rushed to London. There was a new determination and urgency about the girl. It was not that her great rival had been assassinated; it was that, for the first time in their marriage, Charles needed her. Without his faithful Buckingham, the King turned to the only person he could trust, and she, in turn, lavished all her attention on the lonely, isolated man. All the frustrated affection that had been turned on her dwarfs and her dogs was turned instead towards her husband.

Over the course of the next few months, something remarkable happened: the King and Queen fell in love. By Christmas 1628, when the King was away for four nights, the Queen couldn't sleep. She put his portrait on her bedside table.

Soon this new relationship led to an inevitable conclusion. On Christmas Eve a correspondent called George Pory reported: 'We are here putt in some hope that the Queen is with child, she is showing some signs thereof, but a little longer time will make it knowne.'

She was indeed pregnant but the child arrived prematurely. Some people said she was frightened by two dogs fighting in the gallery at Greenwich, one of which tore her dress with its teeth. Others blamed the Queen's passion for shellfish.

Whatever the case, when she went into labour she was far from any professional help. Her ladies brought the local midwife, an old lady who was so terrified at the royalty all around her, she immediately fainted and had to be carried out of the room. In the midst of all this, the Queen gave birth to a baby boy on 13 May 1629. After a brief argument between the King and the Queen's confessor over which baptism rites to use, the child was eventually baptized Charles James, and welcomed into the Church of England. He died an hour later.

The Queen was devastated. Physically, at least, she was never the same again. Ever dramatic, Henrietta Maria was always prone to a certain amount of hypochondria, and several physicians believed that her frequent illnesses were more imagined than real, but from this point on, her life was punctuated with a series of maladies and ailments.

Jeffrey went to Tunbridge Wells with the Queen to complete her convalescence, but Henrietta Maria was so bored that she decided to return home. On her way she stopped at one of her favourite palaces, Oatlands, near Weybridge, Surrey. Charles, hearing of her intention, paid her a surprise romantic visit. A few weeks later, her servants were observed scurrying out to the seafood stalls opposite Denmark House for mussels. The Queen had developed another craving.

This time they were taking no chances and word was sent to the finest midwife in France, Madame Peronne. In truth, she had been 'on call' for the first birth, but the premature delivery took everyone by surprise and Madame Peronne had not even embarked from France. Now she was ordered to make ready in plenty of time.

Some British subjects took it as a personal slight. 'The Queen's majesty, having no fancy, it seems, to our English midwives and nurses, had sent into France for both,' wrote one correspondent. But midwifery was far more advanced in France, where a famous school for midwives had been set up in the Hôtel-Dieu in Paris which included in its curriculum a six-week course on anatomy.

And Henrietta Maria's experiences with what England had to offer were hardly encouraging. The choice between a professionally trained French woman, and an old lady lying in a dead faint on the carpet was not a difficult one. Accordingly, as the time for the Queen's confinement drew nearer, an embassy was prepared to go to France and bring back the midwife.

Among the members of this embassy was Jeffrey. It was to be his first trip abroad, and, sadly, his first taste of imprisonment and loss.

THE
PIRATE CAPTIVE

When one's undone by fire or shipwrack, or goods
taken by Pyrats, what sets him up but the Kings
briefes . . .

The New Yeare's Gift

THE JOURNEY TO FRANCE WAS NOT MERELY TO COLLECT
a midwife. The deputation was concerned not only with
Henrietta Maria's physical well-being, but her spiritual life
as well. There were ten Capuchin friars waiting in Paris to
come to Denmark House, the results of an agreement with
her husband that Henrietta Maria should be allowed to
increase the numbers of her religious establishment to '29
priests and 15 seculars, besides a bishop, a young man
under 30 years old'.

The deputation that left London in late February 1630
was an oddly assorted crew. It was led by Jean Garnier,
Henrietta Maria's master of ceremonies and husband to
the nurse who looked after Jeffrey. Jean had arrived with
Henrietta Maria in 1625 and was a trusted member of her
staff. Later, he was to abuse that trust by carrying on a
scandalous affair with Lady Willoughby, a woman of 'violent and disorderly conduct'. To the outrage of society, the

two lived together as man and wife, paying for their excesses by secretly selling the goods and lands of Lady Willoughby's apparently gullible husband. In the end Garnier was banished from the Court and went to live in France. At the time of this trip, however, he was still very much in favour and he was accompanied by other favourites such as Rocan, the Queen's dancing master, several of her ladies-in-waiting and, of course, Jeffrey.

Historians have since represented this trip as a sign that Jeffrey had been entrusted with some kind of mission. Since he was only ten at the time, it is hard to imagine him being put in charge of any expedition, even one as simple as collecting a midwife. More likely he was being sent partly to enlarge his education, but mainly to show him off to the French Court. Jeffrey was being displayed, sent to France in his familiar role as a rarity of nature.

As such, he was an enormous success. They arrived in France a few days later and Jeffrey was greeted with acclaim. The sumptuous salons of the Parisian Court had never seen anything like this little boy, and he was showered with gifts and attention, especially by Marie de Medici, the Queen's mother, and he was given around two thousand pounds' worth of jewels by the ladies of the Court. It is an astonishing amount for a young boy, who only a few years earlier had been living in a household whose annual earnings cannot have been more than ten pounds.

By mid-March, the embassy was ready to return. Madame Peronne had packed all her equipment, the ten Capuchin monks were ready, the jewels were safely stored away and the other gifts were loaded on to a wagon.

They arrived at Calais on 18 March and boarded a barque. Master Pierre Grielle, the captain of the ship, probably informed them that they would all be back in England within hours.

It didn't quite work out that way. A few hours off the French coast, another sail was spotted, a ship hot in pursuit. It came steadily closer and closer until it could be seen clearly. Hurriedly Garnier rounded up the passengers and herded them below. They were to keep hidden and keep quiet. It was their only chance of escaping the pirates.

Dunkirk, at that time, was an independent Flemish state, making a happy living from the traditional maritime trades of fishing, transportation, piracy, kidnapping and extortion. Throughout the 1620s and 30s the Dunkirkers were the bane of shipping in the Channel. Indeed, piracy was rife everywhere. On 18 March, the very same day that Jeffrey was captured, one Mr Beaulieu wrote to a correspondent:

> Here are daily complaints made of the continual prizes and wrongs done by the Dunkirkers, not only along the coasts, but also within the very rivers of this kingdom, where they have taken divers ships of late.

It was not only the Dunkirkers. To the west the dreaded Barbary Corsairs – pirates from the North African states of Morocco, Tunis and Algiers – were a constant threat, raiding Cornwall, Devon and the Irish coast, capturing ships and even stealing the residents of seaside towns, who were taken off into Africa to act as slaves.

At least the Dunkirkers only stole your money. They might kidnap you for a ransom, but that rarely lasted long. Besides which, the truth was that the French, Spanish and English did exactly the same thing. In times of war between the two countries it was not uncommon for British ships to capture French vessels and vice versa.

For Jeffrey, born and bred miles from the sea, the adventure must have been terrifying. Cowering down below, he could hear the pirates overcome the ship with ease. Footsteps thundered down the stairs and Jeffrey and the terrified ladies were dragged on to the deck. The delighted pirates seized greedily on his marvellous store of gifts.

There was not much resistance. Jeffrey, Madame Peronne, Jean Garnier, Rocan the dancing master and the ship's master were bundled across to the Dunkirkers' ship. The rest were left to fend for themselves. The Capuchins were left behind as they were not thought to be of sufficient value.

The terrified captives were taken back to Gravelines. On 20 March, the mayor of Dover sent a report to London:

> At this very instant arrived at Dover one Nicolas Grellyne, a master of a barque of Calais and other passengers, one of them being servant unto my Lord Edmund, they do all most faithfully affirm that Mr Garnier, the husband unto the Queen's Majesty's nurse, and her majesty's dwarf with four women, the one of them to be the Queen's midwife and one of my Lord Edmund's servants being bound for Dover in a barque of Callais were all taken prisoners by the Dunkirkers and carried into Gravelines on Thursday last ... being the 18th of this instant, and they are detained prisoners, the dwarf carrying at least 2000l [£2000] in jewels and a wagon load of rich goods.

The drama was unfolding fast for, on arrival in Gravelines, it soon became apparent to the Dunkirkers that this group of people was perhaps a little too hot to handle. After a few days in captivity they were released and sent over the border into France. On 27 March, Reverend Joseph Mead related the incident in a letter to Sir Martin Stuteville:

The queen's majesty, having no fancy, it seems, to our English midwives and nurses, had sent into France for both: who, as they were coming, together with a dwarf and, as some say, twelve nuns, were all intercepted and carried away by the Dunkirkers. But I hear, by letters from London that being not found very good prize at Dunkirk, they were released, and are now safely arrived in England.

In fact, the opposite may be more accurate. The party was probably too valuable. The Governor of Calais sent a message to the pirates immediately and in retaliation seized all the Flemish goods and persons in his town. The Dunkirkers must have realized soon that perhaps detaining the Queen's midwife was not a very good idea. The King put up with a lot from them, but if they caused his wife to suffer even he might eventually take action. So they satisfied themselves with appropriating the goods and the jewels and sent the relieved prisoners back to Calais.

It is in this letter that Mead makes the reference to 'Sesquipedal Geoffrey', continuing:

The dwarf taken by the Dunkirkers was Sesquipedal Geoffrey, coming from the Queen Mother out of France with jewels given him by her and the ladies of that Court to the value of 2500l and presents for her majesty of 5000l more.

Two days after they had initially embarked, Jeffrey was back in England. The Queen had been so distraught that one courtier complained that the abduction had 'caused more upset at court than if they had lost a fleet'. She was hugely relieved when her midwife, her master of ceremonies and her faithful dwarf eventually arrived back at Denmark House a few days later.

According to some sources the Queen made good Jeffrey's losses. A later reference indicates that the King might also have issued authorization for payment. He certainly rewarded Madame Peronne when, two months later, after a labour of eight hours, the Queen gave birth to a healthy boy – the future Charles II. The delighted King immediately awarded Madame Peronne one thousand pounds. Jeffrey was probably simply relieved to be home again in Denmark House, where the only danger was falling out of a window.

The adventure had not taken long but it must have been a terrifying ordeal for all involved. For Jeffrey it was to be but the first of many unpleasant experiences on the sea. During future voyages he was to endure storms, bombardment, chases and, unfortunately, more piracy.

Jeffrey's return was a matter of great celebration, not only for the Queen but for the rest of the Court, who had become immensely fond of the little creature and who found in him a huge source of entertainment. It was not long before the trauma was forgotten and the whole affair was being treated as a huge joke. Before long, Jeffrey found himself the star of a poem recounting the adventure.

Jeffereidos, Or The Captivitie of Jeffery is a poem which tells the fictionalized story of Jeffrey's capture. It was written by William D'Avenant, at that time a rising star at the Court. D'Avenant was the son of an Oxford tavern-keeper, albeit one of good family. He was also, as he never tired of telling people, Shakespeare's godson. Indeed, D'Avenant when drunk was prone to claim that the relationship was more along the 'father' lines than the 'god' bit, actively encouraging rumours that he was Shakespeare's illegitimate son. John Aubrey wrote:

Now Sir William would sometimes, when he was pleasant over a glass of wine with his most intimate friends . . . say that it seemed to him that he writt with very spirit that did Shakespeare, and seemed contented enough to be thought his Son. He would tell them the story as above in a way in which his mother had a very light report, whereby she was called a whore.

It is hard to know what to think about a man who would spread tales of his mother's infidelity to enhance his own prestige. And anyway, even if it were true, all it proves is that literary talents are not genetically transmitted.

D'Avenant arrived in London in 1622. An improvident marriage in 1624 left him with a wife and son to support. He had been in the service of Fulke Greville, Lord Brooke, a poet, dilettante and writer of neoclassical dramas, but Brooke's death in September 1628 threw D'Avenant back on his own resources. He decided to turn to literature and Jeffrey's adventure in France offered him a subject too good to miss.

Jeffereidos is a fantasy tale at Jeffrey's expense. It begins with Jeffrey on board an 'old, weary' ship, when the pirates are spotted. He rushes downstairs and hides, but at length the pirates find him:

> At last they found him close, beneath a spick
> And almost span-new-pewter-candlestick.

The pirate captain, who is strangely a Spaniard called Don Diego, interrogates Jeffrey under the belief that he is a spy:

> This that appears to you, a walking-thumbe,
> May prove the gen'rall spie of Christendome.

No information is forthcoming, and Jeffrey is taken to Flanders where the people look on him with emotions that must have been only too familiar to him in real life:

> The people view him round: some take their oath
> He's human issue, but not yet of growth:
> And others (that more sub'tly did conferre)
> Thinke him a small, contracted conjurer.

Finding under their interrogation that he knows nothing he is placed on a dog, an Iceland Shock or Terrier:

> The fleetest Izeland-shock, they then provide;
> On which they mount him strait, and bid him ride:
> He weepes a teare or two, for's jewells lost;
> And so, with heavy heart, to Bruxels post.

On the road to Brussels, however, he is thrown from his dog and attacked by a 'Turkey-cock':

>   . . . for now behold
> A fowle of spacious wing, bloody and bold
> In his aspect; haughty in gate, and stiffe on
> His large spread clawes he stood, as any griffon;
> Though by kinde, a Turkey . . .
>   . . . this fowle (halfe blinde)
> At Jeff'ry pecks, and with intent to eat
> Him up, in stead of a large graine of wheat:
> Jeff'ry (in duell nice) ne're thinks upon't,
> As the Turkeys hunger, but an affront.
> His sword he drew; a better none alive
> E're got from Spanish foe, for shillings five.

The turkey overcomes Jeffrey and he has to be rescued by none other than Madame Peronne:

> A lady-midwife now, he there by chance
> Espy'd that came along with him from France . . .
> 'A heart nurs'd up in war; that ne're before
> This time (quote he) could bow, now doth implore:
> Thou that deliver'd has so many, be
> So kinde of nature, to deliver me!'

The midwife rescues him and D'Avenant ends the poem by promising the publication of a Third Part and the continuation of the story.

Aside from the various elements of farce, D'Avenant also makes use of classical elements in his fictional account. The duel with the turkey-cock is a parody of the ancient fable of the Pygmies and the Cranes. The story goes that the pygmies lived in India where they slaughtered the cranes and seized their eggs and young. The birds vowed to be revenged upon their enemies and a fearful battle ensued, after which the cranes conquered the pygmies. (Interestingly, when James Beattie translated the tale in 1762 he called the pygmies the 'eighteen-inch militia'. 'Sesquipedalian Jeffrey' rides again.)

The poem tells us nothing very much about Jeffrey himself, apart from the fact that he was famous enough to inspire it. D'Avenant describes the boat he sailed on as 'an old weary Pinke', that is a boat with one sail, incapable of the slightest resistance when boarded. Given the amount of valuables that Jeffrey was carrying, and the importance of Madame Peronne, it seems unlikely this was the case.

With the wisdom of hindsight, however, the poem has some more sombre resonances. The duel with the Turkey was to have its real-life counterpart – and with far more tragic consequences for Jeffrey. And D'Avenant describes Jeffrey's captivity in biblical terms:

> Whilst captive-Jeff'ry shewes to wiser sight,
> Just like a melancholy Israelite,
> In midst of 's journey unto Babylon.

This phrase must have rung in Jeffrey's ears in later years, when he truly was a slave in exile, a stranger in a strange land.

Perhaps the most interesting thing about this poem is the way that in subsequent years these flights of poetic fancy were reported as fact; some histories relate that Jeffrey actually did fight a duel with a turkey, and that his preferred mode of transport was a dog. D'Avenant's farce has become documented fact, the pygmies of truth defeated by the cranes of fiction.

The poem was rushed into print and soon became wildly popular. Following his report of the kidnapping, the Rev. Joseph Mead was keen to get hold of the poem. From his Cambridge college on 24 April 1630 he wrote: 'There is a poem which I cannot yet get, called "Geffreidos," describing a combat between Geoffrey, the Queen's dwarf, and a turkey-cock at Dunkirk.'

Although the poem was a popular success, D'Avenant's life at Court was plagued by difficulties. The following year he caught syphilis from a prostitute. According to John Aubrey, D'Avenant 'gott a terrible clap of a Black handsome wench that lay in Axe-Yard, Westminster ... which cost him his nose, with which unlucky mischance many witts were too cruelly bold.'

He was rescued by Thomas Cademan, one of the Queen's physicians, who managed to save his life, even though it cost D'Avenant his nose. It is satisfyingly ironic that

D'Avenant, whose career included laughing at other people's deformities, and who thought nothing of making his mother out to be a whore, should lose his nose through sleeping with a prostitute. In 1633, he killed a servant during a quarrel at a tavern in Braintree and had to flee to Holland. He returned to Court a year later, was eventually pardoned for the homicide and in 1638 was appointed Poet Laureate in succession to Ben Jonson. In later life he became a theatrical impresario, owning the first playhouse in London to feature moving scenery and special effects – a skill no doubt picked up during his experiences creating masques at court.

The Queen was so pleased to have Jeffrey back she immediately commissioned another portrait of him. In June 1630 Mytens painted a 'picture of Jeoffry in a wood' which was placed in the Bear Gallery in Whitehall and now hangs at Hampton Court. The background was done by an associate of Mytens, one Corragio John, and shows a thick, dense wood. It is Mytens' best painting of Jeffrey, capturing for once something of the mystery of the boy.

Jeffrey stands there, alone among the trees, staring straight ahead with a serious, solemn air. Physically, he is still a child; with his blond hair and chubby cheeks, there is something of the toddler about him. But his eyes stare straight ahead with a questioning, almost disturbing intensity. He looks thoughtful, almost suspicious. Perhaps it is because he has seen the world, and the adventure was not all it was made out to be.

Perhaps it is because he was growing up.

THE
LITTLE COURTIER

Hee may be great in spir't though small in sight,
Whilst all his best of service, is delight.
          John Taylor, *The Old, Old, Very Old Man*

THE DECADE BEGINNING IN 1631 WAS THE HAPPIEST
time of Jeffrey's life. His mistress was a charming and
contented wife, and a confident and assured Queen. Jeffrey
grew, if not much in height, then in abilities and accom-
plishments. He learned to ride a pony, to shoot a pistol,
to fence, to play at cards, to dance; in short, all the accom-
plishments expected of a favourite at Court.

The atmosphere of the Court at that time is summed up
in a poem by Thomas Carew:

But let us that in myrtle bowers sit
Under secure shades, use the benefit
Of peace and plenty, which the blessed hand
Of our good King gives this obdurate land,
Let us of Revels sing . . .
Tourneys, Masques, Theatres, better become
Our halcyon dayes.

Safe in the security of Denmark House, Whitehall, and all the other royal palaces, these were, indeed, the halcyon days for Jeffrey and the Court. He was young, he was loved, he was living in an environment which was largely insulated from the murmuring and rumours of discontent elsewhere.

For Charles had eventually solved the problem of a truculent and recalcitrant Parliament by disbanding it altogether and bringing England under his personal rule. Parliament was dismissed in 1629 and for eleven years the King ruled England without its aid, pursuing a foreign policy of appeasement and raising money through a series of unpopular and largely arbitrary taxes.

It was an era, truly, of 'revels, tourneys, masques and theatres'. Secure in his Court, surrounded by a clique of favourites who told him only what he wanted to hear, the King was largely ignorant of the strength of feeling outside the palace walls. The Puritan pamphleteers might spew forth their condemnation, the people might mutter and grumble at the unfair taxes, but in the haven of the royal palaces all was sunny and bright.

And for those whose grumbling grew too discordant, stricter censorship laws would see them imprisoned or fined. In this sunny, self-congratulatory, theatrical world, no one was to be allowed to pull aside the scenery to show the bare walls behind.

Of course, even within this happy family there were arguments. There was the time when various courtiers got the otherwise teetotal poet Edmund Waller drunk, causing the poor man to tumble down the main staircase at Denmark House and suffer a 'cruel fall'. The Queen was most displeased. And there were sharper, more personal rivalries, matters of honour which could only be settled one way.

On 10 January 1631, a quarrel broke out between the Earl of Denbigh and a man named Crofts. Desmond, the Earl's son, had said to Crofts, 'Your hose are too short.' 'So is your nose,' Crofts replied, and thus a fight was born. The Earl's son snubbed Crofts who responded by 'knocking' him in the Queen's presence. Desmond went crying to his father, who challenged Crofts to a duel. The outcome of Crofts versus Denbigh is not clear, but Crofts must have survived for he was involved in another fight a year later, one which, unfortunately, he lost.

Jeffrey must have been aware of the duels and their outcomes, and no doubt looked on when the young man 'knocked' the Earl in the Queen's presence. It was a tragic example of a plague that had infected the Court on and off for many years. James I called duelling 'a vaine that bleeds both incessantly and inwardly', and certainly the first decades of the seventeenth century were times when the 'bewitching duel' claimed many lives.

During the decade, however, duelling in England declined. Crofts, argumentative and headstrong, was the exception rather than the rule. Over the sea in France, duelling was an epidemic, with hundreds, possibly thousands of fights each year. And it was in France that, years later, another duel and another man called Crofts were to change Jeffrey's life.

But these were small clouds on an otherwise unblemished horizon. In November 1631, Henrietta Maria gave birth to another child, a girl, christened Princess Mary. The event called for a celebration, and the Court prepared two masques.

In the five years since Jeffrey had been pulled from the porter's pocket, masques had become less and less about content and more and more about spectacle. Ben Jonson, the great scholar-playwright of the Jacobean age, had always tried to give his masques depth and sophistication. He piled on layers of allusion and classical references and brought to this essentially superficial art form a poet's sensibility.

But now he was fifty-seven and giving every sign of turning into a theatrical relic. His latest play, *The New Inn*, had been badly received with the audience hissing instead of cheering. Rather than let sleeping dogs lie, he responded by writing a long and furious poem to inform the playgoers exactly what he thought of them. Unfortunately the diatribe backfired and his enemies started mocking and parodying him and talking of 'decaying Ben'. Although his supporters rallied round him, many believed that Ben had had his day and the best course of action would be for him to fade into retirement on a Court pension of a hundred pounds a year and an annual cask of canary wine.

He, of course, had no such intention. And 1631 was to be his 'comeback' year. He received a plum commission – the chance to write masques for both the King and the Queen. In collaboration with his old ally, if not friend, Inigo Jones, he produced two masques. His masque for the King, *Love's Triumph Through Callipolis*, was performed on 9 January 1631, a date which engendered some protests from the Earl of Carlisle who thought it unseemly that a masque should be performed on a Sunday. Callipolis was Plato's utopian city, where beauty, truth and goodness dwelt, all of which were personified by King Charles and his followers.

The Queen's masque took place at Shrovetide, 22 February 1631, and was called *Chloridia*, after the goddess of flowers. The preparations were long and exhausting.

On 15 February, Sir Thomas Colpeper wrote to Sir Francis Nethersole, 'for news here is not any but everybody busy about the performance of the Queen's Masque which is to be done on shrovetide'.

Against his better judgement, Jonson had been persuaded to include the antimasque, that strange parade of grotesques and clowns which served as a kind of parody of the main masque itself. Jonson thought such things foreign and unnecessary, but he was aware of their popularity with the audience, and, more importantly; with the designer Inigo Jones.

Jones was a fascinating figure who was to become increasingly influential in the decade beginning in 1630. Jones it was who gave the Stuart Court its style. He was much more than an architect and stage designer, he was the fixer, the dresser; he clothed not only the masquers but the entire age.

Little is known of his early years. He was the son of a clothworker, and is thought to have been apprenticed to a joiner in St Paul's Churchyard. In 1603 he joined the Earl of Rutland's household as 'Henygo Jones, a picturemaker' and two years later he received his first royal commission, designing costumes and settings for a masque to be performed at Whitehall.

He travelled widely abroad, especially in Italy where in Venice, Vicenza, Bologna, Florence, Siena, Rome and Genoa he discovered the great sights of European antiquity as well as more modern architecture, particularly the work of Palladio. In 1615, after the death of the singularly unoriginal Simon Basil, Jones was appointed Surveyor of the King's Works.

As Surveyor, he was the first to be recognized as an architect of considerable skill. He introduced the Palladian style of architecture to England, designed the Queen's House at Greenwich, and built his triumph, the splendid Banqueting Hall at Whitehall.

Although he was a master of so many skills – costume design, stage engineering, architecture and building – he was, ultimately, the greatest ever set designer, a man who built his sets not only in wood and canvas but in stone and brick and marble. Like Albert Speer in the Nazi era, Jones created the backdrop for the age, real-life scenery conveying a subtle and sometimes not-so-subtle message about the actors who inhabited it. It was against his scenery, his backgrounds, that the Court could play out for real the comedies and tragedies of its life.

There is a picture of Jones by Van Dyck, a pencil drawing executed in 1640 when he was sixty-seven. It shows an elderly figure, though still alert. Long, wavy hair descends from under a skullcap, and he has a rather grizzled pointed beard. In his hands he holds a piece of paper, a plan, perhaps, or a design for a new piece of stage machinery. The eyes are still watchful, staring intently. The clothes are plain and unadorned. This is a producer, a maker, a man used to getting things done, a perfectionist whose vision was the only thing that mattered.

In matters of the masque, this was entirely true. When he submitted his costume designs to Henrietta Maria for *Chloridia*, he wrote at the bottom of one sketch, 'The colours are in her Majesty's choice: but I should humbly–' at which point he crossed out the last four words and continued, 'but my opinion is that several fresh greens mixed with gold and silver will be most proper.'

For Jones, at least when it came to masques, there was no need to be humble any more. Small wonder that Henrietta Maria chose him to design her house at Greenwich. She, above all, lived her life as a series of plays – the adolescent victim, the doting wife and mother, the fighting warrior. It was only when the scenery collapsed and the leading actors were brutally replaced that she came to realize that life is not a play with a happy ending.

The set for *Chloridia* was typically ornate. Around the edge of the proscenium arch was a forest of leaves in green and gold with children playing among them. In the middle, a huge garland of flowers spelled out the word, 'Chloridia'.

As usual there had been arguments over precedence. The Spanish ambassador decided to leave town rather than run the risk of coming below the French in the pecking order. Eventually, however, the audience was seated in proper order of importance, the music began to play and the curtains parted.

The scene opened on a serene vista of pleasant hills, tree-studded groves and distant waterfalls. After a pause to allow the audience to 'feast their eyes with the delights of nature', a cloud appeared, driven by a 'plump boy' who played Zephyrus. He sang a gentle song to a maiden in a cloud opposite, playing the role of Spring, before being hoisted off into the wings. Spring descended to the earth to be joined by her fellow Naiads.

Time for a scene change. Scene changes always presented the greatest challenge to the masque designer in the seventeenth century as they were virtually impossible to achieve without the audience noticing. One Italian producer solved this by having stooges at the back of the audience shout 'Help! Fire! Murder!' or snap a piece of wood to simulate the cracking of a gallery support. Whilst the audience turned round to investigate he would change scenery. It was a great idea with only one tiny flaw: there were panics and the whole theatre emptied in the stampede for safety.

Jones solved the problem in a less dangerous way, by inventing a lighting effect – a series of large circles of candles, fitted with reflectors, which when revolved so dazzled the audience they had eyes for nothing else.

Back to *Chloridia*. A crack of thunder broke the air, the stage opened up, and out leapt a 'Dwarfe-post from Hell' who danced and made a speech. This was not Jeffrey, but another, older dwarf, with a large moustache and a rather rakish hat. He was followed by the somewhat strange grouping of Cupid, Jealousy, Disdain, Fear and Dissimulation who performed a dance together, and then it was Jeffrey's turn. The script runs:

> The antimasque. Third entry. The Queen's dwarf, richly apparelled as a prince of hell, attended by six infernal spirits; he first danceth alone, and then the spirits, all expressing their joy for Cupid's coming among them.

Jeffrey is a creature of the otherworld, outlandish, demonic. Unlike the dwarf who played the 'Dwarfe-post from Hell', Jeffrey had no words to speak. Dressed in rich clothes, he capered around the stage, surrounded by six dancers, a freakish, grotesque scene. For a masque-designer like Jones, Jeffrey's tiny size was a gift. Jones took every opportunity to use dwarfs, and Jeffrey featured in three of his masques during the 1630s, always used purely as a visual effect.

For a more sophisticated artist such as Ben Jonson, the emphasis on the visual was trite and superficial. Indeed, *Chloridia* reads like a battle between text and visuals. Ostensibly about spring, it ends with ladies dressed as Fame, Poesie, History, Architecture and Sculpture climbing into a bower. These are not characters natural to the action or the theme of the masque, they are impositions. The designer has forced his vision on the writer. Ben Jonson has been forced to write them in, because Inigo Jones said so.

This conclusion is borne out by Jonson's own comments on the masque. In a scarcely veiled attack, he satirized the masque:

> I have met with those,
> That do cry up the Machine, and the Shows!
> The majesty of Juno in the clouds!
> And peering forth of Iris in the shrouds!
> The ascent of Lady Fame! Which none could spy,
> Not they that sided her, Dame Poetry,
> Dame History, Dame Architecture too,
> And Goody Sculpture, brought with much ado
> To hold her up.

It was to be Jonson's last masque and his last collaboration with Inigo Jones. The rules had changed and the wit and invention which for so long had been his hallmark were now usurped by costume and design. However, Jonson was never going to admit this publicly, and when he published the King's Masque, the title page ran thus:

The Inventors
Ben Jonson   Inigo Jones

Jones was irritated. *He* was pre-eminent, *his* name should have come first. He requested Jonson to make amends in the published version of *Chloridia*. Jonson, with the tact for which he was famous, simply left Jones's name off the title page altogether.

Inigo Jones had had enough. For years he had borne the arrogance and stubbornness of this man whom he described as 'the best of poets but the worst of men'.

There could only be one outcome to the fight. The next Christmas, the commission to write the royal masque went to Aurelian Townsend who, suitably respectful of Jones, pronounced that a masque was 'nothing else but pictures with light and motion'.

Jonson never forgave Jones. He issued a series of scathing verses which showed exactly what he thought of the glorification of scenery over substance:

> O shows! Shows! Mighty shows!
> The eloquence of masques! What need of prose,
> Or verse, or sense, t'express immortal you?

He went on to attack 'wisest Inigo's' emphasis and power:

> Painting and carpentry are the soul of masque.
> Pack with your peddling poetry to the stage,
> This is the money-get, mechanic age.

Finally there is a caustic reference to Jeffrey, complaining how Jones delighted in putting dwarfs on stage, how, just to get a quick response, he would 'paint a Lane, where Thumbe with Geffry meets'.

In Jonson's eyes, Jeffrey was a stage effect, nothing more, nothing less, and in two of his subsequent works a figure called 'Vitruvius Hoop' or 'Colonel Vitruvius' appears; a bossy, pompous figure, who 'will join with no man ... he must be sole inventor'.

Henrietta Maria was the original drama queen. She was certainly theatrical off the stage, delighting in secret plots and intrigues, always trying to get a new storyline going. But nothing pleased her as much as actually taking part in stage productions. In 1632, she began to prepare her most ambitious production yet. *The Queen's Pastoral*, or to give it its proper title *The Shepherd's Paradise*, was a long and complex play, written by Walter Montague, the Queen's Lord Almoner. Later, Suckling was to ridicule the production for its unintelligible plot and incomprehensible language:

> Wat Montague now stood forth for his trial
> And did not so much as suspect a denial;
> But witty Apollo asked him first of all
> If he understood his own pastorall.

The performance took place in the lower courtyard of Denmark House on 10 January. It was a long show according to one exhausted spectator, who wrote: 'This night our queen hath acted her costly pastoral in Somerset House, which hath lasted seven or eight hours.'

For the enemies of Henrietta Maria, this passion for acting merely confirmed the depravity of her court. *The Pastoral*, in particular, had an unfortunate aftermath, for it coincided with the publication of William Prynne's *Histriomastix, or the Player's Scourge*. Prynne's book was an intemperate, densely argued work which attacked, at great length, actors, acting and all things theatrical. In Prynne's eyes, theatricals only served to increase licentiousness and lewdness.

Whether this book was published before Henrietta Maria's appearance in *The Shepherd's Paradise*, or whether, as one source claims, it appeared the day after the marathon performance, it was clearly interpreted as being an attack on the Queen herself.

'Women actors are notorious whores,' wrote Prynne, who went on to quote St Paul's injunction against women speaking in church:

And dares then any Christian woman be so more than whorishly impudent as to act, to speak publicly on a stage (perchance in men's apparel and cut hair) in the presence of sundry men and women?

To be fair to Prynne, many of his English readership would have echoed his thoughts – if not the extremity of his language. It had never been traditional for women to appear on the English stage. But Prynne had insulted the Queen. He was immediately punished; hauled before the Star Chamber and issued with the barbarous sentence of being branded with the letters SL (for 'seditious liar'), placed in the pillory, his books burnt under his nose and to have part of his ears cut off. Given the amount of books and pamphlets he had published, he nearly asphyxiated under the smoke.

To his credit, he never recanted or withdrew his attack. Indeed, he was in almost permanent trouble with the authorities for most of his writing career. What remained of his ears were finally sliced off in 1637 for a further attack, after which he took to wearing his hair long. Prynne, although seen by many as a Puritan martyr, was a Royalist. He was imprisoned by Cromwell, and after his release worked hard for the restoration of the monarchy. He was finally made Keeper of the Records under Charles II and is reported to have been a courteous old man, kind to students, although firmly convinced of the basic immorality of nuns.

Jeffrey was by now a famous figure and in 1633 came the chance to sit for a truly great painter. Mytens's best painting, it is true, shows us something of the mysteriousness of Jeffrey, but when Van Dyck came to be Court painter in 1632, the eye of a genius came to rest on the Queen's dwarf.

Born on 21 March 1599 in Antwerp, Antoon Van Dyck was the son of a textile merchant. His father Frans specialized in importing velvet, satin and silk, the very materials that come to life so thrillingly in Van Dyck's greatest work.

In 1632 Charles I invited him to England. Charles was probably the greatest collector of art of his time. He employed an army of agents to find him great masterpieces, and he patronized and supported a long list of painters, sculptors and craftsmen. He spent huge sums acquiring his collections, but he also had a good eye for a bargain. Art was the one thing about which he was truly enthusiastic. When a consignment of pictures arrived from the Vatican, he excitedly called Henrietta Maria, the Earls of Holland and Pembroke and Inigo Jones to help him unpack it. Together, they spent many happy hours having a competition over who could guess which artist had painted which picture.

The installation of Van Dyck as the 'principall Paynter in ordinary to their Majesties' was his triumph. Van Dyck settled in London in April 1632. Inigo Jones helped him to find a suitable studio with a garden in Blackfriars and on 5 July he was knighted by the King and given an annual salary of two hundred pounds. Never had an artist been so honoured. But then never had a Court had the services of so great an artist as Sir Anthony Van Dyck.

Over the next ten years he was to capture the Caroline Court in all its laced and satined glory. Van Dyck's portraits, with their superb technique and glorious colour, redefined the Court. Under his brush, Charles I changed from a small, aloof, nervous man, to a hero, a warrior astride a huge horse. Henrietta Maria became a wise, serene queen, shimmering with grace and beauty. The Court was suddenly a place where taste and elegance, refinement and wit created a paradise. It was all self-delusion, of course, but who could resist such delicious lies?

Van Dyck was more than a mere propagandist, though; his paintings, above all, are studies in character. When we see the portraits of Charles, we see not only what the King thought of himself, but, lurking behind the eyes, what he really was. He appears majestic, imperious, powerful, but the aloof expression, the hooded eyes, the dispassionate gaze give the game away. This is not a great warrior; it is a shy, small man wearing a costume.

Thus, in most of his Court portraits, Van Dyck was working undercover, as it were; 'Sir Anthony' was painting the subjects in a flattering pose, but 'Van Dyck' was trying to let their true nature show. When it came to painting children, of course, there were fewer restrictions and we see them without the layers of flattery. This natural affinity with children explains, perhaps, some of the power of one of his great masterpieces: *Queen Henrietta Maria with Jeffrey Hudson and an Ape*. Painted in 1633, it is one of the great artworks of the seventeenth century, capturing not only the appearance of the Queen and her dwarf, but also their relationship.

Henrietta Maria is dressed in blue satin, which shimmers with light. She stares straight ahead, confident, calm, one hand resting gently on her pet monkey. She is informal, but in control. The crown sits to her left, on a cloth of deepest gold.

The picture is certainly valuable on the practical level for what it tells us about Jeffrey. His clothes are of a deep scarlet velvet, trimmed with white lace. A gold chain runs diagonally from his right shoulder to his left side, his boots have spurs on them. If these were his real clothes – and there seems no reason to doubt it – he was riding and hunting by the time he was fourteen.

The portrait is so lifelike that it immediately raises the question of Jeffrey's height. He is clearly wearing boots with heels and he rises to no higher than the level of the Queen's waist. We know that Henrietta Maria was tiny herself, less than five feet. Assuming this to be an accurate perspective (and it has to be admitted that is a big assumption, Van Dyck being prone to altering heights and perspectives to enhance the stature of his subjects), Jeffrey would be about thirty-two inches high, or two feet six inches. Rather larger than the eighteen inches of 1627, but then again he is six years older. And as we shall see, his pituitary gland was dysfunctional, rather than completely inoperative.

Jeffrey has brown eyes and shoulder-length fair hair, not blond but very light brown, thin and wispy. As in some of the Mytens pictures, he is in hunting gear, but on his gauntleted hand of cream-coloured satin, there sits not a hawk, but a monkey, held by a thin blue ribbon. In his left hand he holds a pear. In the background is an orange tree.

The presence of the monkey is the source for another of Stonecastle's flights of fancy in his *Universal Spectator* article of 1732:

Her majesty's monkey soon scrap'd Acquaintance with him [Jeffrey], took him for an agreeable playfellow and none were so great as PUG and JEFFREY, though there were some scuffles now and then between them in which JEFFREY could not always keep his Plumbs and his Pears to himself . . . they were painted together by Sir ANTONY VAN DYCK.

The monkey, the fruit, the dwarf, they are all there in this painting, but Van Dyck uses them in an entirely different way. Stonecastle, with his smug joking, turned the presence of the monkey into a farcical jest. Van Dyck uses it as a comment on Jeffrey and the Queen.

For in this portrait Jeffrey is a pet. He looks up anxiously at his royal mistress, gazing at her longingly, desperate for a sign of approval. His whole attention is fixed on her. Is he wondering what she is thinking? Is he waiting for her to tell him what to do? Is he looking for love, hoping that she will pet him as she pets her other animals? Whatever the case, whatever the thoughts in his head, one thing is clear: he is attached to her side, as certainly as if he had been tied to her with the same thin blue ribbon that holds the ape.

Like Pug the monkey, Jeffrey is in thrall. He may be sumptuously clothed, he may be skilled at hunting, he may have all the accoutrements of a courtier, but he still has no will of his own, just a canine-like devotion, like an anxious dog, waiting for his mistress to issue a command or throw a stick.

Yet he is not unhappy. There is anxiety in his eyes, but not fear and not unease. He is looking to please her, to be rewarded for his tricks. He is not still, as she is. All his energy is focused outwards, towards his mistress. He loves her and she loves him.

But their love is not, and never would be, equal.

By 1641, Van Dyck was looking to return home. The King had run out of money and he was no longer being paid. He spent some time in Antwerp in autumn 1641, but by now was seriously ill. He died in London on 9 December 1641, the same day his infant daughter Juliana was baptized. He was buried in the old St Paul's cathedral and a monument was raised over his tomb depicting him as the Genius of Painting. The tomb was destroyed in the great fire of 1666, but it was never his true monument. His real monument is the paintings he made over the course of a decade, paintings which depict a glorious, doomed world in all its finery, in all its glorious, vibrant, tragic, stupid optimism.

In 1999 a huge collection of his works was taken on a world tour. When the exhibition came to London in late 1999 the portrait of Jeffrey and Henrietta Maria was a show-stopper. People stood before it open-mouthed, amazed at the beauty of the Queen and the strange vibrancy of the little figure by her side. As they read their notes and discovered that the little figure was not a child, but a fourteen-year-old dwarf, their surprise must have mirrored all those who saw Jeffrey for the first time.

I sat and looked at it for an hour, maybe more. It explained to me more clearly than anything else who Jeffrey was, what his role was intended to be, and why in later life he was so desperate to cut the ribbon and to break free.

THE
WONDER OF THE AGE

Of subjects, (my dread liege) 'tis manifest,
You have the oldest, the greatest and the least:
That for an Old, a Great, and Little man,
No kingdom (sure) compare with Britain can.
John Taylor, The Old, Old, Very Old Man

In September 1635 another marvel arrived at Court to join the giant knock-kneed porter and the tiny, perfectly formed dwarf.

Thomas Parr – or 'Old Parr' as he was called – was said to be a hundred and fifty-one years old. 'The English Methuselah' was celebrated in verse by the poet John Taylor, in a poem entitled, rather repetitively, *The Old, Old, Very Old Man*, where Taylor refers to him as 'a Monument, I may say, and almost Miracle of Nature . . .'

The poem begins with a dedication to 'the High and Mighty prince Charles' and points out the happy coincidence of Charles having 'the oldest, the greatest and the least' at court; that is, Old Parr, William Evans and Jeffrey Hudson.

Of Evans, Taylor says:

One for his extraordinary stature,
Guards well your gates, & by instinct of Nature
(As hee is strong) is Loyall, True and Just,
Fit and most able, for his Charge and Trust.

Jeffrey, he applauds not only for his size but for his character:

The other's small and well composed feature
Deserves the Title of a Pretty Creature:
And doth (or may) retaine as good a mind
As greater men, and be as well inclin'd:
Hee may be great in spir't though small in sight,
Whilst all his best of service, is delight.

Together, these three were to be known as the 'Three Wonders of the Age'.

Old Parr was discovered by Thomas, Earl of Arundel on a visit to Shropshire. He had the old man carried on a litter to London and presented to King Charles. The old man shuffled in and stood before the King.

'What is the secret of your long life?' asked Charles. The old man paused for a moment.

'Please your majesty,' he replied. 'I did penance for a bastard when I was above a hundred years old.'

There was a frosty silence. This kind of rustic bawdy humour was not to the King's liking at all. But old age must be made allowance for, and Charles kept Old Parr at Court from then to the end of his life. Which, sad to say, was not very long. Evidently the move south had been too much for him, and the old man, who claimed to have been born in the reign of Edward IV, and who could remember a time when 'malt was sold for twelve pence the quarter, and seventeen at the dearest', died soon after his arrival.

The fame of the Three Wonders soon spread beyond the walls of Court, and in 1636 they were brought together in a contemporary print. It is entered in the registers of the Stationer's Company as:

> 6 April 1636 Entred for his Copie a lit[t]le discourse of the three wonders of this age vizt Master JEFFRY HUDSON, WILLIAM EVANS and THOMAS PAR[R]. by master [Thomas] HAYWOOD

There is a copy in the British Museum, where it is bound in with John Taylor's poem on Old Parr and a further engraving of the old man.

In the print, Evans stands, giant, bearded, holding his staff and with no hint of knock-knees or splay feet. Next to him stands Jeffrey, holding a hat with a large feather on it. He has a sword by his side, and the hand on his hip holds a cane. There are fashionably huge rosettes on his shoe buckles. On the right of the picture, Old Parr sits, dozing in a chair.

The engravings are accompanied by short essays on giants, dwarfs and old men, respectively. The essays were the work of Thomas Heywood, a dramatist and hack-writer who had arrived in London in the late 1590s to become an actor and playwright with the Lord Admiral's Company and later the Queen's Players.

His description of the Three Wonders was, presumably, drawn from real-life experience, for in 1633 the Queen appeared in one of his plays. *Love's Mistress, or the Queen's Masque* was a marked success; it was repeated the following year and the Queen was greatly taken with the work of the playwright.

The text under Evans does not tell us much about the man himself, limiting itself mainly to a list of classical giants from Agatho the Athenian to Gogmagog, whose 'statue is still preserved in the Guildhall'. Under Old Parr, we are offered some biblical examples as well as the information that 'his daughter Joan was fain to feed him like a childe, a roasted apple was the last food he received, and soone after dyed and now lies buried at Westminster; and shall have a monument bestowed on him'.

Jeffrey's accompanying text lists the usual classical suspects including Canopes, dwarf to Empress Augusta, various Roman and Greek dwarfs and Molon the actor, before moving on to more modern characters such as Robert Wainman, 'who served M. Willowby in Lincolnshire of an exceedingly low stature, an excellent huntsman, who was after preferred to king James, and served him till his death.'

The article shows how popular dwarfs were, not only among royalty but among the nobility as well:

> Queen Elizabeth had also a she Dwarfe, who lived till she was very aged, the Lady Hatton hath another of the like stature: The lord of Southampton had one of a manly face, but his height not above two cubits, and the lord High Martiall another at this time . . . and also one John Thomson, borne in Yorkshire neere unto Wakefield, being a Smith at this time behind St. Clements Church without Temple-Barre and not any of these exceeding two Cubits.

Heywood then moves on to Jeffrey:

Whosoever then shall look upon Master Jeffrey and his small mistresse who was late living, Her majesties hee and shee-dwarfes, may with the more facility give belief unto these before remembred.

Who Jeffrey's 'small mistresse' is, is not certain. Henrietta Maria's 'hee and shee-dwarfes' were Jeffrey and Sara Holton, but Sara was certainly still alive as late as 1640. Nevertheless, Heywood goes on to give us the first character sketch of Jeffrey himself:

And for him, he is one of the prettiest, neatest, and well-proportioned small men that ever Nature bred, or was ever seene, or heard of beyond the memory of man, for his fine behaviour and witty discourse.

Heywood's text confirms what we learn about Jeffrey from Taylor's poem: that he was known, not only for his stature, but for his behaviour. That he was witty and funny and charming. Heywood ends with an advert for another book:

But concerning Dwarfes, and the praise of little ones, whosoever desires to be instructed therein, let them reade the booke called The New-yeare's Gift, lately come out, (a learned though a little work,) and hee shall be better instructed, and further satisfied . . .

The work he was referring to was entered into the Stationer's Register at the same time as the engraving; indeed it was the work of the same publisher. It was called *The New Year's Gift*, and it was written entirely in praise of Jeffrey Hudson.

The Stationer's Register gives the details of the book as follows:

> 6 April 1636 Entred for his copie vnder the hands of Master HAYWOOD and Master Smethwicke warden a booke called 'a New yeares guift' dedicated to little JEFFERIE the Queenes dwarfe 'in praise of litlenes' by master SLATER.

'Master Slater' is an unknown figure; there is no writer of the time called Slater, and in the book itself the author signs himself under the pseudonym of 'Microphilus'. But Heywood's name in the register, the fact that it came from his publisher, and his advertisement of the book in *The Three Wonders* seem to imply that he was responsible.

There are only two copies of this work in existence, both in the British Museum. Physically, it is a tiny work, measuring only a few inches in both width and height. Stylistically it is simply a game, a *jeu d'esprit*, albeit somewhat laboured at times. The jokes and the theme are evident on the title page which runs:

> The New Yeere's Gift, presented at Court, from the Lady PARVULA to the Lord MINIMUS (commonly called Little Jefferie) Her Majesties Servant, with a Letter as it was penned in short-hand; where it is proved LITTLE THINGS are better than GREAT.

The author of the book is given as Microphilus, a pen-name which roughly means 'lover of smallness'. The book's title indicates that this was commissioned as a gift, a private production which was given out among the traditional New Year's presents on the English New Year of 25 March. It was usual for courtiers and servants to be given gifts at this time. Obviously this present was so successful it was rushed into print a few weeks later.

Mostly it is a mishmash of classical allusion, laboured punning and familiar targets. There are dedicatory poems from fake poets with names like 'T. Little' and 'W. Loe'. Jeffrey is once again linked with William Evans, as the book begins with a poem dedicated 'to his high and mighty friend William Evans, Sirnamed the Great Porter' which runs:

> Will, be not angry this smalle book is read
> In praise of one no bigger than thy head.

And goes on to praise Jeffrey:

> Though hee be small in Body and in Limbe
> Yet wee commend something that's great in him
> The greatnesse of his spirit and his minde
> Whose virtues are not like thy strength confin'd
> Unto his bulke . . .
>   . . . Then be not angry, this small Lord is prais'd
> Since thou by nature, he by wit is rais'd.

If we assume that Heywood wrote it, there still remains the question who commissioned it, for the book claims to be commissioned by a 'Lady Parvula', who also supplies a dedication at the beginning:

> To THE MOST exquisite Epitome of Nature, and compleatest compendium of a Courtier, the Lord MINIMUS; the Lady PARVULA wisheth health and happiness . . .

Parvula means small or little, as in the Rutland motto, Multum in Parvo. The most probable candidate for the role of Lady Parvula was Jeffrey's opposite number, her majesty's 'shee-dwarfe' Sara Holton. The only personal clue we have to Lady Parvula comes at the end of the book where she says that Jeffrey is 'no stranger, but of my owne country an Englishman'.

However, Sara cannot have commissioned the book; that would have been beyond her means. She may have played the role, but the instigator is much more likely to be someone else, someone who always enjoyed creating scenes and playing characters. The affair has Henrietta Maria's fingerprints all over it. We know she admired the work of Thomas Heywood, we know that she adored drama and theatre. It does not take much imagination to picture her delight at the little scene, as Lady Parvula presents Lord Minimus with his New Year's gift, a tiny volume for a tiny man, and full of jokes about the joys of being tiny. How the courtiers and ladies-in-waiting must have applauded the jest.

The book itself tells us little about Jeffrey. There are references to Jeffrey's home:

> Yet you may find Magnum in Parvo, that great excellency in sundry little things.

There are obvious references to his experiences:

> When one's undone by fire or shipwrack, or goods taken by Pyrats, what sets him up but the Kings briefes, and alas, how would many a poore Knight live if he had not a little to keepe him?

'Briefs' in this context refers to 'breves'; letters of authority from the King, which grant the holder power or payment. The pun, of course, is that Jeffrey himself is a human in 'brief' but it may be that following Jeffrey's adventure in

France the King did indeed issue instructions to pay him in lieu of his lost jewels.

Above all, the book treats Jeffrey as an emblem, a wonder to be read for its moral symbolism:

> So little dwarfs (boyes in proportion though perchance men in discretion) being about a Monarch, though silent, yet their very persons are a voice crying; Rex memento te esse minimum: O King remember how thou art little, borne like others little, to teach thee to Heaven, humility, to Earth, humanity.

This is Jeffrey as a kind of *memento mori*, a reminder of man's frailty. Despite the author's efforts to turn Jeffrey into a symbol, it strikes a false note:

> Your little low person (me thinkes) is nature's humble pulpit, out of which shee reads graces diviner lectures to High-Aspiring Mortals: and whereas some in the world (wedded to error) may fondly imagine your residence at Court to bee rather for wonder and merriment then for any use or service, you may require from them no lesse satisfaction then a publique recantation.

Jeffrey, in the end, was not at Court to provide anyone with a philosophical emblem. He was there for curiosity value and to make people laugh. As the book says:

> Had you been Bigge and Great ten to one you never had prooved a Courtier; 'twas onely your littlenesse preferr'd you.

Nevertheless, it is clear that Jeffrey is held in real affection, for several times the book refers to Jeffrey's wit and cleverness. This is courtly language, full of hyperbole and extravagant compliments, but there is an air of genuine affection throughout the book:

> Goe on, goe on therefore (diminutive Sir) with the guide of honour and service of Fortune, your lovelinesse being such as no man can disdaine to serve you, your littlenesse such as no man neede to fear you, the first having put you without hatred, the latter below envy . . .

In the second edition there is a tiny engraving of Jeffrey by Martin Droeshout. The engraving is small, but detailed. Jeffrey is dressed in an embroidered doublet with a lace collar. He stands in front of a curtained balcony, a glove in his hand, his blond hair cut in a kind of bob. He wears all the ornate clothing of a cavalier: the elaborately embroidered, high-waisted doublet, the lace collar, the bucket-topped boots turned down and embellished by flowery 'boot roses'.

Under the engraving is a Latin phrase and its translation:

> Gaze on with wonder, and discerne in me
> The abstract of the world's Epitome.

The word 'epitome' was used several times of Jeffrey. Nowadays we tend to use the word as meaning 'the ideal example', but the original meaning was a 'condensed record or representation in miniature'. Jeffrey was man writ little, that was his appeal. He was a perfect little courtier, witty, endearing and wonderfully detailed down to the tiny roses on his little boots.

Jeffrey was growing up. But in one way, at least, he was still a child. Hypopituitarism – growth-hormone deficiency

– typically affects the development of the child in terms of puberty. Some individuals, particularly boys affected before birth, will have an extremely small penis and undescended testes.

There is no reason to assume this was the case with Jeffrey, but it is likely that puberty was delayed for him. Certainly the portrait by Van Dyck still shows a childish figure, even though he was fourteen.

Stonecastle raises the issue of Jeffrey's sex life in a rather prurient way:

> The ladies were very fond of him. He could make married men Cuckolds without making them jealous and Mothers of the Maids, without letting the world know they had any gallants.

This is salacious nonsense, peddling the idea that Jeffrey, while seen as harmless, was actually fooling the husbands all the time. The truth is we don't know about the presence or otherwise of Jeffrey's sex life. He certainly never married, and the likelihood is that for the first thirty years of his life, at least, it was not an issue. Just as his vertical growth had slowed to a crawl, his physical maturation was similarly slow. His mind was quick to develop, but his body was slow.

Life at Court remained blissfully happy for Jeffrey. The winter months were filled with plays and masques, games and dances; and in the spring and summer the Court would go on 'progress', travels round the country to visit royal palaces and other great homes and cities.

In the summer of 1636, for example, the Court went to Oxfordshire. On 21 August, Jeffrey travelled there in his own carriage, in convoy with the rest of the royal household. Two miles outside Oxford, the convoy stopped and the King and Queen left their carriages. They were officially greeted by Archbishop Laud, in his role of Chancellor of the University, leading a procession of lawyers, doctors, academics and citizens. From there Jeffrey accompanied the Queen to her lodgings while the King went to evensong in Christchurch Cathedral.

That evening they watched a play, *Passions Calmed or the Settling of the Floating Island*, performed by the students of Christchurch. The play, which featured a comic Puritan character called Melancholio, was not a huge success; indeed, one member of the audience described it as the worst performance he had ever seen on a stage (apart from an even worse one he'd witnessed at Cambridge). The next morning, Jeffrey was among the crowd to see the two young Princes receive honorary degrees. Aged six and three they must be among the youngest-ever graduates of Oxford. After that it was a short carriage ride around the corner to St John's to see the new buildings and to hear a short song sung on the steps of the library.

Dinner was enlivened by a selection of baked meats served in the shapes of archbishops, doctors and bishops, although we are not, unfortunately, told what forms these actually took. Then there was *Love's Hospital*, another play, this time performed by students from St John's College and mercifully a lot better than *Passions Calmed*. The play was the work of one Abraham Wright. Thirty years into the future, Abraham was to become vicar of All Saints, Oakham, Jeffrey's home town. Forty years into the future, Jeffrey would sit with Abraham's son, telling his life story, while the young lad scribbled down notes.

This play ended at six o'clock, which gave the Queen just enough time to squeeze in another play, *The Royal*

Slave, which had the benefit of designs and costumes by Inigo Jones. She liked this one so much she borrowed the costumes for one of her own productions.

Early the next morning, Jeffrey was back in his carriage, rolling out of Oxford towards the palace at Woodstock. The Queen had her own chambers at the palace, including a hall for her guards, her own council chamber, a 'neat' chapel where she heard mass, and 'divers other fair and large rooms for the nobility and officers'. The palace was situated on top of a hill, in a fine park which included a labyrinth for the Court's amusement. No doubt Jeffrey and Jerome Gregoire were well provided for.

On the way to Woodstock, they went first to Enstone, a few miles north of the palace, to enjoy the delights of Mr Bushell's water-gardens. Bushell was a miner, engineer and 'master of the art of running up debt', much of which was spent on his magnificent gardens.

Their visit to the water-gardens was supposed to be a surprise visit, but the owner had received enough warning to prepare some rather bad poetry in honour of the King and Queen and have it set to music. After several verses in their honour, and a quick tour round, the King, Queen and courtiers entered a banqueting house built into the side of the hill, like a grotto, where they ate a wonderful meal, while a fountain shaped like a bear's head spouted water into a basin. Above their heads was a painting of the 'woman of Samaria drawing water for our Saviour', and other biblical scenes. On each side of the grotto were smaller caves, draped in black to represent 'the melancholly retyr'd life like a Hermits'.

Below them, in a room of its own, stood a great rock, a huge lump of stone which Bushell had discovered during the excavation of the garden. He had turned it into the centrepiece of a fantastic aquatic display, with masses of pipes and taps that could be manipulated to provide a stunning spectacle.

Water could be made to spout from side to side of the room, or to leap from the stone, supporting a silver ball in its jet. A thin spray could be spread across the room, allowing guests to see an artificial rainbow. Strange flashes of lightning were somehow created, along with artificial nightingales and other 'rarer and audible sounds and noyses'. Best of all, guests who stood too near the stone could be sealed in, caged behind a wall, a 'plash'd fence' of water. Sometimes, to Mr Bushell's delight, fair ladies were caught in this trap, unable to escape without the water 'flashing and dashing their smooth, soft, and tender thighs and knees'.

Outside there was a small pond, where a little artificial duck swam round and round, chased by an equally artificial spaniel. Henrietta Maria, with her love of the strange and unusual, was so delighted with the gardens that she commanded they should henceforth be known 'after her own princely name, Henrietta'. Later on she rewarded Mr Bushell with a rare gift, 'an entire Mummie from Egypt'.

Sadly, the mummy fell to pieces a short while later. As Aubrey recorded: 'The dampnesse of the place has spoyled it with mouldinesse.'

Just before arriving at Oxford, the Queen and her Court had been staying in the Midlands, at Holmby Palace near Northampton. Here she was joined by an emissary from another court, a court which throughout England was viewed with hatred and suspicion. His name was George Con, or Coneo, and he had come from the Pope.

It was bad enough that Henrietta Maria was an actress and dancer. It was bad enough that she was French. What

really angered the populace was 'Queen Mary's' evident
zeal for Catholicism. Despite the King's attempts to limit
its influence, the presence of a strong centre of Catholicism
in London proved a great attraction for many erstwhile
worshippers and new converts.

Indeed, Charles seems never to have correctly judged
the intensity of this feeling. George Con was not the first
emissary from the Pope. Charles had previously allowed
the Pope to send a 'special mediator' to Henrietta Maria,
a Scotsman by birth called Gregorio Panzani. Panzani's
role was to bring some organization to the chaotic Catholic
structure in England, to try to obtain permission for a
Catholic bishop in England, and to arrange for Catholics
to be exempt from all oaths imposed by the government.

The presence of such people and the fact that Charles
agreed that his wife could send a representative of her own
to Rome, only reinforced the dislike of Henrietta Maria
and her Court in the minds of the Puritans – and, more
ominously, in the minds of the London mob.

The offence was only magnified by the presence of a new
and opulent Roman Catholic chapel. Up until 1632 the
Queen had been using a 'spacious room' as a makeshift
chapel but in September of that year, on the Court's return
from Oxford, a ceremony took place in Denmark House
to consecrate the ground for a new chapel to be designed
and built by Inigo Jones.

While a large section of London was drawn to the rich
ceremony and ritual, by far the majority of Londoners were
enraged by this upsurge of popery in the heart of the
capital. Henrietta Maria was, in their eyes, flaunting her
religion before them. It was not just that she was a Catholic,
it was the flamboyance of the faith and the crusading zeal
of its adherents. And while the King did what he could to
prevent his subjects from attending mass at Denmark

House, there was no doubt that the palace served as a nexus of Catholicism in an increasingly Puritan world.

Jeffrey was undoubtedly a Catholic. From the moment he arrived in Denmark House he had been surrounded by Catholics and pro-Catholic sympathizers. His French servants, his nurse, his Queen, his friends were all Catholic; his life was lived in what was, essentially, a Catholic enclave in a Protestant city.

Nevertheless, it is difficult to judge the depth of Jeffrey's faith. Later in life he certainly suffered for it, but that may have been merely a crime of association. The only direct assertion we have from him – indeed, his only recorded utterance – is a curiously ambivalent affair.

It occurred at Holmby Palace and was triggered by the arrival of George Con. Con had been sent by the Pope armed with a huge quantity of relics, medals and rosaries, all blessed by the Holy Father himself. As soon as he arrived he began handing them out, spreading the gospel of Catholicism to the ladies of the Court.

On 8 August, Con entered the presence of the Queen and immediately started to hand out the gifts. He gave to Henrietta Maria magnificent rosaries of 'aloes wood', agate and buffalo horn, all of which were 'curiously worked with cameo medallions'. The other Catholic ladies of the Court were also given these valuable relics, which were handed out by Father Philip, Henrietta Maria's confessor.

Suddenly, Jeffrey realized that he had not received one of these precious gifts. Con recounted the tale in a dispatch back to the Pope:

> The queen's dwarf, who is less and better made than that of Criqui, being present, when all was nearly finished, began to call out, 'Madam, show the father

that I also am a Catholic,' with a manner and gesture that made all laugh.

It is difficult to interpret this event. Jeffrey's assertion of faith is both comic and calculated. There is something that is acquisitive about his attitude here; he is not going to be left out when the gifts are being distributed. Was he serious about his faith? Undoubtedly, for later in life he was to suffer grievously for adhering to the Catholic Church. But that does not appear to be the motive here. Here he is the magpie, performing a trick and hoping to get a trinket in return.

In the end, the episode says less about his Catholicism than his career. As *The New Yeare's Gift* shows, he was witty and clever, acquiring gifts through being adorably funny. Although still notable for being 'less and better made' than the other dwarfs, his ability to accumulate wealth comes about through acting the fool.

In this he had, at least, a good example to follow in Archie Armstrong, the King's jester. Archie had been jester to King James. His position was in many ways very similar to Jeffrey's, for the jester's role was not only to joke, but also to be the butt of jokes. He was often bullied and ill-treated by the friends of the young Prince Charles, who used to toss him 'like a dog' in a blanket.

Such treatment perhaps only made him more determined to exercise what was called the 'privilege of the coat'; the right of the King's jester to tell the truth to the monarch, even if that truth was sometimes bitter. One incident took place at Newmarket, where the elderly King James and his son Prince Charles had been witnessing the racing. As Charles set off to return to London, 'the company, almost universally, turned and accompanied the Prince'. Archie remained with his master, but not before pointing out that the popularity of the son eclipsed the popularity of the reigning sovereign. James wept copiously and the Prince's followers wasted no opportunities for exacting their revenge on the 'fool' who had told the King the truth which everyone knew, but no one else had dared to speak.

Archie never did learn how to read or write, but he still managed to amass a considerable fortune. As one contemporary verse ran:

Archie, by Kings and princes graced of late,
Jested himself into a fair estate.

At the death of James, Archie passed into the service of Charles and remained in place for many years, a familiar figure dressed in his precious jester's coat, speaking the truth. But Charles's Court was a more refined place than the Court of his father, and Archie's jesting, which was always a matter more of buffoonery than wit, was increasingly out of place. Nor did the privilege of his coat help him, for Charles was never much interested in the truth, no matter how humorously conveyed.

In 1637, Jeffrey was to witness Archie's downfall, in a corridor in Whitehall Palace. The Queen, surrounded as usual by her retinue of ladies-in-waiting, negro servants, dogs and monkeys and dwarfs, was in conference with Archbishop Laud. The Archbishop's policy with regards to the prayer book was blamed for leading England into the disastrous war with Scotland. As Archie rounded the corner and spotted the group he shouted out in his best Scottish accent, 'Wha's fool noo?'

Laud did not see the joke. In vain did Archie claim the privilege of his coat. He was hauled before the King in council and, on 11 March 1637, banished from the court:

It is this day ordered by his Majesty, with the advice of the board that Archibald Armstrong, the King's fool, for certain scandalous words of a high nature, spoken by him against the Lord Archbishop of Canterbury, his Grace, and proved to be uttered by Henrietta Maria, by two witnesses, shall have his coat pulled over his head, and be discharged of the King's service, and banished the court, for which the Lord Chamberlain of the King's household is prayed and required to give order to be executed.

To be fair to Laud, it was not just this jest that caused his final quarrel. Archie was reported to have been drunk in a tavern in Westminster, where he was heard to call Laud 'a monk, a rogue and a traitor'. And he had once proposed a grace which ran, 'Great praise be to God and little laud to the devil!'

Archie hung about Westminster Abbey for a bit, dressed in black, but in the end he had no choice. He left Court and retired to Windermere in Cumberland, where he had invested all the 'gifts' that he had been given across the years in land. There he spent his days drinking, counting his money, chasing the local women and watching with glee the downfall and imprisonment of his arch-enemy, Archbishop Laud. He died in 1646 and was buried, appropriately enough, on 1 April.

Archie's career was a salutary lesson for Jeffrey and for all favourites. Store your money, but never overstep the mark. Be funny, be witty, but also be loved.

On 10 December 1636, Jeffrey, like the rest of the Queen's household, went to church. The new chapel at Denmark House was finally complete and the palace was abuzz with people come to attend the opening ceremony.

Accompanying the Queen, he passed through a passage from her lodgings, down a flight of stairs and into the building itself.

A considerable amount of London's nobility was present for the event. Some of them might have harboured a secret yearning for 'the old faith', but mainly it was old-fashioned curiosity about Henrietta Maria and her monks. Gamache, a later chronicler, wrote:

> Persons of quality, ministers, people of all conditions who had never been out of the Kingdom came to see them [the Capuchins] as one goes to see Indians, Malays, Savages, and men from the extremities of the earth.

Inigo Jones had created his greatest stage set, with lights and music designed to make:

> the number of figures double what they were, deceiving by an ingenious artifice not only the eye, but also the ear, all conceiving that, instead of the music, they heard the melody of the angels, singing and playing upon musical instruments . . . there was left nothing but the brilliancy of the lights which caused that place to appear all on fire.

They entered a dimly lit chapel and took their places, at which point the curtains were suddenly drawn back, revealing the splendours within. At the same time the music struck up, and the angels started to sing. 'Thus eye and ear found at the same time gratification in this contrivance of piety and skill,' wrote Gamache.

The interior of the chapel was one of the glories of the Stuart age. A sculptor called François Dieussart built a

'Paradise of glory about forty feet in height', a sculpture which was a setting for the sacrament, supposed to give it a more majestic appearance. Behind the altar were two hundred figures of archangels, cherubim and seraphim, 'some adoring the Holy Sacrament, others singing and playing on all sorts of musical instruments, the whole painted and placed according to the rule of perspective'.

Monseigneur du Peron, the Bishop of Angoulême and grand almoner to the Queen, presided over the occasion. It was a long and impressive event, which was marred only by the crowd problems at the end, where those who were trying to get out ran headlong into a larger group of people trying to get in. The crowds were still coming to see the chapel three days later, by which time Charles decided to have the place cleared of strangers, partly because he wanted to put an end to the number of Protestants going to see the place, but mainly because he wanted to see it for himself.

From then on, the chapel became a regular feature of Jeffrey's life. Every Thursday Catholic doctrine was expounded in French, and every Wednesday and Saturday Jeffrey could join the rest of the household – and a great number of people from outside – in learning about 'the symbols of the faith, the commandments of God and of the Church, the Sacrament, the Lord's Prayer, the way to confess and communicate properly, and to pass the day in a Christian manner'.

It is a supreme irony that perhaps the greatest architectural triumph of Charles I's reign was a Catholic chapel. Indeed, the presence of the Catholic chapel serves as a kind of picture of Charles's reign. Behind the palace walls was a world where Catholicism and High Anglicanism were tolerated, where vestments, liturgy and setting were as rich as the costumes for a masque. Beyond those walls, however, the discontent was growing. An alliance of the wealthy and the zealously puritanical was being formed; disenfranchised without a Parliament, disillusioned by their King and disgusted with their Queen.

It was too much for one Cambridge preacher. 'Lord, open her eyes, that she may see her Saviour, whom she hath pierced with her superstition and idolatry,' he prayed.

It was a heartfelt prayer, shared by many, many subjects, but the King still threw him in jail.

In the summer of 1637, Jeffrey was eighteen. He was an adult and from this moment on, with one exception, there is a different tone to stories of his life. For a start, he went to war.

For some years Spain had been at war with Holland. It was, like so many of the conflicts of the seventeenth century, a religious war, Catholic Spain fighting with Protestant Holland. Indeed, it was one of the main grievances against the King that he did nothing to prevent this war or to aid the Dutch. Instead, he seemed to favour the Spanish, allowing them to reprovision ships on the south coast and even to process the pay for their soldiers through the London goldsmiths. This policy was less directed by diplomacy than by Charles's desperate need for cash, since he took a percentage of the Spanish bullion that was processed.

However, such excuses were lost on the majority of the populace, many of whom went over to Holland to offer the Dutch help, advice and manpower.

In July 1637, instead of joining the Queen on a progress, Jeffrey joined an expedition to Holland, organized by the Earls of Warwick and Northampton, who had volunteered to serve alongside the Dutch leader, Henry, Prince of Orange. They were heading for the siege of Breda, to watch the Dutch troops try (and eventually succeed) to drive the Spanish from the town.

The trip started terribly for the Earl of Warwick, when his son was drowned in a boating accident at Ramekins. However, he was undaunted and, later that same month, they visited the siege.

Their visit was recorded by William Lithgow, a writer and traveller who at that time was serving in the Dutch forces:

> But now, not to bee obvious, I recall, that at the beginning and about the middle time of the siege, there remayned here in the Prince's quarter for certaine dayes these two noble Lords, the Earl of Warwicke and the Earl of Northampton; and with him was the Queenes Majesties Dwarfe, strenuous Jeffrey, that Cycolpian creature, whose Gygantisme body made the bulwarks of Breda tremble.

There follows the usual strained piece of classical allusion, likening Jeffrey to the dwarf Molon mentioned in Pliny. Apparently anyone who wrote anything about Jeffrey was unable to resist showing off their classical education. Nevertheless, Lithgow does say that Jeffrey 'made the whole Army to admire his monstrous smallnesse'. No doubt they were amazed. Here was a tiny man who could ride and shoot, for Jeffrey was a good shot with a pistol – as, later, tragic events would prove.

It is unlikely that he saw any action – he was a visitor come to see the spectacle and one doubts the Queen would have let her favourite courtier take part in anything so dangerous as a battle, but it no doubt served to give him a taste for wider horizons. It was a different way of life. For Jeffrey, instead of the plush surroundings of Denmark

House, here were straw beds and rough living. This was the life of a soldier, the life of a real man, a man's world, with its sweat and its danger and its excitement.

There would come a time when Jeffrey was to experience military conflict for himself, when the hardship he would endure would make a straw bed seem like a luxury. At the siege of Breda, Jeffrey saw warfare for the first time. Here, in front of this Dutch city he saw armies in action and smelled the gunpowder on the air. From his vantage point well behind the action he could hear the shouting and see the dead bodies lying beneath the town walls. And from inside the walls came the acrid smell of death, disease and desperation.

All this Jeffrey saw from the back of his horse, and from a long way away. It was a spectator sport. But the time was coming when he would have to stop watching and join in the game.

He stayed in Holland only a few weeks. By late summer he was back at Denmark House, back in the world of masques and bowling greens and the opulent Catholic mass.

There was building going on in Whitehall. The King was erecting a new Masquing House. Previously Whitehall masques had taken place in the Banqueting House, but now Charles decided that the smoke from the many candles at these entertainments was damaging his precious ceiling panels, painted by Rubens.

Accordingly, he created a new Masquing House which, in honour of Henrietta Maria, was referred to contemptuously by Puritans as 'The Queen's Dancing-Barn'. The building was erected between the Guard chamber and the Banqueting House and was built of 'Fir, only weatherboarded and slightly covered'.

It was a purely temporary structure. 'At the marriage of the Queen of Bohemia I saw one set up there,' wrote George Garrard, 'but not of this vastness that this is, which will cost too much money to be pulled down, and yet down it must when the Masks are over.'

The first masque in the new building was performed by the King and his household. As was now the custom, the Queen's masque took place a few weeks later, on Shrove Tuesday night. It was an unusually efficient operation this time. Inigo Jones with 'high and hearty invention' created 'a variety of scenes, strange apparitions, songs, musick and dancing of severall kinds', all of which were performed 'in shorter time, than anything here hath been done in this kind'.

Indeed, it was almost the sole invention of Inigo Jones. So dominant was he in the production that the author of the songs and verse is not credited. It is generally agreed to be the work of our old friend D'Avenant but, whoever it was, he was working under the control of Inigo Jones. After the battle between words and images that was *Chloridia*, *Luminalia* is almost completely given over to intricate staging, stunning scenery and ravishing costumes, designed solely to give occasion to 'a variety of scenes, strange aparitions, Songs, Musick and dancing of several kinds: from whence doth result the true pleasure of our English masques'. Jeffrey's appearance, as usual, lies squarely in the box marked 'strange aparitions'.

The stage was raised on two large 'basements' adorned with Satyrs bearing baskets of fruit. Pillars framed the stage, featuring women and children picked out in silver, on top of which was yet more fruit.

The curtain rose on a magnificent scene: a wood, and in the distance a river, shimmering in the moonlight. The lighting was just enough for the spectators to make out the scene. As if from far away, the enthralled audience could hear owls hooting and blackbirds singing, 'the voyces of the birds of night'.

Suddenly smoke poured from a hole in the ground and from the depths of the stage came forth a chariot, drawn by two enormous owls, and driven by a lady dressed in the darkest purple, with black wings and a crown. 'Night' had arrived.

She sings a song which tells how the onset of night brings calm:

> Th'adventurous Merchant and the Mariner,
> (Whom stormes all day vex in the deep)
> Beginne to trust the windes when I appeare,
> And lose their dangers in their sleep.

Jeffrey appeared in his usual spot, during the antimasques and performing a grotesque dance. He appears as one of the Captains of the Fairies. The stage direction runs:

> Five Fayries of which Master Jeffrey Hudson, the Queenes Majesties dwarfe, presented Piecrocall, a principall Captaine under King Auberon.

One is reminded inevitably of the little changeling baby displayed at Bartholomew Fair.

Luminalia is one of the most superficial of the masques, remaining blissfully unhampered by any kind of plot or depth of meaning. Each moment is simply an excuse for another stage effect or fantastic costume. Along with the owl-drawn chariot, there were witches, clowns, five feathered men, and a 'morning star', represented by 'a beautiful youth, naked, with a mantle of watchet cypress and a star on his head'. The audience was even treated to a dream sequence, where the city of sleep rose up before the audience, with 'trees of unusual forme, mountaines of gold, Towers falling, Windmills, and other extravagant edifices'.

The whole event is monumentally self-indulgent, a relentless paeon of praise to Henrietta Maria to whom the sun, we are told, has delegated his power and light:

> He hath resign'd the pow'r of making day
> Through this Hemispheare,
> To a terrestr'all beauty here.

Eventually the furthest backdrop is drawn aside to reveal the Queen herself, sitting in a garden, on a magnificent golden throne, with the rest of her ladies sitting 'somewhat lower'. Behind her was a bright sky, and from her presence shone forth rays of light, 'expressing her to be the Queene of Brightness'.

The final scene was a marvel: a cloud appeared thrusting out over the stage, high in the air, full of dancers dressed as clouds and breezes and garlanded with flowers. Undoubtedly this was a triumph of stagecraft which 'for the newnesse of the Invention, greatnesse of the machine, and difficulty of Engining was much admir'd, being a thing not before attempted in the Aire'.

Despite its undoubted technical wizardry, despite the glory of the scenery and the costumes, it is a disturbingly self-indulgent event, the product of a Court which was rapidly losing its grip on reality.

Things were falling apart. The Scots were rebelling against an attempt by the King and the Archbishop to impose the Anglican prayer book on them. The Exchequer was running out of money – just maintaining the Court was costing the King forty per cent of his revenue. And as if that wasn't bad enough, in October 1638 his mother-in-law came to stay.

Marie de Medici had fallen out with her son Louis XIII and been banished from France into exile in Brussels and Holland. She originally suggested coming to take up permanent residence in England at which Charles, with true love and affection, immediately offered the use of the Royal Navy to take her to either Italy or Spain.

The truth was that no one wanted this arrogant, scheming, meddlesome woman, as overbearing as she was overweight. It was not merely her personality that hosts found hard to accommodate; she was also prohibitively expensive.

On her arrival in London, she occupied fifty of the best apartments at St James's Palace. Charles had allocated a hundred pounds a day for expenses, Henrietta Maria spent three thousand more on decorating the palace and supplying new furniture. Even allowing for the fact that she had not seen her mother for thirteen years, it seems rather to be going over the top.

At least Henrietta Maria was pleased to see her. When the coach containing her mother entered the courtyard, Henrietta Maria, although pregnant, could not contain herself. She rushed down from an upper chamber, and hurried forward with trembling fingers to open the carriage door. So unused was she to opening doors of any kind that an assistant had to complete the task. When her mother descended from the carriage, Henrietta Maria fell to her knees. Both were overcome with emotion.

For Jeffrey it was a renewed acquaintance with a generous benefactor, although now she was in no position to shower him with expensive gifts to make up for those he had lost some nine years ago. Now it was Marie who was showered with gifts. She sat for Sir Anthony Van Dyck, who charged Henrietta Maria fifty pounds for the commission. After the King's death, when his paintings were sold, the picture raised three pounds.

Archbishop Laud's suggestion that the Anglican prayer book be forced on the Scots was rebounding on Charles.

The Scots were united in a way that the English could never be. Led by a militant clergy and empowered by centuries of grievances, they flatly refused to comply. Charles decided to impose the prayer book by force and to bring the Scots to heel. He marched against them but, without a Parliament to provide revenue, he could not raise money for an adequate army and his first sortie against them was met with humiliating capitulation at Berwick. Even within his own ranks there had been dissension. During the march north, two officers – Lord Say and Lord Brook – refused to take the Oath of Allegiance. They were arrested and sent home, taking their troops with them.

Charles returned south to lick his wounds and prepare for a second try. His Court attendants, the poets and courtiers, told him that he had not been beaten, instead he had wisely refused to fight. Deep down, Charles must have known the truth: the Scottish campaign was a humiliation.

It was clear that the matter needed a firm hand, so Charles sent for the strongest hand he had: his great lieutenant, Thomas Wentworth.

Wentworth was a doberman, a tough, brutal Yorkshireman who had achieved great success in quelling and controlling the Irish – who were at that time seen as semi-civilized barbarians. He was 'Black Tom the Tyrant', a figure of terror as brutal as Charles was delicate. Charles did not understand men like Wentworth, nor did he really want the man anywhere near him, but he knew he was necessary. Henrietta Maria had similarly ambivalent feelings for him. She was later to describe him as 'ugly, but agreeable enough in person, and had the finest hands in the world'. You could not imagine Wentworth even attending, much less participating in, a masque.

Wentworth might have succeeded in battering Scotland – and then England – into obedience, but he had nothing to batter it with. He had no army. He advised the King that, for the first time in eleven years, Charles would have to call a Parliament.

With the Scots occupying the north of England, with his foreign policy in tatters and his coffers empty, faced with the need to manage a Parliament that would be bitter, resentful and out for revenge, Charles did what he was best at. He held a masque.

Nothing in Charles's Court sums up its fatal ignorance more than the masques, with their hollow phrases, their superficial beauty, their overweening triumphalism when there was absolutely nothing to be triumphant about. The country was dissatisfied, grumbling, discontented; the Scots were at Berwick, but the masques perpetuated the myth that everything in the garden was rosy.

Salmacida Spolia, the last great masque of the Caroline era, was presented on 21 January 1640, probably repeated in February. The words of the masque were written by William D'Avenant and the music was composed by the Queen's musician, Louis Richard. Inigo Jones, once again, was in overall control.

The Court, accompanied by various foreign ambassadors and dignitaries, assembled in the Masquing House – the notorious 'Queen's Dancing-Barn' – behind the Banqueting House at Whitehall. The guest of honour, of course, was Marie de Medici. Because she spoke no English the masque was mainly unspoken, and as all the royal children were present the scenes were short so they would not be bored.

It was, in many ways, Inigo Jones's finest hour, at least in the matter of stage sets. The stage was raised to eight feet to allow for additional machinery beneath. The plot, such as it was, concerned the subduing of certain savage tribes by the Greeks. The tribes were conquered not by force, but by bringing them to visit the fountain of Salmacis where they were so overcome by the beauty and wisdom of the Greeks they immediately laid down their arms.

The allusion was obvious – the rebellious factions, both Scots and English, would come to recognize the joy and wisdom of Charles's government. They would come to Charles, the fount of all good government, and they would voluntarily lay down their arms.

The curtain rose, and the spectators were rewarded with a scene of storm and tempest. Trees swayed in the wind, and in the background moving scenery showed the waves breaking over the rocks. Huge sheets of metal were rattled in the wings to represent the thunder.

The stage was filled with a huge globe – the earth itself. Then, the globe appeared to catch fire, and it broke open to reveal a Fury, 'her hair upright, mixed with snakes, her body lean, wrinkled and of a swarthy colour'. Huge, 'bagging' breasts hung down to her waist and she glared at the audience through 'hollow envious eyes'. She staggered to the front of the stage and declared her intention of visiting carnage and destruction on the otherwise peaceful land of England. She was joined by three more Furies (impersonated by two members of the catering staff and a gentleman of the privy chamber).

There was a scene change. The wings slid back, the two halves of the globe slid into the wings, the waves at the back parted, the dark clouds were hoisted out of sight, and another painted scene appeared.

It was a gentle summer's day. Below the stage, two stage

hands pumped furiously at the device which lowered a silver chariot from the clouds. Two people sat, somewhat unsteadily, inside, singing a duet. They were Concord who was threatening to leave England, and her companion, the Good Genius of the Isles, who was trying to persuade her to stay.

The people might not be grateful, argued the Good Genius, but the King, the wise and good Philogenes, was worth supporting. Concord agreed, and after the chariot landed they parted to persuade the people of the truth.

Their departure was followed by a series of twenty comic dances or grotesque interludes, featuring such characters as Wolfgangus Vandergoose the magician, 'Doctor Tartaglia and two pedants of Francolin' and 'four antique cavaliers'.

Jeffrey appeared in Entry 18 as 'a little Swiss who playd the wag' with two of his countrymen while they slept. By 'Swiss' Jones meant a Swiss guard, well known as mercenary soldiers in the sixteenth and seventeenth centuries.

His costume was a simple one. The stage directions tell us that 'the habit of his majesty and the masquers was of watchet, richly embroidered with silver, long stockings set up of white; their caps silver with scrolls of gold and plumes of white feathers'. Watchet is a cloth of sky-blue, and this formed the basis of Jeffrey's costume. For the rest it was reminiscent of the armour he wore all those years ago in York House; a tiny helmet, and a breastplate with two ribbons strung across in an 'X' shape.

He capered around compliantly, but must have wondered what he was doing there. He was twenty-one years old, there was a war brewing, and here he was engaging in a slapstick dance, while Mr Cottrell, master of ceremonies, and Sir Henry Newton, gentleman of the privy chamber, pretended to sleep.

The antimasques over, the scenery changed again, this time to 'craggy rocks and inaccessible mountains'. The chorus came forward and sang a hymn to Marie de Medici:

> You in whose bosom ev'n the chief and best
> Of modern victors laid his weary head
> When he rewarded victories with rest;
> Your beauty kept his valour's flame alive;
> Your Tuscan wisdom taught it how to thrive.

Whether Henry of Navarre ever availed himself of either his wife's bosom or her 'Tuscan wisdom' is doubtful. But this was masque not biography, and the chorus, having praised the stout, unloved and to the people of England unwelcome Queen Mother, withdrew upstage, calling on their King to appear.

After his appearance, Jeffrey had to nip round the back of the stage and climb to a raised platform, where, joined by the rest of the masquers, he sat obediently and reverently at the foot of the King and Queen surrounded by palm trees and statues of ancient heroes.

He could hear the chorus on the stage, singing the praises of Marie de Medici, and then drawing to either side of the stage. Then the muslin clouds parted, and he found himself gazing out at the audience again as they saw their King sitting on a gold throne, surrounded by his grateful Court.

The King appeared in a magnificent costume of pale blue silk, embroidered with silver thread. Indeed, he was adorned with a lot of silver; his doublet was so heavily embroidered you could hardly see the backing material, and his shoes were almost entirely concealed beneath a massive pair of silver buckles. He wore a silver hat, adorned with ostrich plumes.

At the King's feet were captives, 'bound in several postures' to illustrate the completeness of his victory. 'Murmur's a sickness epidemical,' sang the chorus. 'Tis catching and infects weak common ears . . .'

While the song was being sung, the largest cloud yet descended on strong ropes affixed to hidden pulleys. As it reached mid-air, it slowly opened revealing the Queen and her ladies, dressed in 'Amazonian habits of carnation, embroidered with silver' and illuminated by 'darted lightsome rays'.

Jeffrey looked on as the lords and the ladies came on to the stage and danced together. There was Lady Carnarvon, who declared that she would only join the Queen's masque if it were not performed on a Sunday. There dancing together, but hardly glancing at each other, were Lord and Lady Newport, a one-family civil war, he the Puritan and she who had become a Catholic only two years earlier. Among the lords gathered around the throne were at least three who publicly opposed Charles's policies. And in the middle his Queen, Henrietta Maria, older than her years, a tiny, frail creature dressed as Queen of the Amazons. The warlike posture seemed to suit her. It was not to be many years before she wore the costume for real.

The final scene in the masque was a cityscape, one which Inigo Jones had laboured over for many hours before he got it right. The scenery was made up of parts showing 'magnificent buildings' and even a bridge, over which 'many people, coaches, horses and such like, were seen to pass to and fro'. Jeffrey had seen this town many times in his life. It represented London, the new London which Jones was building. He had seen this city grow restless and threatening, the real city was outside, this was but a stage set.

The masque over, the masquers descended from their

stage and mingled with the audience, still dressed in their flamboyant costumes. The Queen's Dancing-Barn was filled with music and laughter and dancing, and, just for a moment, no one seemed to notice that the clouds outside the windows were real.

THE
MISTAKEN PRINCE

Some (judging by your stature) have taken you to be
a Low-country-man.

The New Yeare's Gift

FEW SUBJECTS IN ENGLISH HISTORY INSPIRE MORE
intense historical debate than the English Civil War. The
eventual outbreak of hostilities was the culmination of a
wide range of constitutional, economic and religious factors over which historians have argued for centuries. So,
there is no room here to do anything other than sketch the
broadest of pictures.

One of the key factors was certainly finance. Charles
inherited a crown that was growing steadily poorer, in a
country that was growing steadily wealthier. As more and
more of the mercantile and land-owning classes became
members of Parliament they began to wonder why their
voice was not listened to; they began to question, in their
own terms, whether they were getting what they paid for.
Charles saw Parliament as a rubber-stamping exercise, a
chore he had to go through in order to get money. Parliament, however, was no longer willing just to stump up the
cash whenever it was asked. They wanted a say in how

the money should be spent, and eventually their demands, and the fact that they controlled the purse strings, forced Charles to end his eleven-year 'personal rule' and reconvene Parliament. As Christopher Hill put it, 'The government was brought down by a revolt of the taxpayers.'

In particular they objected to the vast amounts that the King was prepared to spend on his Court and it is here that the real division between the two sides is to be seen. For the 'Great Rebellion' was not, like later revolutions, a matter of one social class rising against another. There were peers of the realm among the Parliamentarians as well as the Royalists. No, the Civil War was much more a case of Court versus Country; a conflict between those who existed and flourished under royal favour and those who were excluded from power. The latter included a wide range of disenfranchised and disenchanted people. Mrs Hutchinson, wife of one of the Parliamentary generals described them:

> If any were grieved at the dishonour of the kingdom, or the griping of the poor, or the unjust oppressions of the subject by a thousand ways invented to maintain the riots of the courtiers ... he was a Puritan; ... if any gentleman in his county maintained the good laws of the land, or stood up for any public interest, for good order or government, he was a Puritan. In short all that crossed the views of needy courtiers, the proud encroaching priests, the thievish projectors, the lewd nobility and gentry ... all were Puritans.

It was not, however, merely a matter of money, for the role of religion cannot be underestimated. Charles not only ignored the voice of the Parliamentarians on matters of economics and government; he ignored their religious views as well. Throughout his reign Charles simply refused to acknowledge religious views that differed from his own. Indeed, he refused to believe that any view which differed from his was valid in any way. After all, he was the divinely appointed King of England; anyone, therefore, who argued with him was, to some extent, arguing with God. The popular view of the Puritans is that they were zealots who were determined to impose their views on everyone else. If this is so, then they learned it at least in part from Charles. His inflexibility, his determined belief that only he was right, served to widen the schism, for the religious divides at the beginning of his reign were nowhere near as intense as they became later. 'Religion was not the thing first contested for,' said Oliver Cromwell, 'but God brought it to that issue at last.'

Charles, as much as the Parliamentarians, politicized religion. Under his rule William Juxon, the Bishop of London, was made Lord Treasurer, an office which had not been held by a member of the clergy since before the Reformation. When people started questioning Charles's taxes as unlawful, the King instructed the clergy to preach sermons telling their parishioners that it was a sin to refuse the King financial support. All the major religious posts went to the Arminians – the school of religious leaders led by Archbishop Laud. Laud enjoyed vestments and ritual, altars and ceremonial and rejected the severe Calvinist theology of the Puritans.

The 'Puritan' opposition held, in fact, a wide range of differing religious views. But Charles and his policies gave them a focus for their disapproval. It was his inflexibility, his arrogance, his unwavering conviction that he was right, that brought his enemies together.

Perhaps, therefore, the biggest single cause of the English Civil War was Charles himself. Whatever the economic, religious and social causes, the attitude of Charles played a crucial factor in the eventual outbreak of war. For no monarch had a more exalted view of the responsibilities of kingship than Charles I, but few monarchs have been less suited to carry out those responsibilities. He had an almost mystical view of the role and status of kings, but mystics do not make good rulers. Mystics are not practically-minded. Mystics do not know how to quell rebellion.

Towards the end of his life, Laud described Charles as 'a mild and gracious prince who knew not how to be, or be made, great'. And that indeed was his problem. He had such a clear idea of what a divinely appointed monarch should be like, but none of the qualities needed to reach that goal. He was too scrupulous to be a tyrant, and too inflexible not to be one. And it has to be said that few monarchs have demonstrated such an unerring ability to do precisely the wrong thing at exactly the wrong time.

The Parliament in April had lasted only a few weeks – earning it the epithet the 'Short Parliament'. Wentworth – who by now had been made Lord Strafford – believed he could handle Parliament with the same mix of threat and brute force that had succeeded so well in Ireland. He was wrong. The Parliament that met in April 1640 refused to be cowed or intimidated and, more ominously, refused to vote the King any money. They had eleven years of grievances stored up and they were about to take revenge.

Strafford, seeing that he was going to get nowhere, advised King Charles to dissolve Parliament again. He told the King that he was 'loosed and absolved from all rules of government' and could therefore do anything 'that power might admit'. Strafford immediately put these words into effect, arresting three MPs and having their houses searched. Rioting by the city apprentices was punished by the vigilante hangings of two youths – one of whom was tortured before execution. When the City Aldermen refused to loan money to the King, Strafford threw four of them into prison and advised the King to hang one of them. 'Unless you hang up some of them, you will do no good with them,' he advised.

It did no good. Strafford was as much a creature of the past as his master. The English army, marching on Scotland, was beaten again and this time the victorious Scots imposed a subsidy of twenty-five thousand pounds per month on the King, pending the satisfaction of their claims to compensation.

Charles was forced to call another Parliament and in November 1640, amidst great pomp and ceremony he inaugurated what came to be known as the 'Long Parliament'. The person who was eventually to dissolve the Parliament thirteen years later, however, would not be Charles, the divinely ordained King of England, but Oliver Cromwell, Lord Protector of the Commonwealth.

The King's support in Parliament was dismal. He could count on only sixty-four MPs out of four hundred and ninety-three – and even that number was further diminished by the expulsion of sixteen of his supporters for election fraud and other misdemeanours. For a decade he had ignored the voices of discontent, but now the tide had turned. As Thomas Knyvet wrote to a friend, 'I pray God that the violent turning of the tide do not make an inundation.'

The omens were not good. In Cambridge, it was reported that the River Cam turned as red as blood, and angels were seen fighting on the rooftops.

Meanwhile, in London, Parliament was exacting a brutal and lasting revenge. The King was effectively at their mercy and now all their grievances were to be addressed. For eleven years he had ignored them, promoting his cronies and forcing on the country unfair taxes. Now it was their turn . . .

They discovered that Strafford was negotiating overseas for mercenaries and, fearing that he would use them against Parliament itself, immediately impeached him for treason. 'Black Tom' was followed into prison by Archbishop Laud. The House passed the Self-Perpetuating Act, a measure which prohibited the dissolution of Parliament without its consent. It abolished ancient prerogative courts such as the Star Chamber, and passed measures which would henceforth ensure that no taxation could be imposed without Parliament's consent. Strafford's trial presented more of a problem – the old doberman was snarling and fighting for all he was worth. In the end, they fought fire with fire, and passed the despicable Act of Attainder – an act which basically said that a man could be found guilty without proof. Truly, those who fight monsters will become monsters themselves and it is one of the ironies of history that the English Parliament of the mid-seventeenth century, the Parliament that struck such a resounding blow for democracy, ended up being as autocratic and tyrannical as any despot ever was.

Strafford was executed for his 'crimes'. Laud was to die in the same way some years later. And so, of course, was the King.

And still there was no money for the King. Charles needed troops to guarantee his security, but troops cost money and the King was penniless. He was left clutching at the hopes of a rich alliance as a means of raising money.

Accordingly, in January 1641, Charles and the Dutch ambassador, Baron de Heenvliet, agreed a marriage treaty between the twelve-year-old Prince William of Orange, and the nine-year-old Princess Mary, Charles and Henrietta Maria's eldest daughter. In return for the marriage, the Prince of Orange would send money and troops to support the King, should that be necessary.

A month later the young Prince arrived at Whitehall and was taken to meet his bride and future in-laws. It was not a relaxed meeting. Henrietta Maria, who had set her hopes on a French match, refused to kiss the Prince. But despite the problems with his in-laws, on 2 May 1641 Princess Mary and Prince William were rather hurriedly married in the chapel at Whitehall.

The Princess wore silver ribbons in her hair and a gown of silver. Her train was carried by sixteen girls, all dressed in white. As with her refusal to attend the coronation nearly fifteen years before, Henrietta Maria and her mother watched the ceremony 'incognito from a gallery because of the Difference in Point of Religion'.

After the celebratory banquet, the marriage had to be consummated, which, given the ages of the couple, was a strictly symbolic affair. Prince Charles, the Prince of Wales, called at young Prince William's room to conduct the groom, dressed in nightclothes, to the bed of his wife. The room was already full, with the queen standing at one side of the bedstead, the King on the other, and a crowd of people pressing in to watch the proceedings. Next to the the Queen stood Jeffrey, no doubt quietly smiling to himself. The King parted the curtains and the young groom leant forward to kiss the forehead of his bashful new bride.

Then the ladies-in-waiting came forward to pull the covers back, for the formality of the consummation required that the Prince place his unclothed leg against the similarly unclothed leg of his bride. But when the covers were pulled back a trick was discovered – Princess Mary's nightgown went down to her ankles where it had been sewn up as a precaution. The Prince looked around him, bewildered at the laughing faces. How was he to perform the task?

Step forward Jeffrey. For one night only the Queen's dwarf, the lovable, cheeky rogue was back. From beneath his doublet he produced a pair of tailor's shears, handed them to the Prince with a bow, and invited him to cut the gown. The prince did so, legs were pressed, applause filled the room, and everyone filed back to their apartments.

It is Jeffrey's last appearance in his 'jester' role, the last recorded time he was willing to play the fool. To be sure, in the future months he was laughed at, as he had been in the past. But he was never again to collude in the joke; from now on things were to get serious.

The celebrations of the marriage were muted and short-lived. On the very night of the wedding, while Jeffrey was handing Prince William a pair of scissors to cut the threads, Parliament discovered a Royalist plot. Or plots, really, since with typically Royalist inefficiency there had been two distinct conspiracies, one led by Henry Wilmot which aimed to get the leaders of the army to declare for the King against Parliament; the other led by a group of conspirators including William D'Avenant and George Goring, which intended to seize London and capture the Tower. When the plots were revealed to the King and Queen, they appointed the Queen's 'prime servant' and Master of Horse, Henry Jermyn, to act as a go-between between the two parties.

Jermyn was a large, fair-haired man, who had had a very chequered career. He was an immediate success at Court, but his argumentative nature kept getting him into trouble. He was reprimanded for fighting with another man whom he accused of hitting tennis balls at him on purpose. He was imprisoned briefly for carrying a challenge from Lord Holland to Lord Treasurer Weston, as all duelling was strictly banned by Charles. Finally, he was banished for seducing one of the Queen's maids-of-honour. He rather ungallantly refused to marry the girl – who was Eleanor Villiers, niece of the late Duke of Buckingham. Given the King's continuing reverence for the memory of his former favourite, he was unlikely to take a lenient line on the matter and Jermyn was sentenced to eternal banishment. He returned four years later to be appointed Master of Horse to the Queen; evidently eternity was a lot shorter in those days.

The choice of Jermyn to co-ordinate matters was unfortunate. The Queen, wisely for once, objected to his involvement, arguing that if a senior member of her household was found to be involved it would open her up to charges of treason.

This is exactly what happened. When the details of the plots were worked out, one of the chief conspirators, George Goring, realized that he was not going to gain as much as he thought he would. He was a soldier of fortune, a mercenary who, with a selfishness that was only too typical of the Cavaliers, had planned to become Commander of the army. Now it looked as if he would not achieve his ambition. Ruthlessly he contacted Pym, the leader of the House of Commons, and informed him of the conspiracy. On the night of the Royal marriage, Pym revealed the details to the House of Commons. D'Avenant, Suckling and some others were arrested. Jermyn was forced, once again, to flee into France.

Jeffrey was now twenty-one. He had his own allowance from the Queen – fifty pounds per annum allowed for 'his diet and his man'. Jerome Gregoire was still around (although the accounts list him with a rather Disney-like touch as 'Jeremy Criquitt') but he appears to have gained promotion, for Jeffrey's manservant was now Thomas Alexander 'in the room of Jeremy Criquitt'. Thomas was paid twenty pounds per annum out of Jeffrey's allowance, and his wife Elizabeth Alexander looked after little Sara Holton, her majesty's other dwarf.

Considering that most of his living costs were covered by the Court, Jeffrey was comfortably established. He certainly had the means to pursue his own projects and ambitions – but perhaps not any idea of what ambitions to pursue. After all, the job of Court Dwarf was all he knew. Visits to Breda might open his eyes to other possibilities, but as soon as he walked through the gates of Denmark House he was back in his old role – the Queen's Dwarf, the permanent child, the jester.

Now, though, all the old ways were under threat. More than ever, Denmark House felt like a foreign embassy in an enemy country. London was awash with anti-Papist paranoia, most of which centred on the Queen and her heretical Court in the Strand. The London mobs became ever more threatening. A mysterious sign appeared saying that Whitehall Palace was soon 'to be let'. Marie de Medici was the target of death threats, with the King receiving a threatening letter, warning him that the sender would 'chase the Pope and the Devil from St James's where is lodged the Queene, Mother of the Queene'. The eleven-year-old Prince Charles was subject to a series of nightmares and wept for five days. When his father asked him the reason, he replied, 'My grandfather left you four kingdoms, and I am afraid your Majesty will leave me never one.'

Amidst all this, the Queen gave birth to another child,

a boy, christened Henry of Gloucester. He was born at Oatlands on 8 July. Celebrations were muted.

A wise woman would have kept her head down, acted discreetly, done nothing to draw attention to herself and kept away from all intrigues. Henrietta Maria was many things; she was spirited, courageous, doggedly loyal, but she was rarely wise. In times when the very mention of the Pope was enough to incite a riot, she decided to write to him for help. He replied that he would send eight thousand men, but only if her husband became a Catholic. Undaunted, Henrietta Maria wrote to her brother in France, trying to arrange a match with one of her daughters, an offer which was quickly rejected by Cardinal Richelieu. Increasingly desperate, she wrote to Cardinal Barberini, the Pope's nephew, asking for five hundred thousand crowns to bribe members of Parliament. The Cardinal was so amazed that he initially thought the letter a forgery. Her sole aim was to save her husband and to fight on his behalf. It was a shame that so many of her activities – motivated entirely by fierce love – ended up by doing more harm than good.

In the end, Parliament had had enough of her scheming and intrigues. There were threats to impeach the Queen, to make her stand trial. Hurriedly, she was forced to humble herself. She wrote to Parliament apologizing for her actions, for the prominence of her chapel and saying that in future she would be 'careful not to exceed that which is convenient and necessary'. One is reminded of the argument between her and her husband over her household many years before. This time, however, it was not the King who was calling the tune.

Charles never forgave himself for the death of Strafford. And typically, he never forgave himself for the wrong sin. Strafford died because the King could not or would not compromise. But Charles believed that his death was because he made concessions; he thought it was his own weakness that led to Strafford's death and not his own obstinacy. Had the King worked with Parliament then, had he recognized the way that power had shifted and sought to relocate himself, then perhaps blood would not have been shed, but he didn't. Instead he went to Scotland – his opponents only a few months earlier – in a stupid attempt to raise support among the Scottish nobility. It was doomed to failure and for Parliament it merely confirmed that the King could not be trusted.

By the middle of 1641, Henrietta Maria was in a bad way. She wanted to spend some time abroad taking the spa waters in France, but the Commons overruled her, insisting that the great physician Sir Theodore Mayerne examine her. They suspected that since the Queen wanted to take a large amount of plate and jewels with her, she intended to obtain money for the King to raise an army. When Mayerne reported that her illness was, in his opinion, as much in her mind as in her body, the Commons prohibited the Queen's journey.

In August 1641, with Charles in Edinburgh on his futile mission, and her mother finally back in Antwerp, Henrietta Maria and her Court moved to Oatlands. It had always been such a happy place for her, but this summer the atmosphere was oppressive, nervous. There were reports of large numbers of people gathering together, invading the royal parklands and hunting down the deer in the area. Parliament was increasingly exacting. They wrote to the Queen, demanding that she surrender her family into their care, 'lest she should take the opportunity of making papists of them'. She refused, pointing out that the children had individual tutors and other officials specifically to ensure this didn't happen.

There were continual rumours that she was trying to leave the country. Her enemies – although no one ever actually admitted responsibility for this – sent orders to the magistrate at Weybridge, telling him to gather the local militia together at Oatlands where they would be joined by cavalry with 'further orders'.

The magistrate took the order straight to the Queen, who told him that her only wish was to 'do exactly what Parliament dictated, and then to remain tranquil'. She was dissembling, for the moment he left she sent word to every officer she could rely on, entreating them to join her 'before midnight'.

That night, Jeffrey left his room and went to the great hall at Oatlands. All of the household were there, right down to the kitchen scullions. Anyone who could hold a weapon was issued with one, and then, pretending that they were preparing for a masque in Oatlands park, her makeshift troops were positioned at strategic points in the grounds. Jeffrey, like the rest of her household, spent the night hiding in the park, alert for any noise, prepared to defend his Queen with his life. It was a long night. Around midnight, distant hooves were heard and a rumour spread among the defenders that an attack was imminent. But the hooves faded away and by dawn the assault had failed to materialize.

Meanwhile, things were coming to a head. In November news came through of a massive revolt in Ireland. With Strafford gone, the Irish natives rose against the English and Scottish settlers who had taken their land. The slaughter was appalling, with Protestants butchered or stripped naked to die of exposure, and Parliament was outraged. This was exactly what they had been warning of for all these years. Entirely fake letters seemed to imply that the rebellion had been orchestrated by Catholics in London and, although no one actually accused her of involvement, the insurrection came to be known as the Queen's Rebellion. Her confessor Father Philip was arrested and briefly imprisoned by Parliament, largely because when giving evidence he would not swear on the King James Bible.

An army needed to be raised to put down this rebellion, but no one trusted the King to command it. What if he turned back from Ireland and marched on Parliament and London? Parliament informed Charles, who had by now returned from Scotland, that unless he replaced his current advisers with men of their choosing they would put down the revolt themselves.

From here everything started to move with a frightening rapidity. The avalanche which had, for so long, been threatening to descend, was finally set in motion. Charles refused to have his decisions approved by Parliament. In response, Parliament produced the Grand Remonstrance, a lengthy indictment of the King's policy and actions. The Lords finally swung out of the King's control and allowed the Commons to impeach the bishops. There were rumours that the Queen was finally to be sent to trial.

The King decided that he would get his retaliation in first. While he was in Scotland he had discovered that four members of the House of Commons and one of the House of Lords had been in treasonable communication with the Scottish rebels. He decided that he would strike. On 3 January 1642, he sent orders to the Attorney-General to arrest the ringleaders. He went to Whitehall to supervise the arrest himself – a dramatic gesture which completely backfired. When he arrived at the Commons and invaded, the four members had fled. They had been forewarned, perhaps through the indiscretion of Henrietta Maria, who had blurted out details of the plan to her ladies-in-waiting, unaware that one of them, the Countess of Carlisle, was a Parliamentarian sympathizer, who was rumoured to be 'more than friendly' with the arch-Parliamentarian, John Pym. The Countess made her excuses, left the room, and immediately alerted Pym, who escaped with the other accused men. When Charles arrived to arrest them, they had disappeared and he was forced into an ignominious retreat. Whether this was the sole warning Pym received is unlikely, but the Queen never forgave herself for this mistake.

The incident was the final nail in the coffin. With the capital united against him, with mobs running amok, Charles decided the Court must leave London. They climbed into their coaches and made their way out of the city.

It was a mournful exit for Jeffrey and the Court. So many times he had entered cities and towns during royal progresses with the cheers of the citizens ringing in his ears. This time, his carriage made its way through angry crowds of Puritan sympathizers, thousands of people gathered to cheer the Queen's departure. As he looked out of the window he could see that many of them were carrying placards bearing the single word, 'Liberty'.

Charles was not to return to London until 1648, when he went to his trial and execution. Henrietta Maria would not return until 1660, when she was welcomed as the aged Queen Mother of a restored monarch. Jeffrey was not to see London again for nearly thirty years.

They went to Hampton Court first, where it was decided that the Queen should go to Holland, ostensibly to take Princess Mary to join her new husband, but in reality to try to raise money for the now seemingly inevitable war.

She took with her the crown jewels and a huge collection of personal goods and jewellery, embarking from Dover on 23 February 1642. Her company included all her closest friends – Mary Villiers, Duchess of Richmond, Father Philip, two of her favourite Capuchins and, of course, Jeffrey Hudson. After the King and Queen had bid each other a tearful farewell, the anchors were weighed, and their boat, the *Lion*, set out from port. They coasted along the shore for a while, and the King followed them on horseback, waving to his wife all the time.

Jeffrey stood on deck looking at the land fading into the distance. He could see the King, a tiny speck now, standing on the cliffs and waving his hat in farewell. The Queen and her ladies-in-waiting were in tears. The sky was darkening and the wind changed.

The change in the weather was dramatic, and soon the travellers were driven below deck while 'a furious tempest suddenly arose, contrary winds began to roar and drove, tossed and battered the ships with the utmost violence, as if they were bent on sinking them all'. Some ships in the convoy went down in the storm. At length the Queen and her company, all 'very weak and dejected', arrived in Holland. The ship landed at Brielle on 1 March 1642.

She was received with all due pomp and ceremony, but with no great enthusiasm. Henry, Prince of Orange, had made it clear that he did not want the expense or the political complications of having Henrietta Maria in the country.

Nevertheless, he went through the formalities which is more than the burghers and merchants of Amsterdam did. They had no idea how to behave before her. As one observer wrote:

The burgomasters of Holland, nevertheless, showed no great veneration to her royal person; they entered her presence with their hats on, threw themselves on chairs close to her, stared at her from under the brims of their Dutch beavers, and flung out of the room without bowing or speaking to her.

In terms of raising money, the crown jewels were worse than useless, since Parliament had announced that they had, in effect, been stolen, and the Dutch merchants would not touch stolen goods. Still, they bought much of the personal jewellery, although at nothing like the inflated prices that the King and Queen had paid for them. Henrietta Maria, unused to bargaining, found the process repulsive. 'When they know we want money, they keep their foot on our throat,' she wrote to her husband.

Once again, Jeffrey was in a court that was viewed with suspicion by the people. After a while it was evident that the Prince no longer wanted them there, the merchants had got everything they wanted, and the people hated this Catholic Queen. It was just like home. The only person who was glad to make Jeffrey's acquaintance was the Dutch ambassador who kissed Jeffrey by mistake. Henrietta Maria described the incident in a letter to her husband:

> As to the Ambassador who is to go from this country, I had a long conversation with him yesterday. I think he is a very honest man; you have seen him before; he is a tall man, who kissed the hands of Jeffry taking him for my son.

Jeffrey must have been mortified. He was not a child, he was a twenty-two-year-old man. It was time for him to return to England, to prove his worth and to join in the fight.

By the summer of 1642, the Queen had amassed enough money to enable her to start buying arms and ammunition.

She purchased six cannons, a hundred barrels of powder and two hundred pairs of firearms. She later added a thousand saddles to the list as well as a considerable amount of money.

In July, her mother died. Marie de Medici was not much loved, an overbearing, self-important woman, whose advice to her daughter was invariably unhelpful. But she was still a mother, and her daughter grieved for her memory.

Back in England, Charles was still trying to negotiate with Parliament. He was unwilling to strike the first blow, an attitude which infuriated Henrietta Maria. 'Delays have always ruined you,' she wrote. 'You are beginning your own game of yielding everything.' Eventually he made up his mind, finally raising his standard at Nottingham. War had broken out.

The Queen, showing a drive and energy in adversity, was eager to return to aid the fight. For Jeffrey the prospect of war was an opportunity. Here at last was his chance to serve. He might be small, but he could ride and shoot. He was no longer seventeen, as he had been at Breda. He was twenty-two. He was a man. He would fight.

Henrietta Maria decided to go in November, but the north of England was not secure, winter had closed in and she was forced to remain in Holland through to February. Throughout that winter the news from England was scattered and contradictory. Reports told of the first great battle of the Civil War; there were rumours that the King was a prisoner, one man swore that he had touched the lifeless corpse of Prince Rupert, the King's glamorous, dashing nephew. All untrue, but The Hague was rife with rumours. An English lady, enquiring anxiously in a Dutch bookshop for the news from England, had left hurriedly. Onlookers whispered that it was the Queen in disguise.

It could well have been. Henrietta Maria was desperate for news, and desperate to get home. She was deeply unhappy in Holland where she had now completely outlived what little welcome she had in the first place. She was worried about her husband and the children she had left behind. She wrote to her husband complaining of eyepains, which she attributed to too much weeping. She did have some help; the outlawed Jermyn joined her in Holland, resuming his position of responsibility. From now on the Queen was to be ever more reliant on the advice and help of her corpulent Chamberlain.

She was particularly annoyed by the arrival of one Walter Strickland, an 'ambassador' from Parliament, sent over to keep an eye on the Queen's activities and report back to Parliament. She wrote angry letters complaining of the difficulty of the task she had set herself. 'People here are so Parliamentarian,' she wrote, using what must have been one of the most abusive terms she knew. 'I do not wish to remain in this country,' she wrote to her husband. 'I need the air of England, or at least the air where you are.' But finding ships to take them back was proving difficult. She passed the time by trying to write letters to incriminate Sir John Pym.

On 2 February 1643, they finally set out. With some trepidation, given his history of sea-travel, Jeffrey joined his mistress on board the ship, *The Princess Royal*. They left port accompanied by a convoy of eleven transport ships. As was now becoming depressingly routine, as soon as the ships were out of sight of land, the weather changed. This time the storm was atrocious. Experienced sailors, 'sailors who made several voyages to India', swore it was the worst storm they had ever encountered.

The ship was full of noise, people crying, vomiting, shivering with cold and wet. Nobody expected to last the voyage. In the face of imminent death, the Catholics insisted on confessing their sins, even though the Capuchin priests were as ill as anyone. In the horror and commotion the penitents had to shout their confessions, in the full hearing of their fellow passengers. Enemies made up their differences and, according to one historian, 'those who previously hated one another embraced, and all begged forgiveness of each other'. They were tied in their beds for safety.

Only the Queen retained her composure. Indeed, she seems to have found the whole event funny. Her servants still attempted to serve her meals, resulting in food flying everywhere and waiters falling on the floor. Up on deck and leaning against the rudder she assured her frightened ladies that 'Queens of England are never drowned'. She had even persuaded her terrified entourage to go up on deck to take a little fresh air.

Several ships were lost, including one that contained 'a fine piece of the true cross'. All the travellers' personal goods and clothes were lost, as well as their horses, the carriages, grooms and other servants. Although at one point they found themselves only a short distance from Newcastle, they were unable to land and were driven back again, many miles out to sea.

The queen made a vow that if she survived she would visit the church of Our Lady of Liesse and endow masses to be said in perpetuity. It seems to have worked. The wind abated, the sea grew still and the Queen – and Jeffrey – limped back into harbour on the Dutch coast, nine days after they had left it.

Shaking and exhausted, Jeffrey climbed aboard a fishing boat to be ferried ashore. He had hardly slept for nine days. None of the ladies could walk properly, all were cut and bruised. Like all the travellers – including the Queen

– Jeffrey's clothing was so waterlogged and filthy it had to be burnt.

Henrietta Maria took the opportunity of a few days back in Holland to raise more money and supplies and to replace the ships that went down in the storm. They sailed again in late February, and this time, happily, the journey was quick and easy. Accompanied by some Dutch warships under the command of Van Tromp, they soon arrived safely in the harbour of Bridlington. A thousand-strong Cavalier army under the command of the Duke of Newcastle was waiting to meet them and helped them to unload some of the supplies.

When he stepped out of the boat and on to the quay at Bridlington, Jeffrey had been away from England for two days short of a year. It was 22 February 1643. When he left he was still the Queen's Dwarf, but now he was to be her soldier.

THE
CAPTAIN OF HORSE

But rather would I say this Son of *Conopas* made
the whole Army to admire his monstrous smallnesse;
who for his *Bellonean* practice or Champion saw, he
may justly, as Generall, lead an Army of Pigmaes . . .
William Lithgow, *Siege of Breda*

JEFFREY SPENT THE NIGHT IN THE SMALL, SNOW-COVERED
fishing town of Bridlington. At five o'clock in the morning
he woke with a start. There was a huge crash, and then
another one, and another. The village was being attacked.

Six Parliamentary ships had swept into the bay and
began bombarding the village. The darkness was full of
flashes and explosions; everywhere was smoke and rubble.
Jeffrey grabbed his sword and pistol and ran down to
the quayside, along with the other men of the Queen's
household, to repulse an invasion. It was Oatlands all over
again, but this time the enemy was real. The Queen meanwhile was fleeing for her life. The cottage next to the one
she had slept in was reduced to rubble, and two cannon-
balls even arrived through the roof of her house, rolling
down the stairs as she was leaving. Dressed only in their
nightgowns, 'barefoot and bare leg', she and her women

ran into the street. Before they reached safety, however, the Queen remembered her dog. She had forgotten
Mitte, an old, ugly lap-dog, who had been the Queen's
companion for years. With a courage bordering on fool-
hardiness, the Queen turned on her heel, rushed back
down the street and into the house and scooped up the
little animal from the bed where she lay. Then they fled,
creeping through ditches to the edge of town, while all
around them gunfire was exploding. A servant died only
seventy paces from where she stopped. One of her maids-
of-honour became completely hysterical and had to be left
behind.

   Down at the quayside Jeffrey could do little except take
cover and wait for dawn. There was an explosion at sea
and a cannonball flew over his head with a whoosh, landing
in a ditch and covering everyone with earth and stones.
There was nothing to do but wait. As the dim grey light
of day began to dawn, the tide changed and, to his relief,
Jeffrey could see that the Parliamentary ships were being
forced further out of the bay. The firing stopped.

   A strange calm covered the fishing village. The Queen's
forces crept out from their ditches and their shelters, dusted
themselves down, and tried to come to terms with the
reality of what had happened. The Queen of England had
been fired upon by her own subjects. The Civil War was
real. With the guns silenced, the remainder of the supplies
were unloaded and the Queen's forces began to march
inland.

At this stage the Civil War was finely balanced. Only two
battles had taken place, neither of them in any way decisive.
Nevertheless, the Parliamentary forces held much of the
Midlands, with a belt of towns including Northampton,
Leicester and Coventry as well as nearly all of the south-

east, including, of course, London. The Royalist forces held the north, the west, most of the major cathedral cities and the universities. Their headquarters were in Oxford, that most fiercely loyal of cities.

The Queen set up headquarters in York, where she was to remain for three months, while Prince Rupert tried to break through the Parliamentary forces in the Midlands. While she was there news came from Paris; her brother, Louis XIII, was dead, leaving control of the country in the hands of his wife, Anne of Austria, and, more ominously perhaps, in the hands of Cardinal Mazarin, her Italian adviser. Henrietta Maria had had hopes that when Cardinal Richelieu died France would help her cause. This latest news dashed those hopes. Mazarin had no desire to see a strong England. She, her husband, and their supporters were on their own.

Nevertheless, there was a sense of excitement about their company. The Queen, far from being abashed by the rough conditions she found herself in, seemed to be revelling in them. At last they were able to do something. At last the fight was real and in late spring they started to march south.

On 23 May the Queen marched into Newark. On the same day a hundred and thirty miles south, Parliament finally declared Henrietta Maria a traitor.

The Queen wrote to her husband about her army, describing herself as her 'she-majesty Generalissima':

I carry with me three thousand foot, thirty companies of horse and dragoons, and two mortars. Harry Jermyn commands the forces which go with me, as colonel of my guards, and Sir Alexander Lesley the foot under him, and Gerard the horse, and Robin Legg the artillery; and her she-majesty Generalissima over

all and extremely diligent am I, with a hundred and
fifty waggons of baggage to govern in case of battle.

With all these commissions being granted, Jeffrey was not
going to be left out. This was a chance for him to prove
himself, an opportunity to break out of the confines of his
role as jester and freak; to make a name for himself for
his actions rather than his appearance. He successfully
appealed to the Queen to give him a post. He had endured
peril on the seas, he had joined the defence of Bridlington,
he had stayed with her in Holland, he had even been kissed
by the Dutch ambassador. Such fidelity was to be rewarded.
He was made 'Jeffrey Hudson, Captain of Horse'.

That he was an able horseman there is no doubt. Indeed,
later events would prove his skill at riding and shooting in
an emphatic, if unfortunate fashion. Yet it must be ques-
tioned if he would ever have been commissioned in the
King's army, or Prince Rupert's. Probably not, but this was
the Queen's army; the forces of the 'she-majesty Generalissima'. She could appoint whoever she wanted. And after
all, the stout Jermyn was not exactly the ideal figure of a
noble warrior.

Fuller, writing only twenty years later, records Jeffrey's
commission and his courage: 'He was, though a dwarf, no
dastard, a captain of horse in the king's army in these late
civil wars.'

Whether he ever led any troops into battle is a moot
point. On their way south, the Queen's forces met no opposition, merely contenting themselves with a bit of sacking
and looting. There are no records of his involvement in an
actual battle, but then again, troop lists, especially for the
Royalist side, are virtually non-existent. Despite his
undoubted horsemanship, it is difficult to imagine him
commanding a troop of hardened cavalry in the heat of a

battle. What is clear is that for Jeffrey it was an honour that he never forgot. Forty years later, in the last years of his life, in a list of people receiving donations from the King, his name is written *Captain* Jeffrey Hudson.

Travelling in short marches, they evaded the Parliamentary troops and moved south. On 3 July they left Newark, by 7 July they were at Ashby and three days later at King's Norton. On 11 July the Queen's army marched proudly into Stratford-upon-Avon, home of William D'Avenant's 'father', where Prince Rupert was waiting for them. The Queen lodged at New Place, home of Shakespeare's only surviving child, Judith Hall.

Two days later, on 13 July 1643, the weary troops rode and marched into the vale of Keinton. There, at the head of a small force, Jeffrey saw the figure that he had last seen waving his hat on the cliffs of Dover. The King had ridden out from Oxford to meet his Queen.

It was a touching reunion, for the couple were so very much in love. As well as her doting husband, Henrietta Maria was reunited with her sons Charles and James; the Prince of Wales and the Duke of York. In optimistic celebration they rode into Oxford, where they ordered a medal to be struck, showing the happy couple seated on thrones, with the dragon of rebellion dead beneath their feet.

Oxford celebrated Henrietta Maria's arrival by ringing the bells, cheering her arrival and publishing a book of very bad poetry.

'You've come at last!' started one verse, going on to chide the Queen's 'rude' and 'rebellious subjects':

The duteous waves scorned their usurped powers,
And though the ships be theirs, the sea was yours;
In vain to welcome you on shore they sent

By the rude cannon's mouth their compliment,
That which they always meant, but durst not tell,
Yet the bold bullets spoke it plain and well.

The atmosphere was sunny, cheerful, excited. In the very
week the Queen entered Oxford, the Royalists had won a
splendid victory at Roundway Down, where the forces of
Sir William Waller had been almost annihilated. It was the
culmination of a series of victories that gave the King's
supporters real hope.

Jeffrey lodged with his mistress in Merton College. The
College's warden, Sir Nathaniel Brent, had absconded eight
months earlier to join the Parliamentary forces, so his
rooms were rather handily vacant. King Charles was
lodged next door in Christ Church, allowing the royal
couple to visit one another without being seen.

Henrietta Maria's apartments overlooked the great
quadrangle with a staircase allowing direct access to the
main hall. The main room is still known as the Queen's
Room. The chapel with its painted monuments of Bodley
and Sackville was given over to the Queen for the saying
of mass.

In many ways life continued as it had before. D'Avenant
was there, writing verse and organizing plays, and William
Dobson was painting portraits. Music was played and
plays were performed. It was just like Denmark House.

Elsewhere, however, the situation was less comfortable.
With all the Royalists in the city, Oxford was extremely
overcrowded. Fortunately that summer was very warm, so
the soldiers didn't suffer too much through being forced
to sleep in the narrow streets, with canvas slung across
from one side of the road to the other to provide them
with shelter. For a group of people who all their lives had
been used to comfort and space it seemed really quite an

adventure. The wives and daughters of courtiers slept two and three to a bed in poky rooms above shops. Jeffrey spent his time attending mass, visiting the botanical gardens, strolling through the streets, watching the plays that were performed in the college gardens.

After a while, boredom began to set in, and Henrietta Maria's Court took to playing practical jokes. Some ladies of the Court decided it would be a good joke to visit the renowned misogynist Dr Ralph Kettel. This octogenarian eccentric with his 'terrible gigantique aspect, with his sharp grey eies' took one look at Mistress Fanshawe, simpering and giggling on his doorstep, and said to her, 'Madam, your husband and father I bred up here, and I knew your grandfather; I know you to be a gentlewoman, I will not say you are a whore, but get you gone for a very woman.'

Admittedly Kettel was an easy target. He was prone to wander up and down the dining hall with a pair of scissors, attacking the hair of any student he considered effeminate. On one occasion, having lost his scissors, he used the college bread knife. Ultimately the old doctor simply couldn't cope with all these strangers. Kettel, who was used to being obeyed, found himself 'affronted and disrespected by rude soldiers'. He died in July 1643.

The city might have been 'playing' at Court, but they could not be unaware that there was a war going on. The royal mint was set up in New Inn Hall, while in the Astronomy and Music Schools the royal tailors beavered away on uniforms for the army. The royal mill was producing gunpowder and the great quadrangle of Christ Church was turned into animal pens.

No matter how hard everyone tried to re-create the Court at London, there was fighting all around. If Jeffrey did engage in this, then it is most likely that it took place at night, for, as dusk fell, Prince Rupert would leave the town, leading a small strike force of cavalry in nocturnal raids against Parliamentary troops in Thame, Aylesbury and Reading. Night and horseback would have made Jeffrey equal to anyone. It is certainly possible that Jeffrey fought alongside the King and Prince Rupert at the battle of Newbury – a terrible slaughter which both sides claimed as a victory – but the tradition of his presence there only begins with Sir Walter Scott and *Peveril of the Peak*.

Most likely, however, Jeffrey's war was one of skirmishes and lightning raids. Perhaps some nights the streets of Oxford echoed to the sound of horses' hooves as Prince Rupert rode out to strike the enemy, accompanied by Captain Hudson, absconding from the Queen's apartments for a little adventuring of his own.

Amidst all of this, the Queen's circumstances suddenly changed. Her romantic reunion with Charles had led to an inevitable outcome and the she-majesty Generalissima was pregnant.

It was a bad time to bring a child into the world. The news from the battlefront became worse. With the autumn, the city was shrouded in damp mists from the Thames and the crowding which in the summer seemed such an adventure now seemed less exciting. The Cavaliers were, for all their romance, incredibly unhygienic. The Oxford scholar Anthony Wood contrasted their 'gay apparell' with their 'nasty and beastly habits'. When they finally abandoned the city, they left, he claims, 'excrements in every corner, in chimneys, studies, ale-houses, cellars'. Small wonder that a bad outbreak of typhoid swept through the congested city.

Meanwhile, the Parliamentary forces had a new hero, an East Anglian General of Horse whom the Cavaliers called 'Crum-well'. In February an attempted Royalist uprising in London was easily crushed and in subsequent weeks and months the Royalist outposts around Oxford began to crumble. The adventure was over and many believed it was time for the Queen to move on.

D'Avenant summed up the general feeling, addressing the Queen in some of his best verse:

> Fair as unshaded light, or as the day
> Of the first year, when every month was May;
> Sweet as the altar's smoke, or as the new
> Unfolded bud swelled by the morning's dew;
> Kind as the willing saints, but calmer far
> Than in their dreams forgiven votaries are, –
> But what, sweet excellence, what dost thou here?

What, indeed? The Queen, racked by rheumatic pains and the weary pains of pregnancy, decided it was time to go.

The parting came in April 1644. Early in the morning, Jeffrey climbed on his horse to join Jermyn, Frederick Cornwallis, Mitte the lap-dog and the rest of the Queen's faithful household. On 3 April, Charles escorted his beloved wife south to Abingdon. They stayed there for the night, the same place where, during the optimistic days of summer, they had enjoyed boat trips together.

The next morning, in floods of tears, she and her husband said their goodbyes. The King turned back towards Oxford; the Queen set out for Bath.

They were never to see each other again.

It was a doleful journey. Hunted and harried at every turn, the Queen's party seldom experienced a day's peace. Bath turned out to be the least healthy health-spa imaginable, for the city was full of disease, and corpses lay on the street corners. The Queen hoped the spa waters would help her ailment – for by now she was finding every movement a torment – but it was impossible to stay in the city. Jeffrey and his companions headed further west, to Exeter.

Still her illness persisted. Eventually she was so desperate she sent a plea for help to Sir Theodore Mayerne, her old physician from happier days. Mayerne, a pompous, self-righteous man who had never liked Henrietta Maria, refused to go. Eventually Charles sent him a simple, but eloquent plea: 'Mayerne, for the love of *me*, go to my wife.'

The aged physician, to his credit, went to her aid. Accompanied by his assistant Sir Matthew Lister, he found the Queen at Bedford House in Exeter. She was depressed and anxious, complaining that she felt her mind weakening and fearful that she might become crazy. Mayerne, whose bedside manner left a lot to be desired, answered, 'You need not fear it madam, for you are that already.' Whether the Queen appreciated his sarcasm is not recorded.

Despite her frailty, Henrietta Maria gave birth to a beautiful baby girl on 16 June 1644, named Henrietta after her mother. The birth left the Queen very weak and partially paralysed, and in such agony she was begging for death. Even Mayerne believed that she would not survive.

Jeffrey knew that they could not stay in the city long. Exeter was threatened by the Parliamentary forces. The Queen had written to Essex, the Parliamentary General to ask for safe-conduct back to Bath, but he refused. Jermyn, Jeffrey, everyone in the household knew they had only one route left to them: they must escape to France.

Fifteen days after the birth of her daughter, Henrietta Maria left the baby in her cot, gathered up a few things and slipped out of the city at night. She was accompanied by Sir John Wintour, one lady-in-waiting, and her confessor. Throughout the night, small parties of individuals followed her example. The tall figure of Jermyn and the small figure of Jeffrey were each left to make their own escape past the surrounding forces. They were to rendezvous later, in the woods on the Plymouth road.

How Jeffrey left we do not know. It may well be that this was one time when his size was a positive advantage – few soldiers would assume that someone of his height could be anything other than a child – but Henrietta Maria's adventures illustrate only too well how perilous the journey was, for she ran straight into the oncoming army and was forced to hide. For forty-eight hours the Queen lay without food, hiding under a pile of rags and refuse to escape detection. She could hear the soldiers passing by the hut where she was hidden. Later, she told one of her ladies that she heard them swear that 'fifty thousand crowns would be the reward for anyone who captured the Queen'.

Henrietta Maria may have been headstrong; she may have been over-zealous in her faith, unguarded in her opinions and unwise in her counsel, but no Queen has ever shown more courage than she did during those days. Forced to abandon her newborn child, racked with pain, desperately worried for the safety of her husband and sons, she was determined to reach France to bring him help. For herself, she genuinely believed that she would die within a few months. Her only aim appears to have been to aid her husband however she could.

On the third evening, she left her hiding place. The troops were past and the Queen hurried with her advisers to the rendezvous point. In a cabin in the woods she found her faithful friends anxiously waiting her arrival. There on the night of 23 June 1644 she opened the door to find the welcoming faces of Lord Jermyn, Mitte the spaniel and, of course, Captain Jeffrey Hudson.

Six days later the group reached Pendennis Castle in Cornwall. The Queen had been carried in a litter, with the rest of her troop walking alongside her. No horses this time, no carriages to ease their journey, just mile after mile of weary trudging. Francis Basset, a Cornish gentleman who encountered the Queen on her journey, wrote a pitiful description to his wife:

> Here is the woefullest spectacle my eyes ever yet look'd on; the most worne and weake pitifull creature in ye world, the poor Queene, shifting for one hour's liffe longer.

Nevetheless she kept going. The hours turned into days and still the Queen did not give in. A few days later the Queen and her motley entourage boarded a fleet of Dutch vessels and left England.

As usual, the sea was a treacherous place. No sooner had the ships left the harbour than they found themselves pursued by enemy craft. The Queen instructed the captain that, if they could not escape, he was to ignite the gunpowder on the boat and blow the vessel up. Her ladies-in-waiting, hearing this order, began, rather unhelpfully, to scream.

Jeffrey, once again, was in peril on the sea. When they were nearly in sight of Jersey, he felt the ship shudder and list to one side: a cannonball had struck the rigging, bringing down some of the sail. It seemed they would be captured (or blown up) after all. But at this moment, some ships from Dieppe came into sight, took the Queen's little vessels under their protection and the Parliamentary ships abandoned the chase.

It might be thought that by now the Queen and her faithful dwarf deserved a bit of good fortune. It was not to be. The attackers might have been driven off, but a storm blew up, forcing them away from Dieppe and along the French coast. At last, when they were weary, sick and almost drowned, the storm abated enough for the passengers to land. A longboat was put down from the ship and Jeffrey climbed aboard. The boat took them in among the rocks, until they were able to climb out and wade to shore. They were in Brittany. They had escaped.

It was to be many years before any of that oddly assorted landing crew returned to England. When Henrietta Maria went back it was in triumph, as the Queen Mother, the widow of the martyr-King Charles I and the mother of the restored King Charles II.

For Jeffrey it was to be a longer parting. He was not to see his home country for another twenty-five years.

THE
FATAL DUELLIST

. . . and whereas some in the world (wedded to error) may fondly imagine your residence at Court to bee rather for wonder and merriment then for any use or service, you may require from them no lesse satisfaction then a publique recantation.

The New Yeare's Gift

THEY LANDED IN A ROCKY COVE NOT FAR FROM BREST.

Jeffrey was back in France for the first time since his triumphant visit in 1629, when he was showered with gifts and adored by ladies of fashion. But this was not a diplomatic mission or a royal progress; it was a retreat, a surrender, a farewell to a world that had vanished. Now the only thing that he was showered with was the rain.

However, as the boat crunched against the stones, he must have felt that not all was lost. Now twenty-five, he had proved himself amidst hardship and peril; he had aided the Queen during the most perilous weeks of her life. The last time he entered France he entered as a freak; now he was entering the country as a man. Or so, at least, he believed.

It was not an easy place to land. They crossed the rocky

beach and ascended a narrow, perilous path – a journey which must have been as hazardous for the overweight Lord Jermyn as for little Jeffrey. Eventually, tired and exhausted, they found a small village of fishermen's huts where the Queen lay down to rest on a bed of straw.

They were not exactly welcomed with open arms. Within a few minutes a mob of villagers had gathered, in the belief that the party were pirates. Armed with cudgels, axes and whatever they could lay their hands on, the angry Bretons prepared themselves to repel this threat – although quite what threat an exhausted Queen, an obese peer, a dwarf, a pet spaniel and a handful of half-drowned guards presented is not easily imagined. The Queen was forced to rise from her bed and explain to the mob who they really were.

The news spread quickly, and the next morning the little village was abuzz with activity. The Breton nobility, hearing that the daughter of their beloved Henri Quatre was in need, rushed to see her and offer any aid they could.

As Henrietta afterwards observed, she must have seemed like a wandering princess of romance, more than a Queen. But there was nothing fairytale about her situation. After so many months spent under an almost intolerable strain, after the physical dangers and emotional terrors of the last few weeks, she collapsed. Exhausted by her illness, facing the loss of her crown and having been forced to abandon her husband and her newborn daughter, Henrietta Maria was depressed and physically weak. Far from being a glorious and romantic figure, the Queen seems to have undergone a physical and mental breakdown.

Weeping and crying the whole time, unable to move without pain, she was in no state to go straight to Paris for any official reception. Instead, she went south, to Bourbon l'Archambault, where she hoped the natural spa waters would help her recovery.

Madame de Motteville, lady-in-waiting to the Queen of France, was sent to offer help and comfort. She found a sad spectacle awaiting her:

> The Queen of England was much disfigured by the severity of her illness and her misfortunes, no trace remaining of her past beauty . . . She was constantly followed by a great crowd of people running to see her. She was very ill and much changed; her misfortunes had given her such sadness, and her mind was so filled with her sorrow that she wept continually.

Although the French royal family waited for her in Paris, her favourite brother, Gaston of Orleans, rushed to her side. Thankfully, the waters at Bourbon had some effect, for by August she was well enough to make the journey to Paris. A state coach was sent to bring her to the capital. She stopped first at Tours, where the young John Evelyn was given an audience:

> On the 18 came the Queene of England to Towers [sic] newly arrived in France, and taking this Citty in her way to Paris: she was very nobly receiv'd by both people and Cleargy, who went to meet her with all train'd bands: After the Harangue, the Archbish: entertaind her Majestie at his owne Palac, where I did my duty to her. The 20th she set forwards towards Paris.

She arrived in Paris on 21 August where she was greeted by the young King, his mother the Queen-Regent, and the real ruler of France, Cardinal Mazarin. She climbed into the King's coach, and together they made their entry into the city. According to Mademoiselle de Montpensier, who had brought Henrietta Maria from Bourbon, the Queen was still in a 'deplorable' state, so much so that 'no one could look at her without an emotion of compassion'.

France itself was in a period of change. Henrietta Maria's brother Louis XIII had died the previous year, leaving the kingdom in the hands of his wife, Anne of Austria, and, more importantly, Cardinal Mazarin. Mazarin, an Italian by birth, was the most powerful man in the kingdom. So close was he with the queen that in subsequent years there were many rumours that they were actually married – perfectly possible since he had never been ordained as a priest. Louis's successor, his son Louis XIV, was only four. Effectively, Mazarin was in control.

Louis XIV, although young, was perfectly aware of who he was and what he was to be. His earliest recorded statement is typical – when taken before his dying father on 21 April 1643 the King asked, 'Who is it?' 'Louis XIV,' replied the lad. For now, Louis was only a child and Mazarin held the purse strings. Over subsequent years he piled up a huge personal fortune while at the same time keeping the young king permanently short of funds.

Henrietta Maria had reason to be fearful of her reception, she had incurred the displeasure of Anne of Austria by siding with her mother Marie de Medici. She need not have worried. Anne was generous and welcoming and Henrietta Maria was given a set of apartments in the Louvre and an income of twelve thousand crowns per month. Henry Jermyn was put in charge of her household and was responsible for overseeing all items of expenditure. No doubt, Jeffrey had his own room in the Louvre palace, for the building was vacant then, so there was plenty of space available. Received with open arms, provided with money and shelter, perhaps everything would turn out right after all.

Henrietta Maria was still unwell, so she did not stay in Paris for long. After only a few days in the Louvre, the exiled Queen and her entourage left the city for a country residence, the château at St Germain-en-Laye, which had also been donated for her use. There they spent September, in the hopes that the Queen's condition would improve. Unfortunately it became worse, and by October was bad enough to force another move – back to Bourbon to take the waters again.

Thus it was that Jeffrey found himself back in Bourbon on 7 September. They stayed in Bourbon for a few weeks; on 25 September, Evelyn met the Queen again, leaving a description of the medicinal baths:

> . . . some of them excessive hott, but nothing so neatly walled & adorned as ours in Sommersetshire; & inde-ede they are chiefly used to drinke off, our Queene being then lodg'd there for that cause.

A few weeks later, by 11 October, they had moved to more spacious quarters in nearby Nevers. Rumours of her illness reached England. On Wednesday 9 October, an early news-paper called *A Diary or Exact Journal* was disclosing that 'There is a report that the Queene of England is lately dead in France, toomorrow letters from thence are expected either to confirm the report more fully or disclaime it.'

Obviously the letters proved the contrary, and on 11 October another paper, *Perfect Occurrences of Parliament*, reported that 'The French doctors have enjoyned her to drinke Asses milke every morning . . .'

This report is backed up by a letter from the Venetian ambassador in France who wrote: 'The Queen of England, after enjoying the benefits of the waters at Borbon has gone on to Nivers to take the milk.'

Whether the asses' milk did Henrietta Maria any more good than the spa water is debatable. She was still very sick; she could not walk unaided and one of her breasts had to be lanced because of an abscess. At Nevers, she and her Court were esconced in the Hotel de Ville, the ancient home of the Dukes of Bourbon. The castle was large and spacious, but it was also somewhat run-down and the rooms were damp.

By now it was autumn and the cold weather had set in. To a Court used to the splendours of Denmark House and the luxuries of their palaces in England, Nevers must have seemed a dismal place. It was a resort out of season; cold, drab, deserted. The winter winds from the nearby hills had driven most visitors away and the figures of the tiny, stooping Queen, the overweight English peer, her ladies-in-waiting, her dogs and her dwarf must have presented a surreal and pathetic spectacle to the residents.

Before long, however, they were joined by other exiles and a more 'normal' court life began to resume. D'Avenant arrived and William Crofts, her Master of Horse, as well as numerous other escapees from England. It was a strange Court, however, as bitter, cold and cheerless as the weather. The Cavaliers had always reacted to adversity by staging a play or holding a ball or, more frequently, calling for a drink. In the relaxed days of royal power, this might have seemed brave and 'devil-may-care', but in the cold, harsh light of Nevers there is more than a touch of desperation about it. The laughter is jolly, but desperate. As the years went by, this attitude was to harden into a characteristic of the English Court in exile. Far from home, without any ties or responsibilities, they sat in the saloons and drank, because they had no idea how to do anything else.

Things were different now. Jeffrey knew that; Henrietta Maria knew that; but for many of the young blades it was business as usual. In their futile ignorance they simply took up where they left off, with nights of drinking, card-playing, singing and revelry. And, of course, the baiting of Little Jeffrey.

Jeffrey must have looked on with bitterness. Was this what it had all come to? These foolish young men were once again ruling the roost, while he, who had been through shipwreck, bombardment and battle, he who had braved all for the Queen – was he once again relegated to playing the fool? While others who were nowhere to be seen during the Queen's escape from Exeter took posts in her household, he was still Little Jeffrey, the Queen's Dwarf. They had not walked many miles by her side. They had not stood on guard on the quay at Bridlington while the guns roared out at sea. They had not braved the Round-head soldiers on that Plymouth road. But now they were acting as if they owned the place.

So Jeffrey took a decision: he wasn't going to take any more from these people. It was time to stop being the butt of ridicule and the object of witty poems. It was time to make a stand. He let it be known that the next person who insulted him would be invited to a duel. He was no longer prepared to be the subject of snide remarks by courtiers anxious to prove their wit. He was *Captain* Jeffrey Hudson of the Queen's army and he demanded to be taken seriously.

The problem was that although he might have changed, others clearly hadn't. And when word got round about Jeffrey's intentions – that the next person who insulted him would be challenged to a duel – far from stopping the insults, it 'gave promise of high amusement to his tormentors'. It was decided that this was a joke too good to miss.

A volunteer was found – young Charles Crofts, brother of the Queen's Master of Horse, William, Lord Crofts.

Nothing is known of Charles Crofts himself. He left no imprint on history. Indeed, in the accounts of the duel, his first name isn't even given and we can only identify him by a process of elimination. Sir Henry Crofts of Saxham, Suffolk, had five sons. William became Master of the Queen's Horse; John, the second son, became Dean of Norwich; Edmund and Henry died young. That leaves only Charles who was born around 1620 and who was certainly still alive in 1642.

But then again, perhaps the exact identification isn't really so important. Charles Crofts is more of a type than anything else. The whole thing was a joke; his place could have been taken by any of the aimless, rootless, dispossessed young men at Henrietta Maria's Court in exile.

Nevertheless, once a volunteer had been found, the challenge had to be issued. Charles lost no time in seeking out Jeffrey and provoking him. It is not recorded what the insult was, but, as Jeffrey's life proves, it does not take a great intellect to think of ways to insult a dwarf. Jeffrey, true to his word, threw down the gauntlet. The challenge was issued. A duel was arranged in the park that surrounded the castle.

Presumably Henrietta Maria did not know about the duel. Had she known, she would certainly have stopped it; leaving aside her care for Jeffrey, she would not want anyone at her Court to do anything to risk the displeasure of Mazarin.

Only the previous year, Mazarin had issued an edict against duelling, in yet another attempt to curb the epidemic which had gripped France for decades. France was obsessed with duelling, and had been for years. In Richelieu's time, duelling was so common that the streets had become little more than fields of combat. The fights even took place at night under the lights of torches or the stars.

Richelieu attempted to stop the habit by enforcing harsh penalties; even issuing a challenge was enough to deprive a man of his offices, half his property and send him into exile for three years. Those taking part were likely to lose all rights and titles, and, where one of the combatants was killed, the victor was liable to death and total confiscation of goods. Even the dead man lost his property, which might be thought to be adding insult to injury. In 1627 Richelieu put these edicts into practice, executing two noblemen called Bouteville and Deschapelles for arranging and fighting a duel. However, Richelieu's toughness only suppressed the activity for a while. Because the application of these punishments was left in the hands of local magistrates – many of whom were reluctant to offend the nobility – the law was only sporadically enforced, and before long the custom had flared up again.

Richelieu issued another decree against duelling in 1639 and two more in 1640, but nothing seemed to make any difference. His attempts were picked up by Mazarin in the edict of June 1643, which largely repeated previous decrees. This law was no more effective than the earlier ones, and he was forced to issue a further edict in May 1644, only a few weeks before Jeffrey arrived in the country.

Even though the punishments were infrequently imposed, Henrietta Maria was painfully aware of the precariousness of her position in France. She simply could not afford to offend the ruling powers. So it is likely that, had she known, the affair would have been settled without recourse to violence.

But she did not know. And anyway, it was a *joke*.

*　　　*　　　*

Nobody took the duel seriously. Even there, at dawn in the misty light of an autumn morning, there was a light-heartedness among Crofts's seconds. This prank would be the talk of the town, something to brighten the long dull days of the Court in exile.

When the combatants faced each other and were asked to 'name their weapons', young Crofts produced the *coup de grâce* of his jest. From beneath his cloak he pulled out a 'squirt' – a large syringe which served as a seventeenth-century fire-extinguisher. What a priceless joke! It was *Jeffereidos* all over again; then Jeffrey had fought with a turkey-cock, now he was going to fight a duel armed with water-pistols. And if things went really well, little Jeffrey might get a soaking as well! In all the gaiety, no one seemed to have noticed that Jeffrey wasn't laughing.

To Jeffrey, this was the final insult. He had issued this challenge because he was tired of being made to look a fool and Crofts had done the one thing that was guaranteed to stiffen his resolve – he had treated the whole matter as a joke. When the laughter died down, the reality dawned. They came to fight. They would fight. The duel would go ahead.

One can imagine how the laughter drained from the faces of the onlookers. This wasn't what was supposed to happen. What had happened to the little fellow? He had always been such a sport before; always willing to jump out of pies, or dance around in masques, or hide in the pockets of giants. Now he was demanding they fight. With pistols. On horseback. Hurriedly, the squirt was put to one side. Crofts's seconds prepared him and found him a weapon and a horse.

Finally, all was ready. The assailants, mounted on horseback, faced each other, a hundred paces apart. There was nothing but the cold, crisp morning air, the snorting of the horses. A handkerchief was raised and then dropped. The horses began to charge.

Even now, those watching must have believed that it would all end cheerfully, that the danger would disappear as quickly as the early morning mists. The pistols would be discharged, honour would be satisfied, and the affair would be another hilarious episode in the life of Lord Minimus.

They were wrong. When you are only two feet high, it is not enough that you do things as well as the next person; you have to do things better. It is not enough to be competent; you have to excel. 'Captain' Jeffrey Hudson was a good horseman and – as it transpired – a crack shot. He was also a tiny and rapidly moving target. Crofts, cantering towards the dwarf, could hardly even see his opponent. But Jeffrey, racing at full speed, could see Crofts.

All the insults of the years filled those few moments in time; all the jokes, the jests, the patronizing poems and fatuous verse; the capering dances; all the awful triviality of his life.

When he was only a few yards from Crofts, with his horse 'in full career', Jeffrey levelled his pistol and shot the lad through the head.

Poor, stupid young Crofts died on the spot.

The joke was over and no one would ever laugh at Jeffrey again.

The news even quickly reached England. A newsletter called *Perfect Passages* reported the tragic events:

> By letters from France it is certified that Will. Crofts, the queen's great favourite's brother, upon some displeasure conceived against him by little Jeffry, the queen's dwarf, with her in France, was by him slain;

his brother being captain of the queen's lifeguard and master of her horse. It appears the challenge was sent by Jeffry, that they fought on horseback, and Jeffry, running his horse in full career, shot his antagonist in the head, and left him dead on the spot.

They dated the affair as happening on 16 October. A week later a rival publication, *Perfect Occurrences*, had also run the story, reporting how 'Little Jefferies' had 'Pistolled Crofts in the head who fell down dead immediately'.

In the meantime, Henrietta Maria promptly fired off a letter to her sister-in-law the Queen as well as one to the Commander of the Archers, or the police. On 20 October she wrote to Mazarin from Nevers:

> I wrote to the queen, my sister, about a misfortune which has happened to my house of Le Joffroy, who has killed Croft's brother. I have written the whole affair to the commander, in order that you may hear of it. What I wish is that as they are both English and my servants, the queen, my sister, will give me authority to dispose of them as I please, in dispensing either justice or favour, which I am unwilling to do, without writing to you, and asking you to assist me therein as I shall always do in all which concerns me . . .

Mazarin's answer is not recorded, but it is hard to believe he was much bothered by the affair. Henrietta Maria was right; it was a purely internal matter and, as we have seen, Mazarin had enough difficulty stopping the nobles of France from duelling, let alone bothering with some English émigrés. Equally, we know that throughout October he was laid low with a severe bout of fever (probably typhoid) which almost killed him. So it was left to Henrietta Maria to pronounce judgement.

And her judgement was banishment. Jeffrey was told to go; to pack up what few things he had rescued from England and to leave France.

Why? Mazarin, as we have seen, is unlikely to have been too worried about what was viewed as a purely internal matter. Despite Henrietta Maria's anxieties about the Cardinal, he had too much on his mind to risk getting involved. He may, it is true, have insisted that Jeffrey should leave the country just to let the Queen know who was really in charge, but equally he may not have been bothered by the affair. Not when there were Frenchmen dying in the same way every day.

Perhaps Henrietta Maria herself insisted on the punishment, although the fact is Crofts meant little to her, whereas Jeffrey meant a great deal. Jermyn, her Chancellor, was likely to be on Jeffrey's side: he hated William Crofts, the Queen's Master of Horse, and the dead man's brother.

There can be only one explanation. Henrietta Maria, who had first taken Jeffrey in when she was alone and without a husband in England, was now alone and without a husband in France. She had known Jeffrey for some eighteen years. She would have done anything to save him. The truth must be that by sending him away she *was* saving him. By banishing him she was saving his life. The person Jeffrey slew was the brother of a powerful official in her Court. The dead man had many influential, or at the very least impulsive, friends. Would it be likely that these people would let the matter lie? Having slain young Charles, how long would it be before Jeffrey himself was involved in another duel? How many would have to be fought before Crofts was avenged?

So Jeffrey must go. Henrietta Maria's dwarf, Little

Jeffrey, Lord Minimus, had grown up. And a bitter growing it was, too. The dwarf who had spent his life trying to serve his mistress and make her smile, left her Court having only added to her share of woes. Maybe Henrietta Maria thought that, as with Jermyn's 'eternal banishment', it would only be a matter of time before they saw each other again. Just a while, just until everything cooled off.

She could not have known that this bitter parting would be final. The faithful dwarf and his mistress never saw each other again.

It is the supreme irony of Jeffrey's life that his one moment of self-realization cost him everything. Everything he had came about through not standing on his own dignity, through behaving like a fool, a clown, a freak. All that he had gained, he had gained as Jeffrey Hudson, the Queen's Dwarf. The moment he asserted his individuality was the moment he lost everything.

The duel in the park was the most important event in Jeffrey's life. Climbing out of a pie might have defined what others thought of him, but his duel with young Crofts defined what he thought of himself. Not a 'dwarf'; not a freak; not a jester. But a man.

Independence always comes at a cost, and the cost for Jeffrey was everything he had. The life he had known since he was seven was taken away from him. Whatever Henrietta Maria thought of him, the rest of the Court closed ranks. Jeffrey had ruined the joke. He had to leave. Four short years ago he had been on the stage, 'playing the wag' in *Salmacida Spolia*. Now everything was broken. A man lay dead in an obscure French town and Jeffrey's life was about to take another, even more bizarre twist.

At the end of October 1644, he rode out of the castle gates in Nevers, and into a nightmare.

THE
ABANDONED SLAVE

Whilst captive-Jeff'ry shewes to wiser sight,
Just like a melancholy Israelite,
In midst of's journey unto Babylon;

William D'Avenant, *Jeffereidos*

AFTER NEVERS, JEFFREY'S MOVEMENTS BECOME
difficult and sometimes impossible to trace in detail. We
know that he left the town at the end of October, for by
early November Henrietta Maria was back in Paris, and
Jeffrey is no longer mentioned.

He may have travelled in the same direction, heading
north to Paris and then to Le Havre or Dieppe. Equally he
might have gone west, to the Atlantic coast, where the
nearest port was La Rochelle where, so long ago, Buckingham's hopes had come to grief.

Whatever embarkation point he chose, it seems most
likely that, dangerous as it was, he intended to return to
Britain. After all, where else was there for him? He knew
no one in Spain or any of the Italian states. The war,
although not going well for the Royalist cause, was by no
means lost. If he could not join the King's troops, then he
could always return to his roots, back to his family at

Oakham where he might, even in these troubled times, live quietly in the country.

Of course, first he had a more immediate peril to face. It was bad enough that he had killed a man and been banished; now he had to go to sea again.

Few people have ever had worse luck at sea than Jeffrey. In the few voyages that we know of, he was fired on once, kidnapped once, and nearly drowned in storms twice. The voyage he took in the winter of 1644, however, was to beat them all.

The ship was well out to sea when consternation broke out among the crew. There were unidentified sails behind them, and they were closing fast. With a terrible chill, Jeffrey heard the same word that he had heard some fifteen years previously. They were being pursued by pirates.

These were not Dunkirkers, though. Compared to these pirates, the Dunkirkers were amateurs. The ships were sleek, fast, predatory. They sat low in the water and seemed to glide across the surface. They were galleys, propelled not only by the sails, but by banks of oars. As the three ships came close, a sailor standing on the poop of the foremost ship unfurled a flag, a green, crescent-spangled banner. They called out to the captain of the French ship to surrender immediately.

The panic on Jeffrey's boat must have been desperate. Accounts of attacks on other boats tell of passengers and crew fleeing below decks, desperately trying to hide themselves and their belongings. Some even began to swallow coins and jewels, to avoid having them fall into the hands of the pirates. The whole ship would have rocked with a shattering crash, as the leading galley rammed into the merchantman, using its battering ram to smash a hole in the side of the ship. From above their heads came the shattering roar of a cannon, fired from the poop deck of the galley to clear the decks. For a moment, all was strangely quiet, and then there were shouts and screams and the sound of many footsteps as the pirates leapt from their vessel and swarmed on deck.

For the second time in his life, Jeffrey found himself carried roughly up on deck. Meanwhile, a specialist search unit – a prize crew – started to ransack the merchantman and take everything that was valuable.

The figures surrounding Jeffrey appeared like monstrous demons. Dressed in a strange, outlandish garb, they spoke unknown tongues: Turkish, Arabic, Spanish, French, Flemish and English and a weird dialect that seemed an amalgam of all the others. One man, a scribe, was taking notes, marking down the names and condition of all the captured passengers and crew and an inventory of all their goods, his letters a weird series of lines and patterns.

Everything about these men was frightening, from their curved, viciously sharp swords, to their faces, hollowed with greed and malice. They were pitiless, horrifying, relentless. They were Turkish Corsairs, the dreaded Barbary pirates, and they intended to take all their captives into slavery in North Africa.

During the seventeenth and eighteenth centuries, the Barbary Corsairs were the terror of the western seas. Well-trained, swift and deadly efficient, they struck without warning and attacked without mercy. Corsair galleys were faster and lighter than their prey. Scrupulously maintained, carefully cleaned and greased, they could glide through the water, according to the Spanish chroniclers, 'like a fish'.

They were the terrorists of their day, guerrilla seafarers, who would strike fast and get away quickly. Of course, in a fair fight, their ships stood no chance against the firepower of the French, Dutch or English men-of-war. But they didn't fight fair. They chose their victims carefully, followed no set rules of engagement, and struck at the least protected areas. And as the century wore on, their raids grew more and more audacious.

Using renegade English, French, Spaniards or Flemings as guides, they raided the Mediterranean and Atlantic coasts. The Corsairs attacked from Iceland to the Canary Islands, anywhere there might be people to enslave and goods to plunder. They sailed up the English Channel as far as the Isle of Wight. The West Country was particularly hard-hit, with distraught citizens complaining of raids on ships from Devon and Cornwall. In 1640 the mayor of Plymouth complained that vessels had been attacked off the Lizard. In 1636 the shipowners of Exeter, Plymouth, Dartmouth and other West Country ports complained that they could not put to sea for fear of capture, estimating that there were some sixty pirate ships operating in the Channel. Each time it was the same, goods were seized, ships were ransacked and people were taken into slavery.

All the complaints and the pleas came to nothing, for the one thing that might have stopped the pirates – a combined effort on the part of the European powers – was impossible to achieve. Indeed, instead of working together to prevent the piracy, the consuls of various nations – notably England and France – spent their time persuading the Barbary states to break peace with their rivals. Since the pirate states never respected any treaty in the first place, this was something of a redundant effort, but while the other countries were at war with each other, the Corsairs could operate with impunity. And it has to be said that they were doing no more than the European powers commonly did during times of war. It was by no means uncommon for English ships to capture and enslave French merchant vessels during times of conflict, and vice versa, and the French galleys were well known for their hideous enslavement of Turkish and Moorish 'infidels'.

The fear of the pirates was partly, at least, the fear of the unknown. For these Corsairs hailed from that mysterious place, 'Barbary', a country which not only took its name from the Berbers – the indigenous inhabitants of North Africa – but also from 'barbarian', which is how Europe commonly viewed them. The 'Barbary Coast' was a generic term for a group of North African states, most of which were protectorates of the great Ottoman empire of the Turks. Most of the slaves taken ended up in Algiers, but Tunis and Morocco were also highly active.

What made them such a threat was the ruthless professionalism with which they operated. Over the years, the pirates developed highly specialized ships to capture their prey. These galley-ships, the design of which had not changed much since Roman times, were around one hundred and eighty feet long and sixteen feet wide. The horror of these ships is almost unimaginable. The slaves would not – could not – sit during the chase, but would have to leap up to throw their whole weight behind the stroke. It was not unknown for the galley slaves to toil for ten to twenty hours at a stretch, if it meant escaping a foe or capturing a prize. And all the time they were fed only dry rusks or gruel, and given only vinegar and water to drink.

Down the centre of the ship was a raised walkway, where an overseer would stride about, wielding his whip and driving his slaves to even greater exertions. Above him on the poop deck stood the captain, the *raïs*, who was often the owner as well. Generally this was either a European renegade or a Turk; only occasionally was he a Moor.

Once they had secured their victim, the passengers and crew were rounded up and taken on to the deck where a secretary or scribe started to note down the names of the captives. He would also make an inventory of goods, all of which would later be shared out among the pirates according to a carefully worked-out scale. All of their operations were carried out with a businesslike efficiency because that's what the Barbary slave trade was: a business. Expeditions were financed by private individuals and even small corporations, all of whom hoped to capture rich prizes, strong slaves and valuable hostages whom they could ransom to make a profit.

The captives' only hope of release was to be redeemed, bought back out of captivity by the payment of a ransom. Each captured slave, therefore, would work hard to convince the *raïs* that they were not worth much, so that the ransom demand would be kept low.

For Jeffrey it was an impossible task: one look at him alone was enough to demonstrate his value. And if they found out about his royal connections then the ransom would be prohibitive. It was one time in his life when being a rarity of nature was a positive disadvantage. He was obviously special. For Jeffrey there was only one destination: the slave market.

Where Jeffrey was taken no one knows. He described his capture to the historian James Wright:

> After this he was a second time taken Prisoner at Sea, but that was a much more fatal captivity than the first. It was a Turkish Pirate that took and carried him to Barbary, where he was sold, and remain'd a slave for many years.

If his captors were Turkish that means they would probably have taken him to Algiers or Tunis or Tripoli – all of which were under Turkish control.

The likeliest destination, if only statistically, is Algiers. It had the largest fleet and was well used to preying upon English, Norman and Breton shipping. In the 1630s there were an estimated twenty-five thousand slaves at Algiers, seven thousand at Tunis, and a meagre five hundred at Tripoli. In truth, his destination is not important; the slave experience was much the same wherever you went. A slave was a domestic animal, to be traded like cattle. And in the Barbary states, one marketplace was very like another.

He would have spent the voyage in chains, below deck. The first signs that they were close to landing came with the sound of cannon; a salute of guns announcing their return to port. A little later a port official arrived – the *limam raïs* or port captain. He had come out to meet the boat and get particulars of the prizes. He looked the captives over with an experienced eye, preparing to hasten back to the palace to give the details to the Dey.

The boat docked at the quayside. There was the sound of an excited crowd, for the whole city came alive at the arrival of a new slave cargo. Jeffrey was herded on to the deck, blinking in the harsh sunlight. And there before him was a terrible, wonderful, horrifying sight: the city of Algiers.

Rows of whitewashed houses rose up the sides of the steep hill to where the Casbah fortress stood, on the top of the hill, dominating the city. Beyond were distant hills, green with orchards and fields, dotted with country houses. The skyline of the city was broken by an occasional larger building – mosques, public baths, the barracks of the janissaries, the bagnio or slave prison. And there was their first destination: the Jenina or Dey's palace.

The Dey had the right to choose one out of every eight captured slaves. He generally chose the skilled craftsmen, surgeons, carpenters whom he could set to work in the harbour or on the ships. He also chose any person who might prove to be of exceptional worth. Jeffrey, with his unique appearance, might have appealed to the exotic taste of the Dey, but he did not specifically mention the Dey, and he talked to Wright of being 'sold', so it is likely that he was taken out of the palace and down to the Bedestan or slave market. There he was paraded with the other slaves, his degradation complete and his fate a matter of another's whim. Stripped and subjected to humiliating public inspection, Jeffrey was valued by professional brokers, Moorish or Jewish middlemen who knew the precise value of the market. Attention was particularly directed at the state of the teeth – for if bought to be galley slaves they were going to have to survive on the rock-hard ship's biscuit – and of the hands. The latter could reveal whether the men were used to heavy work or were of gentle birth. It is not hard to guess the state of Jeffrey's hands, the hands of a courtier since the age of seven would hardly be workmanlike.

Having set an initial value, the slave would then be walked up and down the street – or occasionally prodded to make him jump or run. The broker would announce the quality and profession of each slave and the last price, until no further offer was made. The first offer never rose very high, as the sale itself took place in the Dey's courtyard, where the slaves were led and put up for auction. Those purchased privately were taken back to their houses and thereafter they were entirely at their new master's mercy.

The fate of a slave depended entirely on his or her owner. In the Dey's household, a clever slave could prosper. The ablest and best-educated slave might rise to the rank of 'Chief Christian Secretary', a hugely important post, for it meant overseeing all the Dey's dealings with European consuls and merchants. Like all slave posts, however, it could be dangerous, for the secretary could be beaten if he were the bearer of bad news, but, if managed well, the job could provide the basis for a bearable living. (At the end of the eighteenth century this post was held by an American called Cathcart who combined his job with running seven taverns.)

In some households lucky slaves were looked after so well that, in the words of one witness, they were 'cared for and cherished like children'. Indeed, some slaves were not over-eager to be set free. If they had a genial master or mistress, life might even be better for them than at home. But this was the exception. Although slave-owners were governed by self-interest and also by Koranic injunctions to treat them humanely, slaves were still routinely beaten and abused.

Although, as a rarity, Jeffrey's ransom value would have been prohibitively high, in another way he was lucky. His size made him completely unsuitable for severe physical work. For those slaves unlucky enough to be assigned to this work, the fate was harsh. They became inhabitants of the government bagnios, or slave prisons, wretched, verminous places each containing around five or six hundred slaves. Bagnio slaves wore iron shackles. Some were sent to the quarries to break stones, some worked in the harbour, scraping the hulls of the galleys or unloading in the docks. Others were harnessed to carts and forced to drag building materials to the various public construction sites. Jeffrey, at least, was spared that fate.

It was up to the slaves to arrange their own ransoms. Communications were slow and unreliable. Frequently letters went astray and their families never even knew of their plight. Should the letter make it through, the family would make over funds to a merchant house that had a factor in

Barbary. The money would generally be used to purchase goods which would be shipped out and sold. Often these intermediaries dragged out the affair, or even simply kept the money, all the while telling the distraught families that 'everything possible was being done'.

If the ransom was slow in coming, or insufficient to satisfy the master's greed, the slave might be fettered in heavy chains, half-starved, mercilessly beaten or immured in a fortress dungeon. The aim was not to kill him – a dead slave was no use to anyone – but to impose maximum pressure on the hapless slave to produce the ransom. Some slaves lived more comfortably. If a slave could convince his master that the ransom was coming, or if he could make some form of monthly payment, then he could be exempted from labour and even from confinement.

One of the mysteries of Jeffrey's time as a Barbary slave is the fact that he was not ransomed earlier. It may be that his letters never reached their destination. Or it may be that there was simply no one to approach. After all, to whom could he plead? His family were poor labourers in Oakham. The King was captured and in prison in London.

The Queen, had she but known, would surely have helped him. Admittedly, during the years she spent in France, she was increasingly hard-up. One observer described how she appeared at the beginning 'with the splendour of royal equipage' including footmen, ladies-in-waiting, coaches and guards. As the years went by, however, 'all vanished . . . and at last nothing could be more mean than her train and appearance'. She was reduced to a scandalous poverty within a few years of arriving in France, but one cannot imagine that she would not have found a way to help Jeffrey – especially later on, when she eventually returned to London to see her son crowned as King.

The truth must be that she did not know. Nor did anyone else. You would have thought that a figure as remarkable as Jeffrey would have excited some attention from visiting tradesmen or consuls. Rumours of the 'tiny slave' would have abounded. But we hear no such thing. He disappears.

After October 1644, it would be a quarter of a century before he emerged, blinking in the light of freedom. Perhaps his letters never reached their destination. Perhaps he went to work at an estate far inland, to one of the great estates high on the hills overlooking Algiers. Perhaps he was simply not allowed to request a ransom. After all, he was still a rarity. Maybe he was a slave whose owner had no intention of releasing him. In any event, no one seems to have known about him. He was a slave, one of thousands, a forgotten remnant of a once great Court; a favourite without anyone to show him favour.

For Jeffrey, the only hope lay in government schemes or escape. The government schemes were a recent introduction. In 1641, the English Parliament persuaded the King to put aside a percentage of revenue from customs to finance expeditions to redeem slaves in Barbary. The expeditions were led by Edmund Cason who arrived in Algiers in 1646 for the first time and ransomed some two hundred and fifty English men, women and children out of the estimated seven hundred and fifty there. It cost him a basic price of thirty-eight pounds a head, but some captives – notably the women – proved more expensive. Elizabeth Mancor of Dundee cost two hundred pounds, Sarah Ripley of London eight hundred, Mary Ripley and her two children a massive one thousand pounds. Cason died in Algiers eight years later. During that time the Treasury had spent some forty thousand pounds on redeeming the slaves from their owners. Schemes went on throughout subsequent years, but most of the lists of those rescued have been lost.

There was always escape, but that was rarely successful. There are examples of slaves escaping, perhaps the most remarkable of which was organized by John Fox from Woodbridge in Suffolk, who lived for fourteen years in captivity, eventually ending up as a barber in Alexandria. He contrived a conspiracy among half a dozen of his compatriots, procured a number of files and improvised weapons and overpowered the guards. They seized a galley and, with two hundred and twenty-eight slaves on board, made off under fire from the port batteries. After eight days at sea the fugitives reached Crete where they were given a triumphant welcome.

Another famous escapee was William Oakley who was captured during a raid on the Isle of Wight in 1639. Oakley was taken to Algiers, where he contracted with his owner to work outside the bagnio selling wine and hardware, and then worked as a weaver. With six other English captives he began secretly to build a boat in a cellar. They smuggled it out in pieces and reassembled it outside the city. After a voyage of five days they reached Majorca and thence to England.

These, however, were the rarities. The punishment was harsh for attempted escape, and the regime was such that most slaves hardly had the energy. No, the only thing to do was wait. Wait and hope for the ransom to come, from your friends, from your family, or from your government.

And that is what Jeffrey did. He waited. For a long, long time.

After a short time in captivity, Jeffrey became used to the culture. He was given a new uniform. Gone were the embroidered and ornate shoe roses, now he wore a simple collarless shirt with wide cuffless sleeves, baggy trousers and a close-fitting red cap. It was not just the clothes that were new, he was surrounded by foreign and unknown tongues. To communicate, he learned the slaves' language, a kind of patois or *lingua franca*, a common language including Italian and Spanish, with a bit of Greek thrown in. It was a vocabulary tragic with meaning, with words like '*usanza*', meaning not just 'tradition', but the fixed, accepted order of things, the terrible, tragic way things were. Another word was '*mangiado*', literally meaning 'eaten' but coming to mean something which was lost, gone, disappeared for ever.

Unsurprisingly, the slave community was not known for its delicate tastes and high morals. Most of the slaves were 'Christian' in name only and, according to one Catholic priest, they were thieves and drunks, their language was profane, and they even took opportunities to 'rejoice at the success and prosperity of the Turks and to jeer at the wretches who are brought in captive'.

They had a prison mentality, cruel and with no room for pity. If one cannot be free, one can at least rejoice in the captivity of others. In the harsh environment of Barbary, it was at least some comfort to know that there was always someone lower down on the food chain. Slaves became hardened, toughened in mind, body and spirit. They lived lives that were precarious, where the merest word or gesture could result in punishment and even death. In such a culture there is no room for sentimentality. There is only some sort of relief when it happens to someone else instead of you. Perhaps Jeffrey's training as a court favourite stood him in good stead here, for he had spent most of his life pleasing his 'owners'. As the time went on, however, the task must have become much harder. He was losing his boyish looks, the ransom was not forthcoming. And, most amazingly of all, he began to grow.

For years, Jeffrey's height remained around two feet,

but in captivity something changed. Something triggered a release of growth hormone, which caused him to shoot up in height. Here is Wright's description, taken from Jeffrey's own testimony:

> I have heard himself several times affirm, that between the 7th year of his age and the 30th he never grew anything considerable, but after thirty he shot up in a little time to that highth of stature which he remain'd at in his old age, viz. about three foot and nine inches. The cause of this he ascrib'd (how truly I know not) to the hardship, much labour, and beating, which he endured when a slave to the Turks.

It seems that Jeffrey was put to work. For the first time in his life, he was employed in physical labour. At Court he had been cosseted and cared for, with the faithful Jerome Gregoire to attend to his every need. He had servants to bring him meals, attendants to open doors for him, tradesmen to bring him whatever he needed. In captivity he had no such luxuries. He had to dig and fetch and carry; he was beaten and mistreated. His diet changed, from fancy refined foods to black bread and vinegar. He spent most of his time outdoors, in a warm climate. All of this combined to trigger some long-dormant growth hormones, adding around eighteen inches to his height.

Sporadic growth is by no means uncommon in sufferers from growth-hormone deficiency. Perhaps the most extreme case is that of Adam Rainer, an Austrian who was only three feet ten inches at the age of twenty-one, but who grew rapidly, reaching the height of seven feet one inch by the time he was thirty-two. The growth so debilitated him that he was bed-ridden for the rest of his life. Jeffrey, it is true, never rose to such great heights, but with his growth went his uniqueness. Three feet nine is not tall, but it is a lot different from eighteen inches or two feet six.

If it is true that hard work precipitated his growth, it raises the question of what would have happened to him had he not lived his life as a pampered favourite. Perhaps if he had been set to work in the fields of Rutland, he would have grown just the same. Maybe all along, it was his treatment as a rarity that kept him so small.

Jeffrey's statement, that he began to grow after the age of thirty, gives us at least a minimum period for his slavery. He was captured in November 1644 when he was twenty-five, so he stayed in North Africa for at least five years. But his absence from any records back in England leads me to believe that he was in captivity for a lot longer than that. For there were occasions over the next two decades where we would expect Jeffrey to have been mentioned, or for him to be present. There were times when, if he was back in England, he would surely have been in evidence, but he is missing.

The first reference to him during his missing years was in 1656, in a catalogue of an odd collection of rarities, curios and strange items. In 1629 John Tradescant began collecting 'curiosities' and plants for his private museum in Lambeth. Tradescant was a renowned gardener, indeed, he had been the gardener to George Villiers, Duke of Buckingham, so he would have been aware of Jeffrey from his very earliest appearance at Court. His son, also called John, continued the collection and together they established it in their house at Lambeth, under the name Tradescant's Ark.

Tradescant's collection, although well known and frequently visited, was not catalogued until 1656 in a book called *Musaeum Tradescantium, or A Collection of Rarities*

Preserved at South-Lambeth neer London. In the section entitled 'Artificial Curiosities as Utensils, Household stuff, Habits, Instruments of Warre used by several Nations, rare curiosities of Art, &c.', Tradescant lists 'Little Jeffreyes Boots' and 'Little Jeffreyes Masking-suit'.

This, evidently, was a costume designed for Jeffrey by Inigo Jones for one of the Court masques of the 1630s. (With unconscious irony, the entry comes right after 'Barbary Spurres pointed sharpe like a Bodkin'.) Tradescant's collection also contained a memento of that other great wonder of the age, William Evans, as it included 'The King's great Porter's Boots'.

The Ark was not the only collection of this kind, for the seventeenth century saw an increased interest in ethnology and anthropology, fuelled by the explorations and discoveries of the New World and other places. As early as 1611, the curious were visiting Drake's ship at Deptford (it was gradually taken to pieces by souvenir hunters) or going to see the slippers of Henry VIII, or viewing 'Harry the Lyon' at the Tower Zoo.

Many people were fascinated by these collections, which were, in a way, the academic equivalent of Bartholomew Fair (indeed, Sir Hans Sloane, one of the great collectors, used to tour the fair to pick up natural history exhibits). Sometimes they included the weirdest objects. Claudius de Puy, a French-Swiss collector who settled in London, had a collection which included a small zoo, some mother-of-pearl shells carved with the story of Lot, a picture of Christ made of feathers, waxworks of Cleopatra, Queen Anne and Queen Eleanor, and, most remarkable of all, Cromwell's head, 'just as it fell down with the spike broke off'.

Indeed, Jeffrey himself may have visited Tradescant's collection, for Charles and Henrietta Maria both visited the Ark, many years before. Perhaps it was then that they promised Tradescant something to commemorate those two great wonders of the age, William Evans and Jeffrey Hudson.

Tradescant's catalogue is irritatingly unspecific, but fortunately we can identify these items with a little more certainty because, in 1662, on the death of John Tradescant the younger, the collection was bequeathed to Elias Ashmole, who put it on display in his museum in Oxford. There, in a catalogue dated 1685, item 218 is listed as 'The costume worn by Charles I's dwarf Geoffrey, made entirely of blue silk. It is in one piece from the chest to the breeches', and item 284 is listed as 'Boots belonging to Charles I's dwarf Geoffrey'.

While we don't know the details of the rest of Jeffrey's costumes for all the masques he was in, we do know about his costume for *Salmacida Spolia*. Jeffrey, you will recall, appeared as a 'little Swiss' and there is a rough drawing which may be his costume. He appears to be wearing a breastplate with two cross-straps and a helmet, but the underlying costume could well be in one piece. And it was made of 'watchet', that is sky-blue silk. Tradescant, it seems, had managed to obtain the costume from the last masque of the age.

Jeffrey's costume and boots are no longer in the Ashmolean. Like so many of the objects directly associated with him, they have disappeared. The catalogue of 1836 makes no mention of them and no one seems to know what has happened to them.

The costume may have simply disintegrated. Masque suits were built for effect, not for longevity. With a delicate material like silk, Jeffrey's 'masking-suit' may have just fallen to pieces. It certainly would not have received the careful treatment it needed, for in the early years of the

Ashmolean Museum the items were roughly handled. Von Uffenbach, a German visitor to Oxford in 1710, was astonished by the fact that visitors to the Ashmolean were allowed to handle the objects. He wrote:

> ... everyone in true English fashion handles them roughly and all persons – even women – are admitted on payment of 6d., who run about and will not be hindred by the sub custos [the custodians].

Probably the costume simply wore away. Despite this, rumours of the survival of his clothing persist. The late-Victorian *Dictionary of National Biography* entry for Jeffrey assures the reader that 'His waistcoat, breeches and stockings are in the Ashmolean Museum, Oxford.' Even as late as July 2000, an article in the *Guardian* newspaper reported that his costume was at Sherborne Castle in Dorset. Alas no. The blue 'masking-suit' has disappeared completely.

The *Dictionary of National Biography* also asserts that Jeffrey returned to England some time before 1658. They base this on the only other mention of Jeffrey in the 1650s – a poem in Heath's *Clarastella,* which was published around this time. Heath is a little-known poet, one of the 'Sons of Ben', the disciples of Ben Jonson. In fact, his book, *Clarastella; Together with Poems occasional, Elegie, Epigrams, Satyrs*, was published in 1650. It consists mainly of some fifty-seven poems concerning a girl called Clarastella. She is the object of Heath's adoration, indeed, some might say his obsession, since we are treated to verses on such subjects as 'On a dust got in Clarastella's eie'; 'To her having a great cold'; and on 'Bleeding at the nose at Clarastella's approach'.

The book includes a poem 'to Jeffrey Hudson' which runs:

Small sir! methinkes in your lesser selfe I see
Exprest the lesser world's epitome.
You may write man, in th'abstract so you are,
Though printed in a smaller character.
The pocket volume hath as much within't
As the broad folio in a larger print,
And is more useful too. Though low you seem,
Yet you're both great and high in men's esteem;
Your soul's as large as others, so's your mind:
To greatness virtue's not like strength confined.

The tone, subject matter and, indeed, most of the content
of the poem are hugely derivative. They seem to have been
taken almost verbatim from the pages of *The New Yeare's
Gift* of 1636. The references to a 'pocket volume' and
'small printing' remind us of the tiny book; the other lines
are almost direct quotes. Compare, for example, the last
two lines of Heath's poem with this couplet from the verse
to William Evans in *The New Yeare's Gift*:

The greatnesse of his spirit and his minde
Whose virtues are not like thy strength confin'd.

And the opening lines of Heath's poem are a version of
the epigram which appeared in *The New Yeare's Gift* under
Jeffrey's picture:

Gaze on with wonder and discerne in me
The abstract of the world's epitome.

Heath may, of course, be 'Microphilus', the anonymous
author of the tiny book. Perhaps this poem is an early

draft. But there is no evidence of Heath's presence at Court. He was probably at Cambridge at the time the book was published, and, anyway, *The New Yeare's Gift*, with its layers of classical allusion, fluent phraseology and repetitive punning strikes one as the work of a seasoned pro.

The likeliest explanation is that Heath was writing about the book rather than the man; that he had somehow got hold of a copy of *The New Yeare's Gift* and was inspired to write a verse, echoing some of what he had seen within.

That is not to say he never saw Jeffrey. Heath was a Royalist who fought, according to his poems, at 'Edgehill' and 'Newberry'. His book contains elegies on friends and associates 'slain in this unhappy Civil Warr'. So he probably saw Jeffrey at Oxford in 1643. But that was many years before publication, for by the time *Clarastella* appeared, Heath wasn't even in the country. The commendatory poem begins, 'Thou'rt gone, and yet thou'rt here', and the rest of the poem implies that Heath is ignorant of the book's publication.

He was probably abroad, with the Court in exile. In all likelihood the book is a collection of Heath's verse written over several years. It includes his youthful infatuation with Clarastella, his celebrations of courtly life and his mournful reminiscences of civil war. His poem to Jeffrey could have been written at any time before 1644. But it couldn't have been written in 1650, for Heath was out of the country, and so was Jeffrey.

So much for the 1650s; just two mentions of Jeffrey in the entire decade: a poem from years earlier and an item in a catalogue of curios. And for most of the 1660s the situation is the same; Jeffrey is notable only by his absence. Nevertheless, his memory obviously lingered on, as is proved by the publication in 1662 of Thomas Fuller's *Worthies of*

England. Fuller's information is largely accurate – although he did not appear to know Jeffrey's surname. (Having said that, Jeffrey was usually referred to as Jeffrey the dwarf, or Little Jeffrey, so perhaps not many people actually knew he had a surname.)

The text is accurate about Jeffrey's early life, but ends after the duel in France. Fuller's information was merely that, following the duel, Jeffrey was 'imprisoned'. He does not know any more than that and merely ends his character sketch by taking his leave of 'Jeffery, the least man of the least county in England'.

Fuller, like many early biographers, was hardly the most assiduous researcher, but had Jeffrey been back at Court, or had his fate been widely known, he would certainly have included it.

For by the time of Fuller's book there was a Court for Jeffrey to return to. And by far the most obvious time for Jeffrey to emerge from obscurity, had he been living in England, would have been in 1660 with the restoration of the monarchy.

The years following Jeffrey's capture by the Turkish pirates were grim for England. Charles and the Royalist forces fought on, but their ragged, ill-disciplined army was no match for Cromwell's well-drilled, highly efficient 'New Model Army'. The defeat of the Royalists at Naseby, despite Charles's confidence that 'God will not suffer rebels to prosper or his cause to be overthrown', was a death-blow to the King's cause. Charles fled to the safety of the Scottish army, which by then was as far south as Newark, but the Scots simply handed him over to Parliament.

He managed to escape as far as the Isle of Wight, where he spent some time 'negotiating' with the Parliamentary forces, while secretly trying to raise an army again. By now, however, all was lost. The army was in charge and

Charles was eventually captured and marched to London to stand trial for his life. The ending has a grim inevitability. On 27 January 1649, sentence was pronounced: Charles I, King of England, was to be executed.

Three days later, he was led from his quarters at St James's, through the cold winter air to Whitehall. He was wearing an extra shirt so that people would not see him shiver and think he was afraid. At Whitehall, there was a long wait for the event itself – so long that Charles agreed to take a piece of bread and a glass of claret, although he had been determined to fast. He was led through the empty, echoing galleries; galleries which had once been rich with pictures and tapestries and sculptures, until he reached a balcony and then stepped on to a scaffold which had been specially built.

After a final declaration of his faith, he lay his head on the block and told the executioner not to strike until he held out his hands. While he was praying the executioner touched his hair to tuck it further under his cap. The King thought he was about to strike. 'Wait for the signal,' he said. A moment later his hands went forward, the axe came down. There, in the shadow of his beloved Banqueting House, with the ceiling paintings which he had been so careful to protect, the final and most gruesome masque of the age came to its inevitable conclusion.

In the gloom of the evening, with the snow falling outside, the King of England was buried without ceremony in the chapel at Windsor. His grave bore no marker and no memorial, and such was the haste of the burial that even the precise spot was forgotten. It was not located until one hundred and sixty-five years later.

The Queen did not hear of her husband's death for over a week. France was racked by its own religious wars – the wars of the Fronde – and fighting was raging all around

Paris, making communication difficult. Jermyn tried to delay telling her, but she knew something was wrong and eventually he was forced to speak. She was so shocked she could not talk for two hours. Eventually the Duchesse de Vendôme approached the Queen and tearfully kissed her hand. Henrietta Maria broke down and wept uncontrollably.

Parliament, or more precisely, Cromwell, was in charge, but the government of the Commonwealth was soon to lose its gloss in the eyes of the people, quickly descending into a morass of petty squabbles and power struggles. Successive Parliaments achieved little. The Puritan movement in opposition was united against the King, but in power it fragmented rapidly and the army which in reality controlled the country was equally divided. Only in foreign affairs did Cromwell make his mark: the wars against Spain and Holland were successful and the Irish were put down with a ferocity that is remembered – and resented – to this day.

But Cromwell's days were numbered. He was old and ill and on 3 September 1658 he died at Whitehall. His body was interred in the unlikely surroundings of the chapel at Denmark House which had now reverted to its original name of Somerset House. There, surrounded by walls of black velvet, the great Puritan leader lay in state in a room which had once been the hated hub of Catholic London.

Less than two years later the revolution was ended. The great experiment had failed and the Prince of Wales returned in triumph from France to take his rightful place as Charles II. He immediately invited his mother to join him and Queen Henrietta Maria once again took up residence at Somerset House.

She had changed much. One of her close associates in France wrote:

> The almost continual suffering she endured gave her much gravity and contempt for life which, to my thinking, made her more solid, more serious, more estimable than she might have been had she always been happy.

Pepys, when he saw her, found her 'a very little, plain old woman, and nothing in her presence in any respect nor garbe, than any other woman'.

Despite her experiences, however, she was still obviously attached to Denmark House. She herself might appear just like any other woman, but she was determined that her old palace should be renewed to its full glory, and she immediately set about its restoration.

Inigo Jones had died some years previously. The old man, out of favour in the dour days of the Commonwealth, was allowed to live in Denmark House, watching sadly while its contents were sold and the building allowed to fall into disrepair. He would stump forlornly through the empty corridors, while the ghosts of courtiers and dancers and his beloved masquers whirled and spun around him. He died in the building he loved in 1652, and was buried in Westminster Abbey.

His influence, however, persevered and the Queen reopened some of the surveyor's old plans. She adorned the front of the house with ornate columns and a new gateway leading to a spacious quadrangle. An Italian garden with paved walks and fountains led down to the Thames through a water gate supported by statues of Thames and Isis. She restocked the interior with the very best furniture and pictures. The floor was inlaid wood in contrasting colours – reputedly the first parquet floor in England.

Perhaps Jones would have been most pleased with the reopening of the chapel, complete with a new set of gold and silver plate, which had once belonged to Cardinal Richelieu; it was a gift from the Cardinal's niece to replace all the plate Henrietta Maria had had to pawn while she was in exile.

The Queen also set about rewarding her faithful servants. Henry Jermyn was created Lord Chamberlain and Lord Steward. They had been so long together that some malicious tongues suggested the relationship was more than merely professional. There is no substance in this rumour. If ever a woman was faithful to her husband's memory, that woman was Henrietta Maria. While she may have been without a husband, in every other respect she tried to re-create the Court of the 1630s, complete with four gentlemen ushers, four pages, eight grooms of the great presence chamber, two cup-bearers, two carvers, numerous ladies-in-waiting, laundresses, nurses, servants – a Court in fact that was virtually identical to the one she had been forced to give up in 1644.

Only one thing was missing: a Court dwarf. In all the stories of Henrietta Maria's return, in all the accounts of the vast expenditure at Denmark House, there is no mention of Captain Jeffrey Hudson.

Had Jeffrey been in the country at the time it is inconceivable he would not have rushed up to London to join the Queen again – and it is equally inconceivable that she would not have welcomed him with open arms. But he did not. There is no mention of him in any of her letters or in any of the accounts of the festivities surrounding the Restoration, no mention of him strutting down the steps to the Thames in the Queen's newly designed livery of black velvet cassocks with gold badges.

Instead, the Queen adopted a Chinese boy – 'a stowaway on an East Indiaman whom she rescued, converted and brought up as carefully as if he had been her own son'. In the absence of Jeffrey he would have to do.

Henrietta Maria stayed in London for four years. During that time she re-created her Court in all its splendour. Eventually she returned to France. She never saw Jeffrey during this time. He was not there to be seen.

He was lost. He was, to use the language of the slaves, '*mangiado*' – eaten, consumed, disappeared.

THE
LOST SON

A heart nurs'd up in war; that ne're before
This time (quote he) could bow, now doth implore:
Thou that deliver'd has so many, be
So kinde of nature, to deliver me!

William D'Avenant, *Jeffereidos*

FROM THE MID-1660S ONWARDS, ENGLAND MADE
renewed efforts to redeem or buy back citizens held in
slavery on the Barbary coast. Diplomats were sent out on
a number of missions and initiated a series of new treaties
with Tunis and Algiers, some of which were occasionally
observed.

In 1668, Thomas Warren went to Morocco, Sallee and
other parts of South Barbary, spending a considerable sum
of money to buy the freedom of English slaves. When he
arrived back in London, he asked the Treasury to repay
him the money he laid out. The Treasury Books record, in
the kind of language that has been a feature of accountants
ever since:

Your majesty is not obliged to reimburse same, he
having no warrant to pay it, so the King cannot allow

it. But he may have a brief to coolect for it if he pleases.

Likewise, another Thomas, Sir Thomas Allen, called in at Algiers and Tunis on his way home around the same time. And Sir William Jennings reported that men of his ship clubbed together to raise money to redeem captives in June 1668:

> The men gave freely for the redemption of slaves one month's short allowance, so with their help I redeemed 7. There are about 30 more which were taken under English colours 4 years since. I inquired not the number of the rest.

Any of these trips could have been the one to rescue Jeffrey, but the exact date of his return is unknown. Whatever the case, eventually Jeffrey's freedom was obtained. Through an official government ransom, through the good offices of a local diplomat, or merely through a collection gathered together by some compassionate sailors, he was granted his freedom.

Now, fifty years old, his life had been almost precisely split in two; twenty-five years at Court followed by twenty-five years in slavery. Half his life had been spent under North African skies; lost, abandoned, forgotten. Now lean, tanned and nearly a foot and a half higher, he was standing on a ship again, heading for home. There must have been a sense of release, but also a sense of foreboding. Like a long-term prisoner being released from jail, he was heading into the unknown.

Wright records his return:

> Being at last redeem'd he came into England, and liv'd in these parts on certain pensions allowed him by the

Duke of Buckingham and other Persons of Honour, for several years.

Wright's testimony is backed up by a document which is the only definite proof of Jeffrey's return to England; a receipt in the Public Record Office dated 9 May 1669. It is the only record we have that comes directly from Jeffrey's own hand and runs:

> May the 9th 1669
> Receiving then from Mr Tunstall and Mr Christian five pounds due to me at Lady day last paste for a pension given to me from the right noble George Duke of Buckingam.

He has signed it 'Geffrie Hudson'.

The handwriting of the signature is shaky. Possibly he did not write the whole receipt itself, it may have been drafted by Buckingham's agents. It was also probably signed in or around Oakham. The Christians were a local family, from Teigh, the other side of Burley on the Hill. The wheel had turned full circle, and Jeffrey, perhaps for the first time in forty years, was back in Rutland. He may well have passed through London on his return, but he would not have seen the Queen. Increasingly frail, she left London in 1665, once again to take the waters in France. There was nothing for Jeffrey in London any more. It was time to go home, back to the beginning. And just like all those years ago, he was once again reliant on the Duke of Buckingham, this time the son of his original patron.

Superficially at least, Oakham had not changed much. The same small town, the same traditional lifestyle. His family was still there – what was left of them. His father John had died while Jeffrey was in captivity. The old butcher was buried in January 1663. He had never escaped his lowly state; he is described in the records as a 'Beadman'; that is, a resident of the almshouses.

Jeffrey's younger sister, Ann, was still alive – she had married one Edward Ullit – but Jeffrey had never really known her; he left Oakham two years before she was born. His elder brother John had died in 1657, and Theophilus in 1642.

There was, however, one person who remembered him – the friend of his childhood, his brother Samuel. Indeed, Samuel was probably the only family member with room to house the returning son. He is recorded in the hearth tax of 1665 as the only Hudson who was charged – meaning that he occupied a home of greater value than twenty shillings annual rent and had goods, chattels or land worth more than ten pounds.

There is also another indication that Samuel would welcome his long-lost brother. It was the custom in families for the first-born son to be named after his father. This was certainly true in Jeffrey's family where his eldest brother was called John, after their father. But when Samuel's first son was born in 1645 he was not christened Samuel. He was christened Jeffrey. There were no other Jeffreys in the Hudson family – it was an obvious tribute to his brother, perhaps remembering their brief friendship of childhood days, perhaps in a tribute to the famous member of the family, Lord Minimus, Little Geffry, the Captain of Horse, lost at sea.

So Jeffrey probably returned, at least for the first part of his stay, to his brother's house at Oakham. There is certainly no record of him living anywhere else. One item that might have given us a clue to his whereabouts at the time is the list of Catholic recusants in the county. Unfortunately, unlike many other dioceses, Rutland did not record individual names. We know that seventy-three were recorded as living in the county, but not who they were.

He was certainly not living back at the great house on the hill. For although Oakham itself had not changed much, the old house at Burley was gone. During the Civil War Parliamentary troops had been garrisoned there and the damage they caused was so extensive as to leave the house a ruin. In 1646 a fire broke out and the entire structure collapsed. In 1651, the shell was described as 'utterly consumed by fire soe that att present there remaines nothing but certaine ruinous parts and pieces of the Walls . . .' Only the stable block remained.

Perhaps Jeffrey would walk up there sometimes, gazing down at the town from the gaunt, skeletal, burnt-out shell. He too had been utterly consumed, taken up and burnt out.

In its place the second Duke was to build a magnificent new house, but at the time when Jeffrey returned to Oakham, Burley on the Hill was a charred ruin. The change was symptomatic of Jeffrey's life; almost everything he had known had been swept away.

So by May 1669, Jeffrey was back in Oakham. Later that year came sad news from Paris. The Queen was dead.

Her decision to leave Denmark House was, as it transpired, a wise one, for she returned to France in 1665, just before the Great Plague began to take a firm grip on London. Nor had the people of England really welcomed her as she might have wished. They were pleased to see her son, the King, but the old Queen Mary was too mixed up with popery for their taste. Pepys with his usual waspishness recorded that, on her return, only three bonfires were lit in celebration.

She stayed in France for what remained of her life. In 1669 her health declined rapidly, and a conference of royal physicians decided on a new regime of medication. The Queen of France's physician, M. Vallot, prescribed three grains of laudanum to be taken at night to help Henrietta Maria to sleep. Henrietta Maria herself was a little uncertain of this – with the true hypochondriac's memory, she recalled that many years earlier Sir Theodore Mayerne had warned her never to take opiates of any sort. Mayerne may have called her mad, but he knew his medicines. Vallot, however, reassured her that had he had any worries, he would never have prescribed laudanum in the first place.

On the last night of her life she dined well, was cheerful and bright and went to bed at ten o'clock. Unable to sleep, she called her doctor and took the laudanum, mixed with the white of an egg.

She fell into a coma and never woke again. The little Queen of England, the she-Generalissima herself, died without regaining consciousness on 21 August 1669.

'She was almost always ill,' wrote her niece. 'They gave her some pills to make her sleep which were so successful that she never woke again.'

She was buried in the crypt of St Denis, but even her afterlife was plagued by revolution. On 16 October 1793, French revolutionaries opened her grave and flung her bones into a common pit.

The news came swiftly to London and a day of national mourning was called for. In Oakham, as he listened to the bell being tolled in her honour, Jeffrey's memories must have been acute. If she had returned to London then he could have gone to her and everything could have been as it used to be. Her majesty and her dwarf, together again.

He knew her better than perhaps anyone else. He had seen her in the early days when she was ostracized by

Buckingham. He had been held in her arms that time when he fell out of the window; he remembered the joy on her face when she rehearsed her masques, and the feeling he had when he made her laugh. He knew her when she was young and vulnerable and looking for someone to love. Those people who had surrounded her in her prime had never really loved her. But Jeffrey did. And Jeffrey remembered.

For seven or eight years, Jeffrey lived quietly in Oakham. He was a familiar figure about the place, the quaint little old man, sitting in the market square, or supping an ale while regaling anyone who would listen with the tales of his life.

One of those who came to listen to him was James Wright, son of Abraham Wright the vicar of Oakham. The vicar had met Jeffrey years before, in 1636, when the Court had come to Oxford. Abraham, then a young student, had written a play, *Love's Hospital*, which was performed before the King and Queen. He had been appointed vicar of All Saints, Oakham in 1645, but because he refused to swear the oaths demanded by the Parliamentarians, he was ejected from his Oxford fellowship and not allowed to take up the living. He eventually became vicar in 1660, in his own little 'Restoration'.

His son, James, was first a law student and then a practising barrister in London. Because of his father's position, James made frequent visits to Oakham, falling in love with the countryside, buying a local manor house, and eventually writing the county's first official history, *The History and Antiquities of Rutland*. As he states in his preface:

As to this undertaking of mine, I must acquaint the reader, that having been above twenty years past, for the most part, resident in the county of Rutland, (though no native of the same) I collected many years ago something of this nature for my own private satisfaction. Which notes, though few and those imperfect, I have since been encouraged by several persons of honour and Quality to complete into just a volume as is now published.

The History and Antiquities of the County of Rutland is the major source for Jeffrey's life. For Wright met Jeffrey, spoke to Jeffrey, heard his story for himself. James it is who gives us the first full picture of Jeffrey's life. His adventures made a compelling tale. The old man, for fifty-five was a reasonably advanced age for the seventeenth century, had such stories to tell. He had survived war, single combat and piracy. He had endured twenty-five years of slavery and abandonment, physical torture, starvation, degradation and disease. Now, it seemed, he was living out his remaining years in quiet, leafy Rutland.

It was obviously too quiet. In 1678 Jeffrey decided to return to London.

Wright does not tell us why Jeffrey left Oakham, simply referring to 'occasions causing him to remove and abide at London', but we can make a couple of guesses as to what caused him to go.

For a start he must have struggled for money. A five-pound pension was not much to start with and the payments were by no means assured. The second Duke of Buckingham was a trivial, superficial man. He had reclaimed his estate in 1660, by virtue of marrying Mary, daughter of the Parliamentarian Lord Fairfax who, purely coincidentally, was the current owner of the property.

It more or less sums Villiers up. He was in love with

luxury and indulgence, and would do anything – or marry anyone – to obtain it. He had inherited his father's love of luxury and extravagance and Lady Mary was the fast route back to comfort and prosperity. However, the son had nothing of the father's ambition. The first Duke may have been a Court favourite, but he did at least covet praise for himself and his achievements – it was just unfortunate that every time he tried to achieve something he ended up even more hated and reviled. His son, on the other hand, made no attempt to be popular. It was as if he had looked at his father's life and decided not to make the effort.

'He had no principles of religion, virtue or friendship,' wrote Burnet. 'Pleasure, frolick or extravagant diversion was all that he laid to heart. He was true to nothing, for he was not true to himself. He had no steadiness nor conduct: he could keep no secret, nor execute any design without spoiling it.'

He was to be immortalized by Dryden as Zimri in the poem *Absalom and Achitophel*:

A man so various, that he seem'd to be
Not one, but all Mankind's epitome.
Stiff in Opinions, always in the wrong;
Was Every thing by starts, and Nothing long:
But in the course of one revolving Moon,
Was Chymist, Fidler, States-Man and Buffoon . . .'

Such a man was not someone to base your long-term income on.

However, a more direct reason for his departure was probably the death of his brother Samuel in July 1676. It left Jeffrey in the remarkable position of being the only one of his brothers still alive. This tiny man had outlived them all. With Samuel gone, there was nothing much left for Jeffrey at Oakham. So, in 1676 he gathered up his belongings, climbed aboard the coach and set off on the long trip south. Back to the city of London.

And back to Court.

THE
WRONGED CATHOLIC

This that appears to you, a walking-thumbe,
May prove the gen'rall spie of Christendome.
William D'Avenant, *Jeffereidos*

IF OAKHAM HAD CHANGED LITTLE, THE SAME COULD
not be said of London. As the coach bearing him crested
the top of the hill, Jeffrey was once again presented with
a view of London, but a London vastly different from that
he had first seen fifty years ago.

Four years before his return from exile the city had been
hit with two devastating calamities: plague, soon to be
followed by fire. True, plague had been common throughout the time that Jeffrey lived at Denmark House; and fire
had always been a risk in the crowded, ramshackle streets
of London, but nothing had ever reached the scale of the
disasters of 1665 and 1666.

The plague that hit London in 1665 killed over one
hundred thousand people. It began in the squalid dockland
tenements and spread rapidly throughout all the capital,
turning London into a necropolis, a city of the dead. Trade
stopped, the streets emptied, grass grew down the middle
of the thoroughfares. Desperate measures were taken: fires

were lit to try to purify the air, all letters passing through the post office were sterilized in the steam of boiling vinegar and the Deanery of St Paul's was smoked twice a week with a mix of pepper, sulphur, hops and frankincense.

Nothing worked, everywhere there was the smell of death, everywhere there were silent, tomb-like houses, their doors daubed with white, chalked crosses and adorned with the simple, desperate plea, 'God have mercy upon us'. This policy of sealing up the houses merely added to the death toll; thousands died through being incarcerated with infected members of their family. In the thirtieth week of the plague there were eight thousand, two hundred and eighty-seven burials and only one hundred and seventy-six christenings in London: one birth for every forty-seven deaths. There were too many dead to bury; they were merely piled into carts and thrown into great pits.

All this was caused by fleas, carried by rats on the ships, but no one knew that, especially not the person who, in an act of kindness, sent a parcel of clothes to Eyam in Derbyshire. The clothes were flea-ridden and in the tiny isolated village, two hundred and fifty-nine out of the three hundred villagers lost their lives.

Gradually the plague abated, and Londoners returned. The city was coming to terms with the scale of its loss and even starting to plan for the future. Conditions were insanitary, buildings unsafe. Something must be done. On 27 August 1666, Christopher Wren, John Evelyn, Hugh May and others met to discuss the perilous state of St Paul's. Like so many buildings in the city it was in urgent need of repair, but the committee was undecided on whether to rebuild or renovate. A week later the decision was made for them.

The fire began on 2 September in the bakery of Thomas Fariner, in Pudding Lane near London Bridge. The weather was hot and dry and unfortunately the local water-engine was out of action, and within minutes the fire started to spread. Five days later, the landscape of the city had altered completely.

Of the four hundred and fifty acres within the city walls, three hundred and seventy-three were devastated. More than eighty churches were destroyed and thirteen thousand houses. In Oxford, Anthony Wood recorded in his diary that clouds of smoke from the distant fire blew over the county. 'The moon was darkened by clouds of smoke,' he wrote, 'and looked reddish.' So great was the devastation that lifelong city dwellers got lost among the charred remains, for there were no longer any landmarks to guide them. They wandered around forlornly, looking for something, anything, that they could recognize. In Evelyn's words they were 'like men in some dismal desert, or rather, in some great city, laid waste by a cruel enemy'.

Within days temporary housing was found; most of the two hundred thousand homeless found accommodation in Islington and Highgate, either in tents or in more permanent, though hurriedly erected, structures. Some moved away to other cities, a lot decided to emigrate. Many stayed where they were, putting up shanty dwellings among the charred ruins of their old quarters.

The great church, St Paul's, had been destroyed, taking with it the monument to Jeffrey's old masque-master Inigo Jones and his portraitist Van Dyck.

Christopher Wren was given the opportunity to direct the rebuilding. He was a man of many parts, a scientist whose theories covered everything from 'A Hypothesis of the Moon's Libation in Solid' to the more useful 'A Way of Imbroidery for Beds, Hangings, cheap and fair'. He invented a 'Perpetual Motion or weather wheel and weather clock compounded', worked out a way to keep hatching eggs at the correct temperature by using lamps and was fascinated by the potential of 'submarine navigation'.

The major house rebuilding did not get underway until the end of 1671, by which time some seven thousand houses had been built. Major public buildings took longer. The foundation stone of the new cathedral was laid in 1675. Wren brought a uniformity to the city skyline, and set a style for its churches and public buildings. By the time Jeffrey arrived in 1678, the city had an entirely new look.

The fire even had an official monument, completed in 1677. A later inscription on the monument blamed the fire on the 'treachery and malice of the popish faction'. The truth of the matter was more prosaic: a dry summer, old wooden houses too close together, and a baker who went to bed without properly closing down his oven. But the inscription showed how enduring even now ten years later, the fear of popery was, for it remained, a smouldering danger and likely to burst into uncontrollable flames.

As Jeffrey rolled into the city there were few landmarks that he would recognize; the Tower, the Inns of Court, half a dozen City churches. Somerset House was still there, but inhabited now by Catherine of Braganza, the forlorn and rather pathetic wife of Charles II.

There was, however, another echo of the past. Fifty years before, in his first weeks in the capital, Jeffrey had shared a stage with William Evans, the giant porter, and still the memory persisted of those two wonders. In the rebuilding of the city an inn along Newgate Street was given a new sign, a small stone relief carving mounted in the front wall of the building. It depicted two people: a gigantic porter and a tiny dwarf.

William Evans and Jeffrey Hudson were, if only in stone,

back together again. The bearded giant leans on a staff, the long sleeves of his porter's gown hanging down by his sides. Jeffrey stands to his right, wrapped in a voluminous cloak. Originally these figures were painted in the King's livery, with red coats and white waistcoats.

The sign was not the only one – there were several 'Porter and Dwarf' signs in the old city – but this was the only one which lasted, for it was still there into the early years of the twentieth century. In 1816 the house over which it stood belonged to a hatter called Payne; by the late nineteenth century, when the street was redeveloped on the widening of King Edward Street, the sign was moved, and set into the balustrade above the central first-floor window of 78 Newgate Street. It was still there in 1909 but now, like Jeffrey's clothing in the Ashmolean, it has disappeared.

Nevertheless, engravings of it survive, and it shows every sign of being contemporary with the rebuilding of the city. Indeed, it may even have been in an earlier building, and survived. Whatever its origin, it was proof that Jeffrey had not been entirely forgotten. He had been remembered – or at least he and the giant had been remembered. The relationship between the two wonders had lingered in people's memories, where it had gradually ripened into myth.

Perhaps he wandered down Cheapside and into Newgate one day, walking among the market stalls, smelling that age-old familiar smell from the Shambles nearby, stopping to gaze up at the sign. He had not been forgotten after all. People still remembered him.

Yes, people still remembered Jeffrey. In fact, as the days to come would prove, they remembered him a little too well.

*   *   *

The Court that Jeffrey came to London to visit was as changed as the city. Charles II was unlike his father, and his Court dwelt in a harsher and more cynical political landscape. He had been restored, it was true, but at the invitation of Parliament. Parliament had given, Parliament could take away. So Charles's policy was to draw a line under the past. The few surviving men who had signed Charles I's death warrant were hanged, and Oliver Cromwell's remains were dug up and disembowelled. His head was stuck on the spikes over the gatehouse on London Bridge, before it fell off, apparently to end up in the collection of M. de Puy.

Charles issued a general proclamation of 'Oblivion and Indemnity', allowing the country to move on and refusing to wallow in recriminations. Indeed, many thought he didn't wallow enough. There was, in the eyes of many Cavaliers, a lack of reward for all they had been through. They had suffered and fought for the crown, but Charles II showed no signs of recognizing their efforts in any tangible way. Those who hoped that the good times would come again, or even that justice would be done, were harshly disappointed.

One anonymous Cavalier writer depicts two 'old rusty Cavaliers' talking sadly of a visit to Whitehall, where everything was different:

Not one, upon my life, among
My old acquaintance, all along
At Truro, and before;
And, I suppose the Place can shew
As few of those whom thou didst know
At York and Marston Moor ...
Old services (by rule of state)
Like Almanacs, grow out of date.

Truro, York, Marston Moor, those great battles, all forgotten now, like an old almanac, yesterday's news. Likewise, the Court had none of the scrupulous refinement of the previous era. Whereas Charles I spent his money on art, sculpture and gorgeous masques, his son preferred to go racing and spend the evening with one of his numerous mistresses. Charles I, it was said, never allowed a drunken word or coarse language in his presence. His son had no such scruples. He paraded his mistresses before the Court and cheerfully admitted to his numerous illegitimate children. His marriage was as loveless as his father's had been loving – or, at least, it was on his side, for the unfortunate Catherine of Braganza made the cardinal mistake of falling in love with her husband. This was a Court of satire and cynicism. Charles II's favourites were men with whom he could gamble and women with whom he could sleep. There was a marked absence of dwarfs and dogs and monkeys.

So Jeffrey arrived in a changed London, to encounter a changed Court. He also managed to arrive at the worst possible time.

It was another man from Oakham who started it all.

In 1678, Titus Oates was widely viewed as 'the saviour of the country'. This was odd, considering he was one of the most malicious and devious liars there has ever been. Because of his lies many men lost their lives and thousands more were thrown into prison. And one of them was Titus's countryman, Captain Jeffrey Hudson.

Titus was born in 1649, in Oakham, Rutland. Later descriptions may have been overdoing his repulsiveness, but he was hardly prepossessing. He had a short, squat body, broad shoulders, a thick neck and bow legs. His forehead was deep and his complexion ruddy. His face was long, with a tiny mouth and a long chin. He had a deep, rasping voice. The engravings of him, even though they were published at a time when he was incredibly popular, show an air of unctuousness. A man so ugly could only be saint or demon, and Oates was certainly no saint.

His mother always thought that there was something wrong with the child:

> ... for his nose always run and he slabber'd at the mouth, and his Father could not endure him; and when he came home at night, the Boy would use to be in the Chimney corner, and my husband would cry take away this snotty Fool and jumble him about, which made me often weep, because you know he was my child.

With a background like this, it is hardly surprising that Oates would create for himself a new world, a world where only he held the secrets, a world where he was loved and listened to and feared.

Like his father, Oates became a clergyman, but he could never do anything without plotting, lying and generally irritating everyone, and he was soon ejected from the parish. His father appointed him curate, but that was a disaster, so his father decided he would be better as the local schoolmaster. There was only one problem: there was already a schoolmaster in post, one William Parker. Unabashed, Oates and his father cooked up a plot against him, accusing him of pederasty, Oates claiming that he had caught Parker committing an indecent act in church with 'a young and tender man-child'.

Unfortunately Titus failed to check his facts. At the very time he claimed to have seen Parker in the act, there were masons at work in the church, and they had seen nothing. Also, Parker had been at a party half a mile away where he stayed for the whole evening. Neither could Titus provide the name or identity of the victim. The case fell apart and Oates, accused of perjury and facing a claim for damages of a thousand pounds, did the only thing he could under the circumstances: he ran away to sea.

The navy proved no better a career for Titus. He was expelled on charges of sodomy, the very charges he had tried to bring against young William Parker. (Throughout his life he was an active homosexual, in a time when the penalties for such activities were severe. Only his exalted influence later in life saved him from being punished.) Adrift in London in 1676, he chanced to fall in with a group of Catholics, and on Ash Wednesday 1677 he was formally received into the Church of Rome. From there he joined the Society of Jesus and before the end of April he was to be found on a ship bound for the English Jesuit Seminary in Valladolid.

Why he became a Catholic – and even more a Jesuit – is uncertain. Perhaps he believed that a Counter-Reformation was inevitable, and that he would be well prepared when England returned to the true faith. Whatever the case, the usual pattern reasserted itself, and after five months he was expelled from the college and shipped home.

Next he tried his luck at another Catholic establishment, the English Jesuit Seminary at Saint-Omer in France, where the boys bullied him and his constant quarrelling led to yet another dismissal. He left Saint-Omer on 23 June 1678, a disgraced Catholic convert. Four days later he arrived in London as a zealous Protestant informer.

He joined forces with Dr Israel Tonge, rector of St Michael's in Wood Street. The Doctor firmly believed that Catholics were plotting the downfall of the kingdom. Pamphlet after pamphlet, speech after speech poured from Tonge in virulent denunciation of these evil subversives.

To Tonge, Oates was an angel of light, confirmation that he had been right all these years, for Oates disclosed to the clergyman the awful truth: the Pope had secretly declared himself Lord of England and the Jesuits were coming to burn down London and kill the King.

Admittedly Oates was a little vague about how the Jesuits were going to achieve this end. They were, he claimed, either going to poison the King, shoot him with silver bullets, or employ four Irishmen to stab him. Possibly all three. Tonge didn't mind and together they prepared a plan to warn the King.

Oates's great success was to divulge his plot at exactly the right time. Many men in England were still wary of the Catholic menace. Charles's commitment to the Anglican Church was questionable, and his brother James, the next in line, was a confirmed Catholic. The mass of the populace were, despite their experiences under the Puritan regime, still virulently anti-Catholic (or anti-French, which amounted to the same thing). Nor was it just in London that these feelings surfaced. In Oxford, for example, a mob surrounded a carriage which they took to contain Charles's French mistress, Louise de Kéroualle. It actually contained another of his paramours, Nell Gwynn, who calmed the mob by shouting out, 'Pray, good people, be civil; I am the Protestant whore.'

It was more than just Catholicism that they feared. It was popery; more than just the different rites and ritual, it was the image of wide-eyed fanatics, Jesuits loyal only to Rome who would stop at nothing to bring down the Protestant religion.

Even so, Charles did not seem to take much notice of the plot – indeed, in interrogating Oates he caught him contradicting himself several times – but he made a huge error of judgement. He went to Newmarket, to the races, and left the Privy Council to interview Oates alone. The inexperienced councillors believed what they heard. Or perhaps they heard what they wanted to believe. Either way they were alarmed. And then, on 12 October 1678, their alarm turned to panic.

Sir Edmund Berry Godfrey, the magistrate to whom Oates had made his first sworn deposition, and who had been given the task of investigating the 'plot', disappeared. His body was discovered a few days later, lying in a ditch. He had been murdered.

A witness came forward who revealed that Godfrey had been murdered at Denmark House – that renowned hotbed of popish rebellion. The public reacted with immediate hysteria. The general belief was that he had been murdered by Catholics for taking Oates's statement. Three entirely innocent people were executed for Godfrey's murder – the truth of which remains a mystery to this day.

Suddenly London was alive with armed men and the air was rife with hysteria. A dagger manufacturer sold three thousand special edition daggers bearing the words 'Remember Justice Godfrey'. (They were particularly popular with the ladies who carried them to ward off potential Jesuit assassins.) Oates continued to produce his revelations, at carefully timed intervals. Despite the obvious contradictions in his story, innocent men were executed for their complicity in the affair. The Duke of York, the King's brother and a prominent Catholic, was forced to leave the country. On 30 October, Parliament asked the King to banish all Papists from a radius of twenty miles around London.

The Catholics, for the most part, had beaten them to it; as many as thirty thousand Catholics were said to have fled London. Those that could took ships to the Continent. The rest were rounded up by mobs and thrown into jail.

Catholic books, relics and artefacts were burnt in the streets. Catholic merchants were ruined, their stock looted, their custom destroyed.

Jeffrey was an obvious target. If he had come to London to seek preferment from Court, he would naturally have made much of his past connections with Henrietta Maria. Now these connections were to come to haunt him. The fact was that he *was* remembered, his past had not been forgotten. He was identified by the mob, hunted down and dragged out of his lodgings. He was taken to Westminster where he was thrown into the Gatehouse prison.

Wright describes Jeffrey's plight in a few short sentences:

> But occasions causing him to remove and abide at London, he was there in the late troublesome times, which began in the year 1678 and being known to be a Roman Catholick, he was taken and clapt up in the Gate-House, where he lay a considerable time . . .

The Gatehouse was a terrible place; two wings of a crumbling, antiquated building. It was situated near the west end of the Abbey, and was generally used not only for debtors, but for those accused of theft and even treason. Sir Walter Raleigh was imprisoned there, immediately before his execution. The Cavalier Richard Lovelace was also an inmate, using his time to compose the poem 'To Althea, from Prison' which contains the lines, 'Stone walls do not a prison make, / Nor iron bars a cage'.

Perhaps Jeffrey would have recalled the case of Viscountess Purbeck who was discovered 'in an intrigue' with Sir Robert Howard in 1635. She was sent to the Gatehouse before performing her sentence of standing in a sheet in the Savoy church and then going barefooted to St Paul's. She managed, however, to break out of the Gatehouse in man's apparel and escaped to France. For Jeffrey there was no such hope of escape.

The winter was a bitter one, full of ice and snow. Many Catholics perished in the terrible conditions. Seized by mobs, dragged through the streets, beaten, manhandled, terrified, they were thrown into prison without spare clothing or money. They had nothing to live on in prison, except the goodwill of friends and relatives.

Prison life in the seventeenth century was harsh. The prisoners were kept in irons and had to sleep on nothing but boards. There was no heating and no defence against the cold. For Jeffrey the effect must have been devastating. He was not a young man and the effect on him both physically and psychologically cannot be imagined. He had survived twenty-five years in servitude in North Africa, now he was to be locked up in his own country – a country, moreover, which he had fought for.

Jeffrey spent his sixtieth year, as he had spent his thirtieth and fortieth, in chains.

Still the hysteria rose.

At the beginning of November strange knocking noises were heard in the House of Commons. A committee was hurriedly appointed to investigate the digging, fearing another gunpowder plot. They found nothing, but Sir Christopher Wren reported that the roof of the House of Commons was so rotten it would very likely fall down in the next high wind. A French Papist called Choqueux was discovered storing gunpowder in the next street. He was thrown into jail, despite explaining that he was, in fact, the King's firework-maker.

The rumours continued to fly. Spaniards had landed in Ireland, the French fleet was at Milford Haven, the English shipyards at Chatham had been attacked and burnt.

Only Oates was prospering. He was seen at the most fashionable houses, and preached to packed congregations. Clothed in sumptuous robes, he was granted a huge allowance for food, lodgings and the payment of expenses for his 'witnesses'. In 1679 he earned nearly a thousand pounds. He began to describe himself as 'England's Saviour' and invented ever wilder revelations to support his theories, even going so far as to accuse Queen Catherine of complicity in the plot. She was unpopular with the people and, indeed, with her husband and he obviously thought that made her a good target, but the King showed a surprising loyalty to her. He even had Oates arrested, but others begged the King not to imprison the one man who knew the truth. Oates, realizing he had gone too far, allowed the accusation to die down.

The richer, well-connected Catholic land-owners were out of prison by early 1679. Others, like Jeffrey, without friends or supporters, lingered on, through another year, another winter and into 1680.

Finally, the plot began to run out of steam. Under pressure of cross-examination, Oates's lies became apparent. His friends started to desert him, and the King, sensing a shift in popular opinion, ordered him to leave Whitehall. He ran into debt and even his own brother Samuel began to speak out and turned against him.

Oates was not to be called to account for his crimes until 1685, after the death of Charles II and during the brief reign of the Catholic James II. He was found guilty, and sentenced to be led from prison, wearing a paper hat bearing the words 'Titus Oates, convicted upon full evidence of two horrid perjuries'. He was set in the pillory and savagely whipped, so harshly that according to one witness he endured 'what would have killed a great many others'. He was imprisoned in the King's Bench prison in Southwark for three years, eventually being freed on the accession of William of Orange. Later in life he became a Baptist minister. He was thrown out after a year for trying to con one of his congregation out of fifteen hundred pounds.

The plot did have one curious and lasting consequence. Bedlow, one of Oates's fellow conspirators, said that he had letters to say that Irish outlaws were coming to kill Oates. These assassins were called *tóraidhe*, meaning 'pursuer' in Gaelic. Oates was much amused by this – mainly because he knew it was a pack of lies – and thereafter called any enemy of his a *tóraidhe*, which is pronounced 'Tory'. The name stuck and became a generic name for the conservative, Stuart-supporting party in government. It comes as something of a surprise to find out that the English Conservative Party is actually named after a bunch of imaginary Irish assassins.

Dryden, who satirized the plot in *Absalom and Achitophel*, wrote:

> This plot, which failed for want of common sense,
> Had yet a deep and dangerous consequence.

For Jeffrey, the consequences were indeed 'deep and dangerous'. The imprisonment was his last and most perilous adventure. He was released in 1680, a tired and defeated old man. There was some sympathy for him, however, and his case was evidently brought before the King, for Charles gave orders that the dwarf should receive some money.

The accounts are found in details of Charles II's 'Secret Service Payments'. The title is misleading – Jeffrey was no spy and many of the monies entered in the book are simple ex-gratia payments to courtiers and servants in need. The first payment was recorded on 7 June 1680: 'To Capt. Jeffery Hudson, as of free gift and bounty £50'.

Ironically it is preceded by a payment of forty-eight pounds to Dr Oates, who at that time, despite the holes in his stories, was still under 'contract' to the Crown.

The second and final payment was made ten months later: 'To Capt. Jeffery Hudson, as of free gift £20'. The first payment had run out. But the second was not as great. Charles's sympathy obviously had its limits.

Some chroniclers report that Jeffrey died in the Gatehouse. Maybe they are right. For even though he was released, his experience was the final nail in the coffin of the past. He was no longer the little fellow who charmed the court, he was a tired old man, hated by the mob and imprisoned for a crime he did not commit. He had been physically attacked and scared witless. He had lived for two years in appalling conditions. Those final payments, welcome though the money must have been, only underlined the truth. They were not rewards for his grace, or his appearance or his witty remarks; they were gifts to a feeble old man, made out of pity.

The money was probably quickly used up. There were debts to pay to those who had supported him during his time in the Gatehouse; there were living expenses to be found, and, in all probability, medical bills as well.

After his release from prison, says Wright, 'he lived not long after and died about two years ago.' Wright, clearly, did not know the date of Jeffrey's death. And neither does anyone else. But since Wright's book was published in 1684, it is usually assumed that 'two years ago' means Jeffrey died in 1682. Wright, however, must have finished the book earlier, and the payment in 1681 is the last record we have of Jeffrey, so there is every reason to suppose that he died some time in the second half of 1681.

The date and the place of his death remain a mystery. There is no burial record in London, nor in Rutland. No grave has ever been found, no record of his last moments. No will exists, for there was nothing left to leave. He was existing on loans and payments and handouts. In the end, the gifts ran out.

It would be nice to think that Jeffrey was buried in splendour and ease, that he was given the last rites and extreme unction from a Catholic priest, before being taken to the chapel of Somerset House, where his body was laid in the grave. Or that he returned to his home county, to lie in a country churchyard, unnoticed by the records, resting peacefully beneath the Rutland skies.

Alas, the truth is probably less romantic. In all probability, Jeffrey Hudson died alone and in poverty, unremarked and unremembered. If he was buried according to Catholic rites it would have been surreptitiously and swiftly, for despite the decline of the plot, London was still not a safe place for Catholics. In such threatening times, nothing was done in the open. The Catholic burial service was read over the body while the corpse lay in the house. In the light of a guttering candle, a handful of blessed earth was thrown into the winding sheet. Otherwise, in the graveyard of the heretic Anglicans, the body would lie in unconsecrated ground.

Then, like thousands of paupers, he was hurriedly taken away and buried, either in his cheap casket, or simply tipped into a communal grave.

No headstone, no entry even in the burial register. Nothing to mark the death of Lord Minimus, the Queen's Dwarf.

*   *   *

He has faded away into darkness.

So much of Jeffrey's life has disappeared. His sky-blue 'masking suit' is gone, worn away to shreds, or stolen, or lost. His only 'gravestone', a shop sign on an old house in Newgate Street, has disappeared without trace. The palaces and grand houses where he lived – Burley, Denmark House, Whitehall, Oatlands – have all gone, torn to pieces in wars or allowed to fall into a slow decline, until all that is left are fragments. There are no letters, no will, no documents, just one receipt, signed in his twilight days, by a frail old man.

Still, there is enough to remember him by. If we need a monument, then we can look at the paintings by Van Dyck and Mytens; we can examine the engravings and imagine the masques; we can read the poems by D'Avenant and Heywood and the two brief eulogies by Wright and Fuller.

Jeffrey left these for us. And put together they tell the story of a remarkable man – a man who braved everything for honour, a man who lived a life packed with adventure, a man who, in the end, became more than a mere curiosity. Jeffrey Hudson was a man praised for his wit and cleverness, whose greatness of spirit was as much commented on as his size.

Indeed, it is this spirit that, I think, is apparent throughout his life. Those who wrote about Jeffrey were always fond of referring to him as some kind of symbol, as 'nature's humble pulpit' demonstrating the need for humility and the frailty of man. But if Jeffrey's life is a sermon, then it is a sermon about strength, not frailty, about endurance rather than delicacy, for this 'exquisite Epitome of Nature' survived blows which would have felled most men twice – or even three times – his size. If he is a symbol, therefore, he is a symbol of determination and courage and, above all, the greatness of the human spirit.

He was the smallest man in England. He was one of the wonders of the age. He was Captain Jeffrey Hudson.

He deserves to be remembered.

APPENDIX ONE
Fuller's Biography of Jeffrey Hudson

The text is taken from Fuller's *History of the Worthies of England*, 1662.

JEFFERY WAS BORN IN THE PARISH OF OAKHAM IN this county, where his father was a very popular man, broad-shouldered and chested, though his son never arrived at a full ell in stature. It seems that families sometimes are chequered, as in brains so in bulk, that no certainty can be concluded from such alterations.

His father, who kept and ordered the baiting bulls for George Duke of Buckingham (a place, you will say, requiring a robustious body to manage it) presented him, at Burley on the Hill, to the Duchess of Buckingham, being then nine years of age, and scarce a foot and half in height, as I am informed by credible persons then and there present, and still alive.* Instantly Jeffery was heightened (not in stature) but in condition, from one degree above rags into silk and satin, and two tall men to attend him.

He was, without any deformity, wholly proportionable, whereas often dwarfs, pigmies in one part, are giants in

* John Armstrong of Cheshunt.

another. It was not long before he was presented in a cold baked pie to King Charles and Queen Mary at an entertainment; and ever after lived (whilst the court lived) in great plenty therein, wanting nothing but humility (high mind in a low body) which made him that he did not know himself, and would not know his father, and which by the king's command caused justly his sound correction. He was, though a dwarf, no dastard, a captain of horse in the king's army in these late civil wars, and afterwards went over to wait on the queen in France.

Here being provoked by Mr Crofts, who accounted him the object not of his anger but contempt, he shewed to all that habet musca suum splenum [even a fly has its temper] and they must be little indeed that cannot do mischief, especially seeing a pistol is a pure leveler, and puts both dwarf and giant into equal capacity to kill and be killed. For the shooting of the same Mr. Crofts he was imprisoned. And so I take my leave of Jeffery, the least man of the least county in England.

APPENDIX TWO
James Wright's Account of Jeffrey Hudson

The text is taken from Wright's *The History and Antiquities of the County of Rutland*, 1684.

LET ME ALSO REMEMBER ANOTHER MAN OF REMARK who was born here in this last age, and the rather because Dr. Fuller in his book called the Worthies of England hath already placed him in the list of memorable persons, tho he knew but little of his story. It is Jeffrey Hudson, the Dwarf, memorable on several accounts.

He was the son of one John Hudson, a person of very mean condition, but of a lusty stature and so were all his children, except this Jeffrey, born in the year 1619. Being above seven years old and scarce 18 inches in highth, he was taken to the Family of the late Duke of Buckingham at Burly on the Hill, in this county, as a Rarity of Nature: And the Court being about that time in Progress there, he was served up to the Table in a cold Pye.

After the marriage of King Charles the First with the Excellent Princess Henrietta Maria of France, he was presented to that Queen and became her Dwarf; and being sent over into France to fetch the Queen's Midwife, in the journey he was taken at Sea by a Flemish Pirate, and carryed Prisoner into Dunkirk: Of which captivity there is in Print an very pleasant Poem consisting of three Canto's writ by Sir William D'Avenant and call'd Jeffreido's.

Afterwards, when the Rebellion broke out he became a Captain of Horse in the King's service, till he went over with his Royal Mistress into France: during his abode there it was his unhappiness to kill Mr. Crofts (Brother to the Lord Crofts) in a combat on horseback; for which he was expell'd the Court.

After this he was a second time taken Prisoner at Sea, but that was a much more fatal captivity than the first. It was a Turkish Pirate that took and carried him to Barbary, where he was sold, and remain'd a slave for many years. Being at last redeem'd he came into England, and liv'd in these parts on certain pensions allowed him by the Duke of Buckingham and other Persons of Honour, for several years.

But occasions causing him to remove and abide at London, he was there in the late troublesome times, which began in the year 1678 and being known to be a Roman Catholick, he was taken and clapt up in the Gate-House, where he lay a considerable time; from whence being at last enlarged, he lived not long after and died about two years ago.

But that which in my opinion seems the most observable is what I have heard himself several times affirm, that between the 7th year of his age and the 30th he never grew anything considerable, but after thirty he shot up in a little time to that highth of stature which he remain'd at in his old age, viz. about three foot and nine inches. The cause of this he ascrib'd (how truly I know not) to the hardship, much labour, and beating, which he endured when a slave to the Turks. This seems a Paradox how that which have been observed to stop the growth of other persons should be the cause of his, But let the Naturalists reconcile it.

APPENDIX THREE
Sir Geoffrey Hudson and *Peveril of the Peak*

JEFFREY'S APPEARANCE IN *PEVERIL OF THE PEAK* inadvertently provided much source material for later historians.

He appears at the end of chapter 33 when the hero of the book, Julian Peveril, is thrown into a cell in the Gatehouse prison:

> Julian at first glance, imagined from the size that he saw a child of five years old; but a shrill and peculiar tone of voice soon assured him of his mistake.
>
> 'Warder,' said this unearthly sound, 'What is the meaning of this disturbance? Have you more insults to heap on the head of one who hath ever been the butt of fortune's malice? But I have a soul that can wrestle with all my misfortunes; it is as large as any of your bodies . . . I who was the favoured servant of three successive sovereigns of the crown of England, am now the tenant of this dungeon and sport of its brutal keepers. I am Sir Geoffrey Hudson.'

Jeffrey is depicted in the book as a comic character; Scott for the most part follows Fuller's characterization of the

dwarf as 'wanting nothing but humility'. Scott describes
him as:

> . . . a dwarf of the least possible size, had nothing posi-
> tively ugly in his countenance, or actually distorted in
> his limbs. His head, hands, and feet were indeed large,
> and disproportioned to the size of his body, and his
> body itself much thicker than was consistent with sym-
> metry, but in a degree which was rather ludicrous than
> disagreeable to look upon.

The novelist also equips him with a large moustache,
'which it was his pleasure to wear so large [it] almost
twisted back amongst and mingled with, his grizzled hair'.

He describes all the well-known adventures, inventing
the fact that the Duke of Buckingham thought it a jest to
warm the pie before serving it; and giving a fictional
account of Jeffrey fighting alongside Prince Rupert at Newbury, where the soldiers would cry, 'There goes Prince
Robin and Cock Robin!' Throughout his story, Jeffrey is
a pompous, but heroic figure. He even fights against the
mob in a later chapter. As far as I can tell, Scott is the first
person to make Jeffrey into a knight – and he only does
this so that the diminutive Sir Geoffrey can be confused
with Julian Peveril's father, Sir Geoffrey Peveril.

Scott takes the bulk of his information from Walpole's
account in his *Anecdotes of English Painting*. Like Walpole, his biographical note of Jeffrey at the back of the
book gets the order wrong, claiming he fought the duel
and was captured by the Corsairs before the Civil War.
Most of his account is invention, but then again, he *was*
writing a novel.

Nevertheless, at one point, Scott does come close, I think,
to what Jeffrey really must have felt. In recounting to Julian

his duel with Crofts, the old dwarf tells the lad how he felt in the instant after the gunshot:

> I would not wish on my worst foe the pain which I felt when I saw him reel on his saddle, and so fall down to the earth! – and when I perceived that the life-blood was pouring fast, I could not but wish to Heaven that it had been my own instead of his. Thus fell youth, hopes and bravery, a sacrifice to a silly thoughtless jest; yet, alas! Wherein had I choice, seeing that honour is, as it were, the very breath in our nostrils; and that in no sense can we be said to live, if we permit ourselves to be deprived of it?

Jeffrey's portrayal in Scott's book raised his profile among the Victorians, and the 'hero of the pie' was a popular topic for magazines and journalism. There is even a huge porcelain statue of Jeffrey, emerging from the pie, sword in hand. It was featured on the BBC programme, *The Antiques Roadshow*, and stands as the centrepiece in the public bar of the Boat Inn at Portumna, County Galway. Following this theme, recent years have seen Jeffrey immortalized in the form of a teapot, and on the label of a prizewinning beer, JHB, or Jeffrey Hudson Bitter, brewed by the Oakham Brewery.

He has not been forgotten.

SOURCES

1. MAIN SOURCES

The fundamental sources for Jeffrey's life are the accounts by Fuller and Wright (see Appendixes 1 and 2).

Fuller's is found in his *History of the Worthies of England*, 1662. He also gives us a brief biography of William Evans. Wright's account can be found on page 105 of his *Histories and Antiquities of the County of Rutland*, 1684. He adds some information about Oakham, Burley and the Duke of Buckingham.

The other main account is Henry Stonecastle's article in *The Universal Spectator and Weekly Journal*, 30 Dec. 1732, No. 221, excerpts of which are also in *The Gentleman's Magazine*, Dec. 1732, p.1120.

2. GENERAL ACCOUNTS OF JEFFREY

The following books contain brief accounts of Jeffrey's life, mostly drawn from those mentioned above:

James Caulfield, *Portraits, Memorials of Remarkable Persons from Ed.III to the Revolution* (London, R.S. Kirby, 1813)

Dictionary of National Biography, Vol. X (London, 1885–1904) pp.149–50

James Doran, *The History of Court Fools* (London, 1858)

F. W. Fairholt, *Eccentric and Remarkable Characters* (London, Richard Bentley, 1853)

J. Granger, *A Biographical History of England* (London, Baynes and Son, 1824)

C. Northcote Parkinson, 'Charles I's Dwarf', *History Today*, Vol. XXVII, No. 6 (June 1977)

Rutland Magazine, Vol. V (n.d. c.1910), p.21

Walter Scott, *Peveril of the Peak* (London, Hurst Robinson, 1822)

John Southworth, *Fools and Jesters at the English Court* (Stroud, Alan Sutton, 1988)

Horace Walpole, *Anecdotes of Painting in England* (London, John Major, 1826–8)

E. J. Wood, *Dwarfs and Giants* (London, Richard Bentley, 1868)

3. GENERAL HISTORIES AND OTHER WIDELY USED SOURCES

GENERAL POLITICAL HISTORY

For the background history, especially about the Civil War and the political events of the age, I have drawn heavily on the following:

Charles Carlton, *Charles I: The Personal Monarch* (London, Routledge & Kegan Paul, 1983)

Christopher Hill, *The Century of Revolution 1603–1714* (London, Abacus, 1961)

J. P. Kenyon, *The Stuarts* (London, Batsford, 1958)

C. V. Wedgwood, *The King's Peace, 1637–1641* (London, Collins, 1955)

C. V. Wedgwood, *The King's War, 1641–1647* (Collins, London, 1958)

Blair Worden, ed., *Stuart England* (Oxford, Phaidon, 1986)

Most of the letters quoted come from Thomas Birch, *The Court and Times of Charles I, inc. memoirs of the mission in England of the Capuchin friars, with Cyprian de Gamaches*, ed. R. F. Williams (London, Henry Colburn, 1849).

HENRIETTA MARIA

For events in the life of Henrietta Maria, the most detailed account is that found in H. Strickland, *Lives of the Queens of England* (London, Henry Colburn, 1845) but I have also drawn substantially from Carola Oman's *Henrietta Maria* (London, Hodder & Stoughton, 1936) and Quentin Bone, *Henrietta Maria, Queen of the Cavaliers* (London, Peter Owen, 1973).

Her letters are to be found in *Henrietta Maria, Letters inc. Her Private Correspondence*, ed. M. A. E. Green (London, 1857) while a contemporary account is to be found in the *Memoir on Life of Henrietta Maria* by Mme de Motteville, ed. M. G. Hanotaux, Camden Society Miscellany, Vol. VIII (London Camden Society, 1880).

Other accounts of her life consulted include:

Comte de Baillon, *Henriette-Marie de France* (Paris, 1877)

Elizabeth Hamilton, *Henrietta Maria* (London, Hamish Hamilton, 1976)

Rosalind K. Marshall, *Henrietta Maria – The Intrepid Queen* (London, HMSO, 1990)

I. A. Taylor, *Queen Henrietta Maria* (London, Hutchinson, 1905)

For the social background I have been particularly indebted to Elizabeth Burton, *The Jacobeans at Home* (London, Secker & Warburg, 1962) which is a superbly informative and interesting book.

4. SOURCES FOR PARTICULAR CHAPTERS

THE BUTCHER'S SON
Details of Jeffrey's family are to be found in the Oakham
Parish registers, available in the Leicestershire Record Office.

Information on Oakham comes from the Rutland volume in the Victorian County History series. I have also
drawn heavily on the *Rutland Record* (1980–2000). The
poem about Burley is taken from Wright's *Histories and
Antiquities of the County of Rutland*.

The information on bull-baiting comes from F. W. Hack-
wood, *Old English Sports* (London, T. Fisher-Unwin,
1907) while the accounts of English fairs, particularly Bartholomew Fair, are to be found in C. McKechnie, *Popular
Entertainments Through the Ages* (London, Sampson Low
& Co., 1932).

Information on 'Jeffrey's Cottage' can be found in the
Rutland Magazine, Vol. III (c.1910) p.158 and in contem-
porary travel guides such as Bryan Waites, *Rutland Trails*
(Oakham, 1997).

The account of other dwarfs of Jeffrey's height comes
from Wood, *Dwarfs and Giants*.

THE DUKE'S GIFT
An excellent account of the original mansion at Burley can
be found in Anne Blandamer, 'The Duke of Buckingham's
House at Burley on the Hill', in *Rutland Record*, No.18
(1998), pp.349–60. Also in P. Finch, *History of Burley on
the Hill* (2 Vols, London, 1901).

Biographical details about George Villiers can be found
in Carlton, *Charles I*. Various contemporary portraits of
him are collected in David Nichol Smith, ed., *Characters
from the Histories and Memoirs of the Seventeenth Century* (London, OUP, 1918).

The account of York House is drawn from Thomas Peacham, *The Compleat Gentleman* (London, 1634) and Oliver Millar, *The Age of Charles I, Painting in England, 1620–1649* (London, Tate Gallery, 1972). *The Survey of London: Charing Cross, London* (London, Country Life, 1935) also contains some information, particularly regarding the surviving water gate.

The skyline of London can be clearly seen in Visscher's engraving of 1616. My copy of this is in Henry B. Wheatley, *Mediaeval London* (London, Dent, 1922). I have also consulted Robert Carrier and Oliver Lawson Dick, *The Vanished City* (London, Hutchinson, 1957).

The accounts of the Duke's banquets of November 1627 can be found in Birch, *The Court and Times of Charles I* (Vol. I); the banquet I have suggested for Jeffrey's arrival is described on p.392. General information on Stuart banquets has been taken from Burton, *The Jacobeans at Home* and from C. Anne Wilson, ed., *'Banquetting Stuffe'* (Edinburgh, Edinburgh University Press, 1991). Information about the 'presentation' of other dwarfs is taken from Wood, *Dwarfs and Giants*.

THE QUEEN'S DWARF
The history of Somerset House (a.k.a. Denmark House) is taken from Raymond Needham and Alexander Webster, *Somerset House, Past and Present* (London, Unwin, 1905). This also contains an account of Jeffrey's fall, but the actual letter describing the event is in the Public Record Office (PRO SP 16/67/53) and also in the Calendar of State Papers Domestic (CSPD) Charles I, 1627–28, p.222.

Other information on Denmark House has been taken from Norman Brett-James, *The Growth of Stuart London* (London, Allen & Unwin, 1935) and Neville Williams,

The Royal Residences of Great Britain, A Social History (London, Barrie & Rockliffe, 1960).

Jeffrey's first appearance in the masque is mentioned in the Dramatic Records of the Lord Chamberlain's Office, reprinted in *Malone Society Collections*, Vol. II, No.3 (1931), pp.332–34.

The Household Books of Queen Henrietta Maria, which include the payments to her servants, are at the Public Record Office (PRO E 101/438/7; E 101/438/14).

The plays and masques of 1627–28 are described in Birch, *The Court and Times of Charles I*, Vol. II, pp.4, 70.

THE PIRATE CAPTIVE

There are two accounts of Jeffrey's capture by the Dunkirkers. One in the Public Record Office (PRO SP 16/163/25; CSPD, 1629–31, pp.217–18, 278, 310) and the other in a letter from Mead to Stuteville in Birch, *The Court and Times of Charles I*, Vol. II, pp. 69–70. This is the 'sesquipedal Geoffrey' letter.

Madame Peronne and the state of English and French midwifery is discussed in Antonia Fraser, *The Weaker Vessel, Woman's Lot in Seventeenth-Century England* (London, Weidenfeld & Nicholson, 1984).

Jeffereidos is reprinted in *Sir William D'Avenant, The Shorter Poems and Songs from the Plays and Masques*, ed. A. M. Gibbs (Oxford, Clarendon Press, 1972). I have also drawn on a biography, A. H. Nethercot, *Sir William D'Avenant* (Chicago, University of Chicago Press, 1938) as well as John Aubrey's account of the dramatist in *Brief Lives*, ed. Oliver Lawson Dick (London, Secker & Warburg, 1949). There is more on D'Avenant in Frederick S. Boas, *An Introduction to Stuart Drama* (Oxford, OUP, 1946) and Douglas Bush, *English Literature in the Earlier Seventeenth Century* (Oxford, OUP, 1945).

The Mytens pictures are listed in the *Burlington Magazine* (Vol. XVII, p.162; Vol. LXXXV p.304; Vol. LXXXIX pp.245–7) and also in Oliver Millar, *Tudor, Stuart and Early Georgian Pictures in the Collection of H.M. The Queen* (2 vols, London, Phaidon Press, 1963) plates 50, 59, 314).

THE LITTLE COURTIER

The account of the halcyon days of the Court is largely based on C. V. Wedgwood, *Poetry and Politics Under the Stuarts* (Cambridge, CUP, 1960).

The duel between Crofts and Denbigh is recounted in Birch, *The Court and Times of Charles I*, Vol. II, p.87. Information on Ben Jonson and Inigo Jones can be found in Marchette Chute, *Ben Jonson of Westminster* (New York, Dutton, 1953) and in *Ben Jonson's Plays and Masques*, ed. Robert Adams (New York, Norton Critical Editions, 1979).

Information on masques in general has been drawn from Frederick. S. Boas, *An Introduction to Stuart Drama* (Oxford, OUP, 1946) and David Lindley, ed., *Court Masques, Jacobean and Caroline Entertainments 1605–1640* (Oxford, OUP, 1995).

William Prynne's career is detailed in H. J. C. Grierson, *Cross Currents in English Literature of the Seventeenth Century* (London, Chatto & Windus, 1929).

The text of *Luminalia* can be found in *Luminalia*, ed. A. B. Grosart in *Miscellanies of the Fuller Worthies Library*, Vol. IV (Blackburn, Privately Printed, 1872–6) pp.609–30, while the authorship is discussed in Edith S. Hooper, 'The Authorship of Luminalia', MLR, Vol. VIII (1913), pp.541–3.

The record of the Queen's carriages can be found in the Public Record Office (PRO SP 16/375/10).

Information on Van Dyck and the King's love of painting comes from Carlton, *Charles I.*

THE WONDER OF THE AGE
The account of Old Parr is taken from John Taylor, *The Old, Old, Very Old Man* (1636). He is also depicted along with Jeffrey and William Evans in Thomas Heywood, *The Three Wonders of the Age* (1636). The two can be found together in one volume in the British Museum.

Also in the British Museum are the two copies of *The New Yeare's Gift* by 'Microphilus' (1636; 1638).

Accounts of Thomas Heywood can be found in Arthur Clark, *Thomas Heywood* (Oxford, Basil Blackwell, 1931), A. W. Ward, 'Thomas Heywood', in *Cambridge History of English Literature*, Vol. VI (Cambridge, CUP, 1910).

Details of the Court's visit to Oxford can be found in Carlton, *Charles I* and Oman *Henrietta Maria.* The account of the water-gardens comes from John Aubrey's biography of Thomas Bushell in his *Brief Lives* and also from Burton, *The Jacobeans at Home.*

The incident at Holmby Hall is recounted in Green, ed., *Henrietta Maria, Letters inc. Her Private Correspondence*, under the title, 'The Dwarf and the Rosary'.

Archie Armstrong's career is outlined in Doran, *Court Fools* and Southworth, *Fools and Jesters at the English Court.*

Details of the chapel at Denmark House come from Raymond Needham and Alexander Webster, *Somerset House, Past and Present* (London, Unwin, 1905).

The account of Jeffrey at the siege of Breda comes from Walter Lithgow, *A True and Experimentall Discourse upon the beginning, proceeding and Victorious event of this last siege of Breda* (1637), p.45, and also from the CSPD Charles I, 1637–38, p.308.

The text of *Salmacida Spolia* can be found in David Lindley, ed., *Court Masques, Jacobean and Caroline Entertainments 1605–1640* (Oxford, OUP, 1995). It was originally published as William D'Avenant and Inigo Jones, *Salmacida Spolia. A masque. Presented by the King and Queenes Majesties; at Whitehall on Tuesday the 21 day of January 1639* (London, Thomas Walkley, 1639–40). There is a superb reconstruction of the event by C. V. Wedgwood in 'The Last Masque' in *Truth and Opinions* (Oxford, OUP, 1962).

THE MISTAKEN PRINCE

The general outline of the events and causes of the Civil War is taken from Hill's superb *The Century of Revolution 1603–1714*.

The accounts of the marriage of Princess Mary and Prince William can be found in Green, ed., *Letters of Queen Henrietta Maria*. There is a good account in Stephen Coote, *Royal Survivor – A Life of Charles II* (London, Hodder & Stoughton, 1999).

Jeffrey's allowances and servants are listed in *Horace Walpole, Letters*, ed. W. H. Lewis, Vol. 1 (London, OUP, 1937), pp.28 & 41.

The events at Oatlands, the flight from London and the journey to Holland are primarily from Oman, *Henrietta Maria*, and Wedgwood, *The King's War*. I have also drawn on Cyprien de Gamache, 'Memoirs of the Mission in England of the Capuchin Friars', in Birch, *The Court and Times of Charles I*, Vol II, pp.291 ff.

THE CAPTAIN OF HORSE

Henrietta Maria's return to England, march south and escape to France are detailed in Strickland, *Lives of the Queens of England* and also in Oman, *Henrietta Maria* and in Bone, *Henrietta Maria, Queen of the Cavaliers*.

The Court at Oxford is described in the biographies of Henrietta Maria and Charles and also in Burton, *The Jacobeans at Home* from where I have taken Anthony Wood's comments. An account of Ralph Kettell can be found in Aubrey's *Brief Lives*. The poem comes from *Musarum Oxoniensium* (Oxford, 1643). I have also drawn on Christopher Hobhouse, *Oxford* (London, Batsford, 1939) and Jan Morris, *The Oxford Book of Oxford* (Oxford, OUP, 1978).

The letter from Francis Basset is quoted in *Polwhele, Traditions and Recollections* (London, 1826), p.17.

The sea battle is also described, albeit from a Parliamentarian viewpoint, in *A True Relation of the Queen's Departure from Falmouth*, (London, 1644).

THE FATAL DUELLIST

The Queen's arrival in France and the chronology of her first few months is drawn from Oman, Bone and Strickland.

The account of the Queen's appearance is taken from de Motteville, *Memoir on Life of Henrietta Maria*. I have also used the Calendar of State Papers Venetian, 1644, pp.101, 119, 143.

The picture of the Cavaliers in exile comes from Wedgwood, *Poetry and Politics Under the Stuarts*.

For information on duelling in France I used Norman A. Bennetton, *Social Significance of the Duel in Seventeenth Century French Drama* (London, Johns Hopkins Studies in Romance Literatures and Languages, 1938).

The various newspaper accounts quoted can be found in the following:

The Diary or Exact Journal, No. 8 (11 July); No. 10 (29 July); No. 22 (9 Oct. 1644)

Perfect Diurnall of Some Passages in Parliament, No. 65 (21 Oct. 1644)

Perfect Occurrences of Parliament (2 Aug. 1644); No. 10 (11 Oct. 1644)

Perfect Passages of Each Days Proceedings in Parliament, No.1 (16 Oct. 1644); (18 Oct. 1644)

Information on the unfortunate Charles Crofts can be found in 'Who Was Crofts?' in *Notes and Queries*, 11th Series, Vol. 6, (1912), pp.369, 433, 475.

Henrietta Maria's letter to Mazarin can be found in Strickland and in her *Letters*, ed. Green.

THE ABANDONED SLAVE

The reconstruction of Jeffrey's capture is based on the account by Emanuel D'Aranda, *Relation de la Captivité à Alger* (Leyden 1671). This account – and most of the information on which I have relied for this chapter can be found in Stephen Clissold, *The Barbary Slaves* (London, Paul Elek, 1977). The other standard book on the Barbary pirates is Lieut Colonel R. L. Playfair, *The Scourge of Christendom* (London, Smith Elder & Co., 1884). I have also consulted J. F. P. Hopkins, trans., *Letters from Barbary, 1576–1774* (London, British Academy, 1982) and T. Pellow, *The Adventures of Thomas Pellow, Mariner* (London, 1739), p.103.

The mentions of Jeffrey's boots and 'masking-suit' are found in John Tradescant, *Museum Tradescanteum or A Collection of Rarities Preserved At South-Lambeth Near London* (London, 1656) and in the Ashmolean Catalogue of 1675.

The poem 'To Jeffrey Hudson' can be found in Robert Heath, *Clarastella* (Gainsville, Gainsville Fac. Edn, 1970).

THE LOST SON

Journeys to redeem slaves are described in Clissold, *The Barbary Slaves*. There are specific references in government records; Treasury Books, 1668, p.382, and CSPD 1668, p.423.

Jeffrey's receipt for the gift from Buckingham can be found in the Public Record Office PRO SP 29/441/51; (CSPD Addenda 1660–1685, p.293) and PRO SP 29/450/137 (CSPD Addenda 1660–1670, p.734). The sketch of the second Duke of Buckingham is drawn from accounts in David Nichol Smith, ed., *Characters from the Histories and Memoirs of the Seventeenth Century* (London, OUP, 1918).

The Rutland Hearth Tax is detailed in Bourne and Goods, eds, *The Rutland Hearth Tax, 1665* (Rutland Record Society, 1991) while Anne Whiteman, ed., *The Compton Census of 1676* (Oxford, OUP, 1986) contains information about recusants in Rutland.

THE WRONGED CATHOLIC

The plaque of the Porter and the Dwarf is mentioned in many accounts of London including Philip Norman, *London Signs and Inscriptions* (London, Eliot Stock, 1893), p.21, Thomas Pennant, *Some Account of London* (London, 1813) and Thomas, *Ancient Remains of London*, Vol. II, (London, Sears & Co., 1830), p.235. Its fate is discussed in *Notes and Queries*, 10th Series, Vol. II, (1911), pp.194, 236.

All information about Titus Oates and the Popish Plot comes from Jane Lane, *Titus Oates* (London, Andrew Dakers, 1949), J. P. Kenyon, *The Popish Plot* (Heinemann, 1972) and Stephen Coote, *Royal Survivor – A Life of Charles II* (London, Hodder & Stoughton, 1999).

The Westminster Gatehouse is described in Henry B.

Wheatley, *London Past and Present*, Vol. II (London, J. Murray, 1891), pp.88–90.

The plague and the fire are brilliantly described in Liza Picard, *Restoration London* (London, Weidenfeld & Nicolson, 1997) and also in Burton, *The Jacobeans at Home*.

The final mentions of Captain Jeffrey Hudson can be found in J. Y. Akerman, ed., *Moneys Received and Paid for Secret Services of Charles II and James II*, (London, Camden Society, 1851), pp.14, 28.

INDEX

Algiers 71, 184–188, 190–191, 206–207

Anne of Austria 155, 169

Anne of Denmark 48, 51

Armstrong, Archie 113–115

banquets, 40, 41–42

Barbary 71, 181–190, 192, 195, 206, 238

pirates 71, 181–5

Bartholomew Fair 24–25, 122, 195

Bassompierre, François de, 33, 39

Bourbon l'Archambault 167-168, 169, 170

Breda 118–120, 141, 149, 153

Buckingham, Katharine, Duchess of 26–27, 65

Buckingham, George Villiers, First Duke of, 1, 2, 14–15, 16, 17, 26, 28–30, 32, 33–35, 38–40, 43, 44–45, 51, 53, 63–65, 140, 180, 194, 212, 214, 235, 237, 241

Buckingham, George Villiers, Second Duke of, 208, 213–214, 238

bull baiting 17–19, 54

Burley on the Hill 6, 14, 16, 26–28, 34–36, 208, 210, 233, 235, 237, 243

Bushell, Thomas 109–110

Capuchins 69–70, 72, 116, 147, 151

Catholicism, Catholics 30–31, 49, 110–113, 115–118, 141–142, 219, 224–228, 232, 238

Charles I, 15, 28–36, 38, 39–41, 44–45, 48, 51, 53, 54, 56–59, 64–66, 74, 81, 83, 92–98, 104–105, 108–109, 111, 113–114, 117–118, 120–143, 145–149, 157–158, 160–162, 165, 189, 190, 195–196, 200–201, 212, 221–222, 236–237

Charles II 6, 74, 91, 108, 138, 141, 157, 165, 202, 219, 221–222, 225, 229–231

childbirth 12, 66–68

civil war 132–135, 149, 153–160, 199, 200–202

Coneo, George 110–112

Crofts, Charles (duellist in France) 173, 175–179, 236, 238

Crofts (duellist in England) 82

Crofts, William, Lord 171, 173, 178, 238

Cromwell, Oliver 57, 91, 134, 136, 161, 195, 200, 202, 221

D'Avenant, William 74–79, 121, 126, 139–140, 157–158, 161, 171, 233, 238

D'Avenant, William – *cont.*
  Jeffereidos 74–78, 175, 180,
    206, 216 (*see* masques)
Denmark House 34, 45–51,
    54–55, 60, 62, 67, 69, 74, 81,
    90, 111, 112, 115, 120, 141,
    158, 171, 202–204, 210, 216,
    219, 226, 232, 233
Dryden 214, 230
duelling 81–82, 173–174
dwarfs, dwarfism, 7, 20–22,
    61–62, 106, 192–193 (*see*
    growth-hormone deficiency)

Evans, William 49–52, 97,
    99–100, 103, 195–196, 198,
    219
Evelyn, John 168, 170, 217–218

Fuller, Thomas 5, 13–14, 16,
    19–21, 23, 26–27, 35, 50,
    52–53, 58, 156, 199–200,
    233, 235–237

Garnier, Jean 69–70, 72
Garnier, Françoise 55–56, 69
Gibson, Richard 56–57
Godfrey, Sir Edward Berry
    226–227
Goring, George 52, 139–140
Gregoire, Jerome 55, 109, 141,
    193
growth-hormone deficiency
    20–21, 106–107, 193–194

Heath, Robert 16, 197–199
Henrietta Maria, Queen 1–2,
    30–36, 39, 43–47, 48–51,
    53–60, 62–67, 69, 72–74,
    79–86, 89–96, 99–101, 104,

    108–112, 114–126, 130–131,
    138–150, 153–158, 160–165,
    166–174, 177–80, 195,
    201–205, 210–212, 227, 236,
    237
Henrietta, Princess 162–163
Henry, Prince 142
Henry, Prince of Orange 118, 147
Heywood, Thomas 20, 26,
    99–104, 233, 250
  The New Year's Gift 46, 69,
    101–106, 113, 132, 166,
    198–199
Holton, Sara 56, 101, 104, 141
Hudson, Ann, 209
Hudson, Jeffrey
  birth and family 10–13, 19–20,
    22–23, 25, 208–210
  height and medical condition
    19–22, 94, 106–107,
    192–194
  in Rutland 13–14, 24, 26–7,
    34–35, 208–213
  presentation at banquet 1–3,
    38–43
  at Denmark House 48–50,
    55–56, 60, 140–141
  as 'jester' 60–62, 74, 87, 89,
    113, 138–139, 172
  in masques 50–53, 82–83,
    86–88, 89, 121–123,
    126–131, 196–197
  portraits of 62–63, 79, 91–95,
    96, 106, 219–220
  sea journeys of 70–74,
    146–147, 150–152, 164–165,
    180–182
  Catholicism 112–113,
    115–117, 209–210, 227–228
  in Holland 118–120, 146–150

in civil war 146, 153–154,
    156–160
escapes with Queen 161–164
in France 70, 166–168,
    170–172
fights duel 172–179
taken to Africa 182, 185–192,
    204–205
returns to England 205–213
returns to London 213–215,
    219–220
imprisoned 227–228, 230
released 230–231
death 231–233
accounts of 5–7, 74–78,
    98–106, 197–200, 212–213,
    235–242
'myths' about 27–28, 60–62,
    78, 94, 240–242
Hudson, Joan 11, 25
Hudson, John (Father) 6, 10–14,
    17–19, 22–23, 26–27, 58,
    208–209, 237
Hudson, John (Brother) 25
Hudson, Lucy 7, 12, 19
Hudson, Mary 11
Hudson, Samuel 25, 209, 214,
    229
Hudson, Theophilus 25, 209
hypopituatirism (see growth-
    hormone deficiency)

James I 14, 17, 28, 29, 35, 48,
    82, 100, 113, 114, 145, 213
James, Prince (later James II) 157,
    225, 226, 229
Jermyn, Henry, Earl of St Albans,
    139–140, 150, 155–156,
    161–164, 167, 169, 178–179,
    202, 204

Jones, Inigo 46, 54, 83–89, 92,
    109, 111, 116, 121, 126–128,
    130, 195, 203, 204, 218 (see
    masques)
Jonson, Ben 37, 42, 47, 50, 79,
    82–84, 87–89, 121, 197 (see
    masques)

Laud, Archbishop William, 98,
    104, 108, 114–115, 125,
    134–137
Lithgow, William 119, 153
London 12, 32, 36–38, 46–47,
    61, 64, 66, 75, 79, 92, 95–96,
    111, 124, 130, 136, 139, 141,
    146, 155, 161, 195, 201–205,
    208, 211, 216–222, 226, 232,
    238
Louis XIII 63, 124, 155, 169
Louis XIV 168–169

Marie de Medici 30, 33, 70, 73,
    124, 126, 129, 141, 149,
    169
Mary, Princess 82, 138, 146, 251
masques, 50–53, 80, 85–89,
    120–123
  Chloridia (Jonson) 83, 85–88,
    121
  King's Masque (1627) 53
  Neptune's Triumph (Jonson) 42
  Queen's Masque (1626) 51–52
  Love's Triumph Through
    Callipolis (Jonson) 83
  Luminalia (D'Avenant)
    121–122
  Salmacida Spolia (D'Avenant)
    126–131, 179, 196
Mayerne, Theodore 143, 162,
    211

Mazarin, Cardinal 155, 168–169, 173–174, 177–178, 253
Morocco 71, 184, 206
Mytens, Daniel 62–63, 79, 91, 94, 233, 249

Nevers 170–171, 177, 179–180
New Year's Gift, The (*see* Heywood, Thomas)

Oakham 10–11, 13–14, 16, 24–25, 27–28, 58, 108, 181, 189, 208–213, 215–216, 222, 235
Oates, Titus 13, 222–226, 229–231
Oatlands 67, 142–144, 153, 233
Oxford 61, 74, 107–111, 155, 157–158, 160–161, 196–197, 199, 212, 218, 225

Parliament 29, 64, 81, 118, 121–126, 132–137, 139, 142–146, 148–150, 190, 200, 202, 221, 226
Parr, Thomas, 97–100
Peronne, Madame 67, 70, 72, 74, 77, 248
Philip, Father 112, 145, 147
plague 34, 210, 216–217, 255
plays, 55, 80–81, 89–91, 99–100, 108–109
Prynne, William 90–91
Puritans, puritanism 29, 120, 130, 133–134, 202, 225
Pym, John 140, 146, 150

Richelieu, Cardinal 142, 155, 173–174, 204
Richmond, Mary Villiers, Duchess of 147

Rochelle 63–64, 180
Rubens, Peter Paul 38–39, 54, 120
Rupert, Prince 7, 149, 155–157, 160, 241
Rutland 7, 10, 13, 15, 36, 84, 103, 194, 208–209, 212–213, 222, 232, 237

Scott, Walter 6–7, 114, 144–145, 160, 200, 240–242
Shakespeare, William 42, 74–75, 157
Shepherd, Anne 56–57
Somerset House (*see* Denmark House)
St. Pauls Cathedral 36–37, 48, 90, 95, 217, 227
slavery, 185–192, 206–207, 238
Stonecastle, Henry 6, 19, 22–23, 27–28, 35, 60–61, 94–95, 107
Strafford (see Wentworth)

Taylor, John 80, 97, 99, 250
Tonge, Israel 224–225
Tradescant, John 16, 194–196
Tunis 71, 184–186, 206–207

Van Dyck, Sir Anthony 85, 91–95, 107, 124, 218, 233, 250
Vanderwort, Abraham 56

Wentworth, Thomas, Earl of Strafford 125–126, 135–137, 142–144
Westminster 36, 48, 54, 78, 100, 115, 227
Gatehouse 227, 231, 238, 240, 254

Whitehall 45, 51, 54–55, 62, 79, 81, 84, 114, 120, 126, 138, 141, 145, 201–202, 221, 229, 233

William, Prince of Orange 138–139

Willoughby, Lady 69–70

Wood, Anthony 61, 160, 218, 252

Wren, Christopher 217–219, 228

Wright, James, 5–6, 22, 26, 34, 185, 187, 193, 207–208, 212–213, 227, 231, 233, 237

Wright, Abraham 108, 212

York House 35, 38, 40, 46, 128, 247